ISBN 978-1-330-10695-2
PIBN 10027448

English
Français
Deutsche
Italiano
Español
Português

www.forgottenbooks.com

Mythology Photography **Fiction**
Fishing Christianity **Art** Cooking
Essays Buddhism Freemasonry
Medicine **Biology** Music **Ancient
Egypt** Evolution Carpentry Physics
Dance Geology **Mathematics** Fitness
Shakespeare **Folklore** Yoga Marketing
Confidence Immortality Biographies
Poetry **Psychology** Witchcraft
Electronics Chemistry History **Law**
Accounting **Philosophy** Anthropology
Alchemy Drama Quantum Mechanics
Atheism Sexual Health **Ancient History**
Entrepreneurship Languages Sport
Paleontology Needlework Islam
Metaphysics Investment Archaeology
Parenting Statistics Criminology
Motivational

AUTOBIOGRAPHY

OF

LEIGH HUNT.

WITH

Reminiscences

OF FRIENDS AND CONTEMPORARIES.

"Most men, when drawn to speak about themselves,
Are moved by little and little to say more
Than they first dream'd; until at last they blush,
And can but hope to find secret excuse
In the self-knowledge of their auditors."

WALTER SCOTT'S *Old Play.*

IN TWO VOLUMES.

VOL. I.

NEW YORK:

HARPER & BROTHERS, **********,

329 & 331 PEARL STREET.

FRANKLIN SQUARE.

1860.

THE

AUTOBIOGRAPHY

OF

LEIGH HUNT,

WITH

Reminiscences

OF FRIENDS AND CONTEMPORARIES.

"Most men, when drawn to speak about themselves,
Are moved by little and little to say more
Than they first dream'd; until at last they blush,
And can but hope to find secret excuse
In the self-knowledge of their auditors."

WALTER SCOTT'S *Old Play.*

IN TWO VOLUMES.

VOL. I.

NEW YORK:

HARPER & BROTHERS, PUBLISHERS,

329 & 331 PEARL STREET,

FRANKLIN SQUARE.

1860.

PREFACE.

BEFORE the reader looks any further into these volumes, I would entreat him to bear in mind *two things*.

And I say "entreat," and put those two words in italics, not in order to give emphasis to the truth (for truth is, or ought to be, its own emphasis) but to show him how anxious I am on the points, and to impress them the more strongly on his attention.

The first is, that the work, whatever amusement he may find in it (and I hope, for the publishers' sake, as well as my own, that it is not destitute of amusement) was commenced under circumstances which committed me to its execution, and would have been abandoned at almost every step, had those circumstances allowed.

The second is, that the life being that of a man of letters, and topics of a different sort failing me toward the conclusion, I found myself impelled to dilate more on my writings, than it would otherwise have entered my head to contemplate.

It is true, that autobiography, and autocriticism also, have abounded of late years in literary quarters. The French appear to have set the example. Goldoni and Alfieri followed it. Goethe and Chateaubriand followed them. Coleridge's *Literary Life* is professedly autocritical. With autocriticism Wodsworth answered his reviewers. And editions

of Collected Works have derived new attractions from whatever accounts of them their authors have been induced to
supply.

Example itself, however, while it furnishes excuse in proportion to the right which a man has to follow it, becomes
reason for alarm when he knows not the extent of his
warrant. Others will have to determine that point, whatever he may be disposed to think of it ; and perhaps he may
be disposed not to think of it at all, but wholly to eschew its
necessity. Such, at all events, was the case with myself. I
would have entirely waived the autobiography, if a sense of
justice to others would have permitted me to do so. My
friend and publisher, Mr. Smith, will satisfy any one on that
head, who is not acquainted with my veracity. But Mr.
Smith's favorable opinion of me, and his own kindly feeling,
led him to think it would be so much the reverse of a disadvantage to me in the end that he took the handsomest means
of making the task as easy to me as he could, through a long
period of engagements over due, and of interruptions from ill
health ; and though I can never forget the pain of mind
which some of the passages cost me, yet I would now, for
both our sakes, willingly be glad that the work has been done,
provided the public think it worth reading, and are content
with this explanation. The opportunity, indeed, which it
has given me of recalling some precious memories, of correct-
ing some crude judgments, and, in one respect, of discharging
a duty that must otherwise have been delayed, make me
persuade myself on the whole, that I *am* glad. So I shall
endeavor, with the reader's help, to remain under that comfortable impression. I will liken myself to an actor, who

though commencing his part on the stage with a gout or a headache, or, perhaps, even with a bit of heartache, finds his audience so willing to be pleased, that he forgets his infirmity as he goes, and ends with being glad that he has appeared.

One thing, perhaps, may be said in greater excuse for me, than for most autobiographers; namely, that I have been so accustomed during the greater part of my life to talk to the reader in my own person, or at least to compare notes with him by implication on all sorts of personal subjects, that I fall more naturally into this kind of fire-side strain than most writers, and therefore do not present the public so abrupt an image of individuality.

So much for talking of myself at all. The autocriticism I would rank, at due distance, in the category of those explanations of their thoughts and feelings, their designs, or idiosyncrasies, with which poets have occasionally accompanied their verses, from the times of Dante and Petrarch downwards. At least, this was the example, or instinctive principle, on which I acted, owing to my intimacy with the old Italian writers, and to my love of the way in which their prose falls a talking of their poetry; for I have not entered into the nature of such autocriticism itself, or given my reasons as I might have done, and I think to good effect, for the desirableness of poets giving an account of their art. I came unexpectly on the subject, while at a loss for my next autobiographical topic; and I was so perplexed what to find, that I had not time even to make choice of my instances. I would make the same excuse for going into details on other points, or on any points, especially those most relating to myself: for I have lived long enough to discover, that autobiography may

not only be a very distressing but a very puzzling task, and
throw the writer into such doubts as to what he should or
should not say, as totally to confuse him.   What conscience
bids him utter, for the sake of the world, may be clear
enough ; and in obeying that, he must find his consolation for
all chances of injury to himself.

The autobiography includes all that seemed worth retaining of what has before been written in connection with it, and
this has received the benefit of a maturer judgment.   The
political articles from the *Examiner*, curious from the consequences attending them, are republished for the first time ;
several hitherto unpublished letters of Thomas Moore appear in the work, in addition to those which the public
have already seen ; and the whole work will be new to by
far the greater number of readers, not only because of the new
reading generations that have come up, but because times are
altered, and writers are willingly heard now, in the comparative calm of parties, and during the anxiety of all honest men
to know what it is best to think and to do, whom, twenty or
thirty years ago, every means would have been taken to
suppress.

      *   *   *   *   *   *

Let me close this preface with thanking two members of a
profession, which literature has always reason to thank and
to love ; the one my old and distinguished friend Dr. South
wood Smith, the friend of his species, whose attentions to my
health enabled me to proceed with the work ; and the other,
my new and, if I am not greatly mistaken, hereafter to be
distinguished friend, Dr. Francis Sibson, a young physician,
who is not unworthy to be named at the same time, and who

did me the like cordial service when I could no longer prevail on myself to interrupt a public benefactor.

And so Heaven bless the reader, and all of us: and enable us to compare notes some day in some Elysian corner of intuition, where we shall be in no need of prefaces and explanations, and only wonder how any of us could have missed the secret of universal knowledge and happiness.

READER (smiling and staring about him).—Where is it?

AUTHOR.—Ah, we must get into the confines of Elysium first, in order to know.

READER.—And where is Elysium?

AUTHOR.—Why, a good old Divine of the Church of England says, the approach to it is called Temper.—" Heaven," says Dr. Whichcote, " is first a temper, and then a place."

CONTENTS OF VOL. I.

CONTENTS.

CHAPTER XII.

LITERARY WARFARE.

CHAPTER XIII.

THE REGENT AND THE EXAMINER.

CHAPTER XIV.

IMPRISONMENT.

AUTOBIOGRAPHY OF LEIGH HUNT.

CHAPTER I.

THE AUTHOR'S PROGENITORS.

Fetching a man's mind from his cradle.—Transmission of family faces and qualities.—Childhood a favorite theme in after-life.—The author's ancestors and father.—Perils of the latter during the American Revolution.—Compliment paid him by the father of Sheridan.—His answer to a bishop, and general character and career.—Becomes tutor to the nephew of the Duke of Chandos.—Accidental death of that nobleman, and affecting end of his duchess.—Misfortunes in the author's family.—His mother and her connections.—Her behavior during her voyage to England; admirable conduct on various other occasions; and love of the sunset during her decline.

THE circumstances that led to this Autobiography will transpire in the course of it. Suffice it to say for the present, that a more involuntary production it would be difficult to conceive; though I trust it will not be found destitute of the entertainment which any true account of experiences in the life of a human being must of necessity, perhaps, contain.

I claim no importance for any thing which I have done or undergone, but on grounds common to the interests of all, and to the willing sympathy of my brother-lovers of books. Should I be led at any time into egotisms of a nature that seem to think otherwise, I blush beforehand for the mischance, and beg it to considered as alien from my habits of reflection. I have had vanities enough in my day; and, as the reader will see, became aware of them. If I have any remaining,

1 hope they are only such as nature kindly allows to most of us, in order to comfort us in our regrets and infirmities. And the more we could look even into these, the less we should find in them for self-complacency, apart from considerations that respect the whole human race.

There is a phrase, for instance, of " fetching a man's mind from his cradle." But does the mind begin at that point of time ? Does it begin even with his parents ? I was looking once, in company with Mr. Hazlitt, at an exhibition of pictures in the British Institution, when casting my eyes on the portrait of an officer in the dress of the time of Charles the Second, I exclaimed, " What a likeness to B. M. !" (a friend of ours). It turned out to be his ancestor, Lord Sandwich. Mr. Hazlitt took me across the room, and showed me the portrait of a celebrated judge, who lived at the same period. "This," said he, "is Judge So-and-so ; and his living representative (he is now dead) has the same face and the same passions.". The Hazlitt then of the same age might have been the same Hazlitt that was standing with me before the picture ; and such may have been the case with the writer of these pages. There is a famous historical bit of transmission called the " Austrian lip ;" and faces, which we consider peculiar to individuals, are said to be common in whole districts : such as the Boccacio' face in one part of Tuscany, and the Dante face in another. I myself have seen, in the Genoese territory, many a face like that of the Bonapartes ; and where a race has strong blood in it, or whatever may constitute the requisite vital tendency, it is probable that the family likeness might be found to prevail in the humblest as well as highest quarters. There are families, indeed, of yeomen, who are said to have flourished like old oaks, in one and the same spot, since the times of the Anglo-Saxons. I am descended, both by father's and mother's side, from adventurous people, who left England for the New World, and whose descendants have retained the spirit of adventure to this day. The chances are, that in some respects I am identical with some half-dozen, or perhaps twenty of these ; and that the mind of some cavalier of the days of the Stuarts, or some gentleman or yeoman, or "roving blade," of those of the Edwards and Henrys, perhaps the gallant merchant-man, " Henry Hunt" of the old ballad—mixed, alas ! with a sedentary difference, is now writing these lines, ignorant of his former earthly self and of his present ! I say earthly, for I speak it with no disparagement to the existence of an individual " soul"—a point in which I am a firm believer ; nor would it be difficult to reconcile one opinion with the other in ears accustomed to such arguments; but I must not enter upon them here.

The name of Hunt is found among the gentry, but I suspeet it is oftener a plebeian name ; and though my immediate progenitors were clergymen, and Bryan Edwards's History of the West Indies contains a map of Barbados (their native place) with one of the residences designated by it—apparently a minor estate—yet it does not appear either in the old map in the History of Barbados by Ligon, or in the lists of influential or other persons in that by Sir Robert Schomburgck. There is a " Richard Hunt, Esq.," in the list of subscribers to Hughes's Natural History of Barbados, which contains also the name of Dr. Hunt, who was Hebrew and Arabic professor at Oxford, and whose genealogy the biographer can not discover. Perhaps the good old oriental scholar belongs to our stock, and originated my love of the Arabian Nights ! The tradition in the family is that we descend from Tory cavaliers (a wide designation), who fled to the West Indies from the ascendency of Cromwell ; and on the female side, amidst a curious mixture of quakers and soldiers, we derive ourselves not only from gentry, but from kings—that is to say, *Irish* kings !—personages (not to say it disrespectfully to the wit and misfortunes of the sister-island) who rank pretty much on a par with the negro chief, surrounded by half a dozen lords in ragged shirts, who asked the traveler what his brother kings thought of him in Europe. I take our main stock to have been mercantile.

I have begun my book with my progenitors and with childhood, partly because " order gives all things view," partly because, whatever we may assume as we grow up respecting the " dignity of manhood," we all feel that childhood was a period of great importance to us. Most men recur to it with delight. They are in general very willing to

dilate upon it, especially if they meet with an old schoolfellow; and therefore, on a principle of reciprocity, and as I
have long considered myself a kind of playmate and fellow-
disciple with persons of all times of life (for none of us,
unless we are very silly or naughty boys indeed, ever leave
off learning in some school or other), I shall suppose I have
been listening to some other young gentleman of sixty or .
seventy years of age over his wine, and that I am now going
to relate about half as much respecting my existence, as he
has told us of his own.

My grandfather, himself the son, I believe of a clergyman, was Rector of St. Michael's in Bridge-town, Barbados.
He was a good-natured man, and recommended the famous
Lauder to the mastership of the free-school there; influ-
enced, no doubt, partly by his pretended repentance, and
partly by sympathy with his Toryism. Lauder is said to
have been discharged for misconduct. I never heard that;
but I have heard that his appearance was decent, and that
he had a wood enleg : which is an anti-climax befitting
his history. My grandfather was admired and beloved by all
his parishioners for the manner in which he discharged his
duties. He died at an early age, in consequence of a fever
taken in the hot and damp air, while officiating incessantly
at burials during a mortality. His wife, who was an O'Brien,
or rather Bryan, very proud of her descent from the kings
aforesaid (or of the kings from *her*), was as good-natured and
beloved as her husband, and very asssiduous in her attentions to the negroes and to the poor, for whom she kept
a set of medicines, like my Lady Bountiful. They had
two children besides my father; Anna Courthope, who died
unmarried; and Elizabeth, wife of Thomas Dayrell, Esq.,
of Barbados, father by a first marriage of the late barrister
of that name. I mention both of these ladies, because they
will come among my portraits.

To these their children, the worthy rector and his wife
were a little too indulgent. When my father was to go to
the American Continent to school, the latter dressed up her
boy in a fine suit of laced clothes, such as we see on the little gentlemen in Hogarth : but so splendid and costly, that

when the good pastor beheld him, he was moved to utter an expostulation. Objection, however, soon gave way before the pride of all parties; and my father set off for school, ready spoilt, with plenty of money to spoil him more.

He went to college at Philadelphia, and became the scapegrace who smuggled in the wine, and bore the brunt of the tutors. My father took the degree of Master of Arts, both at Philadelphia and New York. When he spoke the farewell oration on leaving college, two young ladies fell in love with him, one of whom he afterward married. He was fair and handsome, with delicate features, a small aquiline nose, and blue eyes. To a graceful address he joined a remarkably fine voice, which he modulated with great effect. It was in reading, with this voice, the poets and other classics of England, that he completed the conquest of my mother's heart. He used to spend his evenings in this manner with her and her family—a noble way of courtship; and my grandmother became so hearty in his cause, that she succeeded in carrying it against her husband, who wished his daughter to marry a wealthy neighbor.

My father was intended, I believe, to carry on the race of clergymen, as he afterward did; but he went, in the first instance, into the law. The Americans united the practice of attorney and barrister. My father studied the law under articles to one of the chief persons in the profession; and afterward practiced with distinction himself. At this period (by which time all my brothers, now living, were born) the Revolution broke out; and he entered with so much zeal into the cause of the British Government, that, besides pleading for the loyalists with great fervor at the bar, he wrote pamphlets equally full of party warmth, which drew on him the popular odium. His fortunes then came to a crisis in America. Early one morning, a great concourse of people appeared before his house. He came out—or was brought. They put him into a cart prepared for the purpose (conceive the anxiety of his wife!), and, after parading him about the streets, were joined by a party of the revolutionary soldiers with drum and fife. The multitude then went with him to the house of Dr. Kearsley, a

stanch Tory who shut up the windows, and endeavored
to prevent their getting in.   The doctor had his hand
pierced by a bayonet, as it entered between the shutters
behind which he had planted himself.   He was dragged out
and put into the cart, all over blood; but he lost none of
his intrepidity; for he answered their reproaches and out-
rage with vehement reprehensions; and, by way of retaliation on the "Rogue's March," struck up "God save the
King."   My father gave way as little as the doctor.   He
would say nothing that was dictated to him, nor renounce a
single opinion; but, on the other hand, he maintained a
tranquil air, and endeavored to persuade his companion not
to add to their irritation.   This was to no purpose.   Dr.
Kearsley continued infuriate, and more than once fainted
from loss of blood and the violence of his feelings.   The
two loyalists narrowly escaped tarring and feathering.   A
tub of tar, which had been set in a conspicuous place in one
of the streets for that purpose, was overturned by an officer
intimate with our family.   My father, however, did not
escape entirely from personal injury.   One of the stones
thrown by the mob gave him such a severe blow on the
head, as not only laid him swooning in the cart, but
dimmed his sight for life, so as to oblige him from that time
to wear spectacles.   At length, after being carried through
every street in Philadelphia, the two captives were deposited,
in the evening, in a prison in Market-street.   What became
of Dr. Kearsley, I can not say.   My father, by means of a
large sum of money given to the sentinel who had charge of
him, was enabled to escape at midnight.   He went immediately on board a ship in the Delaware, that belonged to
my grandfather, and was bound for the West Indies.   She
dropped down the river that same night; and my father
went first to Barbados, and afterward to England where he
settled.

My mother was to follow my father as soon as possible,
which she was not able to do for many months.   The last
time she had seen him, he was a lawyer and a partisan,
going out to meet an irritated populace.   On her arrival in
England, she beheld him in a pulpit, a clergyman, preach-

ing tranquillity. When my father came over, he found it impossible to continue his profession as a lawyer. Some actors, who heard him read, advised him to go on the stage; but he was too proud for that, and went into the church. He was ordained by the celebrated Lowth, then bishop of London; and he soon became so popular that the bishop sent for him, and remonstrated against his preaching so many charity sermons. He said it was ostentatious in a clergyman, and that he saw his name in too many advertisements. My father thought it strange, but acquiesced. It is true, he preached a great many of these sermons. I am told, that for a whole year he did nothing else : and perhaps there was something in his manner a little startling to the simplicity of the Church of England. I remember, when he came to that part of the Litany where the reader prays for his deliverance "in the hour of death and at the day of judgment," he used to make a pause at the word "death," and drop his voice on the rest of the sentence. The effect was striking; but repetition must have hurt it. I am afraid it was a little theatrical. His delivery, however, was so much admired by those who thought themselves the best judges, that Thomas Sheridan, father of the late Sheridan, came up to him one day after service, in the vestry, and complimented him on having profited so well from his Treatise on Reading the Liturgy. My father was obliged to tell him that he had never seen it.

I do not know whether it was Lowth, but it was some bishop, to whom my father one day, in the midst of a warm discussion, being asked "if he knew who he was?" replied, with a bow, "Yes, my lord; dust and ashes." Doubtless the clergyman was warm and imprudent. In truth, he made a great mistake when he entered the profession. By the nature of the tenure, it was irretrievable; and his whole life after was a series of errors, arising from the unsuitability of his position. He was fond of divinity; but it was as a speculator, and not as a dogmatist, or one who takes upon trust. He was ardent in the cause of Church and State; but here he speculated too, and soon began to modify his opinions, which got him the ill-will of the Government.

He delighted his audiences in the pulpit; so much so, that he had crowds of carriages at the door.   One of his congregations had an engraving made of him; and a lady of the name of Cooling, who was member of another, left him by will the sum of £500, as a testimony of the pleasure and advantage she had derived from his discourses.

But unfortunately, after delighting his hearers in the pulpit, he would delight some of them a little too much over the table.   He was extremely lively and agreeable; was full of generous sentiments; could flatter without grossness: had stories to tell of lords whom he knew; and when the bottle was to circulate, it did not stand with him.   All this was dangerous to a West Indian who had an increasing family, and was to make his way in the church.   It was too much for him; and he added another to the list of those who, though they might suffice equally for themselves and others in a more considerate and contented state of society, and seem born to be the delights of it, are only lost and thrown out in a system of things, which, by going upon the ground of individual aggrandizement, compels dispositions of a more sociable and reasonable nature either to become parties concerned, or be ruined in the refusal.   It is doubtless incumbent on a husband and father to be careful under all circumstances: and it is very easy for most people to talk of the necessity of being so, and to recommend it to others, especially when they have been educated to that habit.   Let those fling the first stone, who, with real inclination and talent for other things (for the inclination may not be what they take it for), confine themselves industriously to the duties prescribed them.   There are more victims to errors committed by society themselves, than society suppose.

But I grant that a man is either bound to tell them so, or to do as they do.   My father was always, theoretically speaking, both for the good of the world, and for that of his family (I remember a printed proposal which he drew up for an academy, to be entitled the " Cosmopolitical Seminary"), but he had neither uneasiness enough in his blood, nor, perhaps, sufficient strength in his convictions, to bring his speculations to bear; and as to the pride of cutting a figure above his neighbors, which so many men mistake for a better principal of action, he could dispense with that. As it was, he should have been kept at home in Barbados. He was a true exotic, and ought not to have been translated. He might have preached there, and quoted Horace, and been gentlemanly and generous, and drunk his claret, and no harm done. But in a bustling, commercial state of society, where the enjoyment, such as it is, consists in the bustle, he was neither very likely to succeed, nor to meet with a good construction, nor to end his pleasant ways with pleasing either the world or himself.

It was in the pulpit of Bentinck Chapel, Lissen Green, Paddington, that my mother found her husband officiating. He published a volume of sermons preached there, in which there is little but elegance of diction and a graceful morality. His delivery was the charm; and, to say the truth, he charmed every body but the owner of the chapel, who looked upon rent as by far the most eloquent production of the pulpit. The speculation ended with the preacher being horribly in debt. Friends, however, were lavish of their assistance. Three of my brothers were sent to school; the other, at her earnest entreaty, went to live (which he did for some years) with Mrs. Spencer, a sister (I think) of Sir Richard Worsley, and a delicious little old woman, the delight of all the children of her acquaintance. My father and mother took breath, in the mean time, under the friendly roof of Mr. West the painter, who had married her aunt. The aunt and niece were much of an age, and both fond of books. Mrs. West, indeed, ultimately became a martyr to them; for the physician declared that she lost the use of her limbs by sitting in-doors.

From Newman-street my father went to live in Hampstead-square, whence he occasionally used to go and preach at Southgate. The then Duke of Chandos had a seat in the neighborhood of Southgate. He heard my father preach, and was so pleased with him that he requested him to become tutor to his nephew, Mr. Leigh, which my father did, and remained with his Grace's family for several years.

The duke was Master of the Horse, and originated the famous epithet of "heaven born minister," applied to Mr. Pitt, which occasioned a good deal of raillery. I have heard my father describe him as a man of great sweetness of nature and good-breeding. He was the grandson of Pope and Swift's Duke of Chandos. He died in 1789, and left a widow, who survived him for several years in a state of mental alienation. I mention this circumstance, because I think I have heard it said in our family, that her derangement was owing to a piece of thoughtlessness, the notice of which may serve as a caution. She was a woman of great animal spirits; and happening to thrust aside the duke's chair, when he was going to sit down, the consequences were such that, being extremely attached to him, she could never forgive herself, but lost her husband and senses at once. The duchess had already been married to a gentleman of the name of Elletson. She was daughter of Sir Richard Gamon, and mother of an heiress, who carried the title of Chandos into the Grenville family.

To be tutor in a ducal family is one of the roads to a bishopric. My father was thought to be in the highest way to it. He was tutor in the house, not only of a duke, but of a state-officer, for whom the king had a personal regard. His manners were of the highest order; his principles in Church and State as orthodox, to all appearance, as could be wished; and he had given up flourishing prospects in America, for their sake; but his West Indian temperament spoiled all. He also, as he became acquainted with the Government, began to doubt its perfections; and the king, whose minuteness of information respecting the personal affairs of his subjects is well known, was most likely prepared with questions, which the duke was not equally prepared to answer.

My father, meanwhile, was getting more and more distressed. He removed to Hampstead a second time: from Hampstead he crossed the water; and the first room I have any recollection of is a prison.

Mr. West (which was doubly kind in a man by nature cautious and timid) again and again took the liberty of representing my father's circumstances to the king. It is well known that this artist enjoyed the confidence of his majesty in no ordinary degree. The king would converse half a day at a time with him, while he was painting. His majesty said he would speak to the bishops ; and again, on a second application, he said my father should be provided for. My father himself also presented a petition ; but all that was ever done for him, was the putting his name on the Loyalist Pension List for a hundred a year ; a sum which he not only thought extremely inadequate for the loss of seven or eight times as much in America, a cheaper country, but which he felt to be a poor acknowledgment even for the act-ive zeal he had evinced, and the things he had said and written ; especially as it came late, and he was already in-volved. Small as it was, he was obliged to mortgage it ; and from this time till the arrival of some relations from the West Indies, several years afterward, he underwent a series of mortifications and distresses, not without reason for self-reproach. Unfortunately for others, it might be said of him, what Lady Mary Wortley said of her kinsman, Henry Fielding, " that give him his leg of mutton and bottle of wine, and in the very thick of calamity he would be happy for the time being." Too well able to seize a passing mo-ment of enjoyment, he was always scheming, never perform-ing : always looking forward with some romantic plan which was sure to succeed, and never put in practice. I believe he wrote more titles of non-existing books than Rabelais. At length he found his mistake. My poor father ! He grew deeply acquainted with prisons, and began to lose his graces and his good name, and became irritable with conscious error, and almost took hope out of the heart that loved him, and was too often glad to escape out of its society. Yet such an art had he of making his home comfortable when he chose, and of settling himself to the most tranquil pleas-ures, that if she could have ceased to look forward about her children, I believe, with all his faults, those evenings would have brought unmingled satisfaction to her, when, after settling the little apartment, brightening the fire, and bring-ing out the coffee, my mother knew that her husband was going to read Saurin or Barrow to her, with his fine voice, and unequivocal enjoyment.

We thus struggled on between quiet and disturbance, between placid readings and frightful knocks at the door, and sickness, and calamity, and hopes, which hardly ever forsook us. One of my brothers went to sea—a great blow to my poor mother. The next was articled to an attorney. My brother Robert became pupil to an engraver, and my brother John apprentice to Mr. Reynell, the printer, whose kindly manners, and deep iron voice, I well remember and respect. I had also a regard for the speaking trumpet, which ran all the way up his tall house, and conveyed his rugged whispers to his men. And his goodly wife, proud of her husband's grandfather, the bishop; never shall I forget how much I loved her for her portly smiles and good dinners, and how often she used to make me measure heights with her fair daughter Caroline, and found me wanting; which I thought not quite so hospitable.

As my father's misfortunes, in the first instance, were owing to feelings the most respected, so the causes of them subsequently (and the reader will be good enough to keep this in mind) were not unmixed with feelings of the kindest nature. He hampered himself greatly with becoming security for other people; and, though unable to settle himself to any regular work, his pen was always at the service of those who required it for memorials or other helps. As to his children, he was healthy and sanguine, and always looked forward to being able to do something for them: and something for them he did, if it was only in grafting his animal spirits on the maternal stock, and setting them an example of independent thinking. But he did more. He really took care, considering his unbusiness-like habits, toward settling them in some line of life. It is our faults, not his, if we have not been all so successful as we might have been: at least it is no more his fault than that of the West Indian blood of which we all partake, and which has disposed all of us, more or less, to a certain aversion from business. And if it may be some vanity in us, at least it is no dishonor to our turn of mind, to hope, that we may have been the means of circulating more knowledge and entertainment in society, than if he had attained the bishopric he looked for, and left us ticketed and labeled among the acquiescent.

Toward the latter part of his life, my father's affairs were greatly retrieved by the help of his sister, Mrs. Dayrell, who came over with a property from Barbados. My aunt was generous; part of her property came among us also by a marriage; and my father's West Indian sun was again warm upon him. On his sister's death, to be sure, his struggles recommenced, though nothing in comparison to what they had been. Recommence, however, they did; and yet so sanguine was he in his intentions to the last, and so accustomed had my mother been to try to believe in him, and to persuade herself she did, that not long before she died he made the most solemn promises of amendment, which by chance I could not help overhearing, and which she received with a tenderness and a tone of joy, the remembrance of which brings the tears into my eyes. My father had one taste well suited to his profession, and in him, I used to think, remarkable. He was very fond of sermons; which he was rarely tired of reading, or my mother of hearing. I have mentioned the effect which these used to have upon her. When she died, he could not bear to think she was dead; yet retaining, in the midst of his tears, his indestructible tendency to seize on a cheering reflection, he turned his very despair into consolation; and in saying " She is not dead, but sleeps," I verily believe the image became almost a literal thing with him. Besides his fondness for sermons, he was a great reader of the Bible. His copy of it is scored with manuscript; and I believe he read a portion of it every morning to the last, let him have been as right or as wrong as he pleased for the rest of the day. This was not hypocrisy; it was habit, and real fondness: though, while was no hypocrite, he was not, I must confess, remarkable for being explicit about himself; nor did he cease to dogmatize in a sort of official manner upon faith and virtue, lenient as he thought himself bound to be to particular instances of frailty. To young people, who had no secrets from him, he was especially indulgent, as I have good reason to know. He delighted to show his sense of a candor in others, which I believe he would have practiced himself, had he been taught it early. For many years before his death, he had greatly relaxed in the orthodoxy of his religious opinions. Both he and my mother had become Unitarians. They were also Universalists, and great admirers of Mr. Winchester, particularly my mother.* My father was willing, however, to hear all sides of the question, and used to visit the chapels of the most popular preachers of all denominations. His favorite among them, I think, was Mr. Worthington, who preached at a chapel in Long Acre, and had a strong natural eloquence. Politics and divinity occupied almost all the conversation that I heard at our fire-side. It is a pity my father had been so spoilt a child, and had strayed so much out of his sphere ; for he could be contented with little. He was one of the last of the gentry who retained the old fashion of smoking. He indulged in it every night before he went to bed, which he did at an early hour ; and it was pleasant to see him sit, in his tranquil and gentlemanly manner, and relate anecdotes of " my Lord North" and the Rockingham administration, interspersed with those mild puffs and urbane resumptions of the pipe. How often have I thought of him under this aspect, and longed for the state of society that might have encouraged him to be more successful ! Had he lived twenty years longer he would have thought it was coming. He died in the year 1809, aged fifty-seven, and was buried in the churchyard in Bishopsgate-street. I remember they quarreled over his coffin for the perquisites of the candles ; which put me upon a great many reflections, both on him and on the world.

My grandfather, by my mother's side, was Stephen Shewell, merchant of Philadelphia, who sent out his " argosies." His mother was a Quaker, and he, himself, I

---

* " The Universalists can not, properly speaking, be called a distinct sect, as they are frequently found scattered among various denominations. They are so named from holding the benevolent opinion, that all mankind, nay, even the demons themselves, will be finally restored to happiness, through the mercy of Almighty God."—*History of all Religions and Religious Ceremonies*, page 263. What an impiety toward " Almighty God," that any body could ever have thought the reverse !

believe, descended from a Quaker stock.   He had ships
trading to England, Holland, and the West Indies, and used
to put his sons and nephews in them as captains, probably
to save charges ; for, in every thing but stocking his cellars
with provision, he was penurious.   For sausages and " botargoes" (first authors, perhaps, of the jaundice in our blood),
Friar John would have commended him.   As Chaucer says,

> " It snewèd, in his house, of meat and drink."

On that side of the family we seem all sailors and rough
subjects, with a mitigation (on the female part) of Quaker-
ism ; as, on the father's side, we are creoles and claret-
drinkers, very polite and clerical.

My grandmother's maiden name was Bickley.   I believe
her family came from Buckinghamshire.   The coat of arms
are three half moons ; which I happen to recollect, because
of a tradition we had, that an honorable augmentation was
made to them of three wheat-sheaves, in reward of some
gallant achievement performed in cutting off a convoy of pro-
visions by Sir William Bickley, a partisan of the House of
Orange, who was made a banneret.   My grandmother was
an open-hearted, cheerful woman, of a good healthy blood,
and as generous as her husband was otherwise.   The family
consisted of five daughters and two sons.   One of the
daughters died unmarried ; the three surviving ones were
lately wives and mothers in Philadelphia.   They and their
husbands, agreeably to the American law of equal division,
were in the receipt of a pretty property in lands and houses ;
our due share of which, some inadvertence on our parts
appears to have forfeited.   I confess I have often wished, at
the close of a day's work, that people were not so excessively
delicate on legal points, and so afraid of hurting the feelings
of others, by supposing it possible for them to want a little
of their grandfather's money.   But I believe I ought to blush
while I say this ; and I do.   One of my uncles died in England, a mild, excellent creature, more fit for solitude than
the sea.   The other, my uncle Stephen, a fine handsome
fellow of great good nature and gallantry, was never heard
of, after leaving the port of Philadelphia for the West Indies

He had a practice of crowding too much sail, which is supposed to have been his destruction. They said he did it " to get back to his ladies." My uncle was the means of saving his namesake, my brother Stephen, from a singular destiny. Some Indians, who came into the city to traffic, had been observed to notice my brother a good deal. It is supposed they saw in his tall little person, dark face, and long black hair, a resemblance to themselves. ' One day they enticed him from my grandfather's house in Front-street, and taking him to the Delaware, which was close by, were carrying him off across the river, when his uncle descried them and gave the alarm. His threats induced them to come back ; otherwise, it is thought, they intended to carry him into their own quarters, and bring him up as an Indian ; so that, instead of a rare character of another sort—an attorney who would rather compound a quarrel for his clients than get rich by it —we might have had for a brother the Great Buffalo, Bloody Bear, or some such grim personage. I will indulge myself with the liberty of observing in this place, that with great diversity of character among us, with strong points of dispute even among ourselves, and with the usual amount, though not perhaps exactly the like nature, of infirmities common to other people—some of us, may be, with greater, —we have all been persons who inherited the power of making sacrifices for the sake of a principle.

My grandfather, though intimate with Dr. Franklin, was secretly on the British side of the question when the American war broke out. He professed to be neutral, and to attend only to business ; but his neutrality did not avail him. One of his most valuably laden ships was burnt in the Delaware by the Revolutionists, to prevent its getting into the hands of the British ; and besides making free with his botargoes, they dispatched every now and then a file of soldiers to rifle his house of every thing else that could be serviceable : linen, blankets, &c. And this, unfortunately, was only a taste of what he was to suffer ; for, emptying his mercantile stores from time to time, they paid him with their continential currency, paper-money ; the depreciation of which was so great as to leave him, at the close of the war, bankrupt of every thing but some houses, which his wife brought him; they amounted to a sufficiency for the family support : and thus, after all his cunning neutralities, and his preference of individual to public good, he owed all that he retained to a generous and unspeculating woman. His saving grace, however, was not on every possible occasion confined to his money. He gave a very strong instance (for him) of his partiality to the British cause, by secreting in his house a gentleman of the name of Slater, who commanded a small armed vessel on the Delaware, and who was not long since residing in London. Mr. Slater had been taken prisoner, and confined at some miles' distance from Philadelphia. He contrived to make his escape, and astonished my grandfather's family by appearing before them at night, drenched in the rain, which descends in torrents in that climate. They secreted him for several months in a room at the top of the house.

My mother at that time, was a brunette with fine eyes, a tall, lady-like person, and hair blacker than is seen of English growth. It was supposed that Anglo-Americans already began to exhibit the influence of climate in their appearance. The late Mr. West told me, that if he had met myself or any of my brothers in the streets, he should have pronounced, without knowing us, that we were Americans. A likeness has been discovered between us and some of the Indians in his pictures. My mother had no accomplishments but the two best of all, a love of nature and of books. Dr. Franklin offered to teach her the guitar; but she was too bashful to become his pupil. She regretted this afterward, partly no doubt for having missed so illustrious a master. Her first child, who died, was named after him. I know not whether the anecdote is new; but I have heard that when Dr. Franklin invented the Harmonica, he concealed it from his wife till the instrument was fit to play; and then woke her with it one night, when she took it for the music of angels. Among the visitors at my grandfather's house, besides Franklin, was Thomas Paine; whom I have heard my mother speak of, as having a countenance that inspired her with terror. I believe his aspect was not

captivating ; but most likely his political and religious opinions did it no good in the eyes of the fair loyalist.

My mother was diffident of her personal merit, but she
had great energy of principle. When the troubles broke out,
and my father took that violent part in favor of the king, a
letter was received by her from a person high in authority,
stating, that if her husband would desist from opposition to
the general wishes of the colonists, he should remain in security ; but that if he thought fit to do otherwise, he must
suffer the consequences which inevitably awaited him. The
letter concluded with advising her, as she valued her husband's and family's happiness, to use her influence with him
to act accordingly. To this, "in the spirit of old Rome and
Greece," as one of her sons has proudly and justly observed (I
will add, of Old England, and, though contrary to our royalist
opinions, of New America too), my mother replied, that she
knew her husband's mind too well to suppose for a moment
that he would so degrade himself; and that the writer of
the letter entirely mistook her, if he thought her capable of
endeavoring to persuade him to an action contrary to the convictions of his heart, whatever the consequences threatened
might be. Yet the heart of this excellent woman, strong as
it was, was already beating with anxiety for what might
occur ; and on the day when my father was seized, she fell
into a fit of the jaundice, so violent as to affect her ever afterward, and subject a previously fine constitution to every ill
that came across it.

It was nearly two years before my mother could set off
with her children for England. She embarked in the
Earl of Effingham frigate, Captain Dempster, who, from
the moment she was drawn up the sides of the vessel with
her little boys, conceived a pity and respect for her, and paid
her the most cordial attention. In truth, he felt more pity
for her than he chose to express ; for the vessel was old and
battered, and he thought the voyage not without danger.
Nor was it. They did very well till they came off the
Scilly Islands, when a storm arose which threatened to sink
them. The ship was with difficulty kept above water.
Here my mother again showed how courageous her heart

could be by the very strength of its tenderness. There was a lady in the vessel who had betrayed weaknesses of various sorts during the voyage; and who even went so far as to resent the superior opinion which the gallant captain could not help entertaining of her fellow-passenger. My mother, instead of giving way to tears and lamentations, did all she could to keep up the spirits of her children. The lady in question did the reverse; and my mother, feeling the necessity of the case, and touched with pity for children in the same danger as her own, was at length moved to break through the delicacy she had observed, and expostulate strongly with her, to the increased admiration of the captain, who congratulated himself on having a female passenger so truly worthy of the name of woman. Many years afterward, near the same spot, and during a similar danger, her son the writer of this book, with a wife and seven children around him, had occasion to call her to mind; and the example was of service even to him, a man. It was thought a miracle that the *Earl of Effingham* was saved. It was driven into Swansea Bay, and borne along by the heaving might of the waves into a shallow, where no vessel of so large a size ever appeared before; nor could it ever have got there, but by so unwonted an overlifting.

Having been born nine years later than the youngest of my brothers, I have no recollection of my mother's earlier aspect. Her eyes were always fine, and her person ladylike; her hair also retained its color for a long period; but her brown complexion had been exchanged for a jaundiced one, which she retained through life; and her cheeks were sunken, and her mouth drawn down with sorrow at the corners. She retained the energy of her character on great occasions; but her spirit in ordinary was weakened, and she looked at the bustle and discord of the present state of society with a frightened aversion. My father's danger, and the war-whoops of the Indians which she heard in Philadelphia, had shaken her soul as well as frame. The sight of two men fighting in the steets would drive her in tears down another road; and I remember, when we lived near the park, she would take me a long circuit out of the way rather than

hazard the spectacle of the soldiers.   Little did she think of
the timidity with which she was thus inoculating me, and
what difficulty I should have, when I went to school, to sus-
tain all those fine theories, and that unbending resistance to
oppression, which she inculcated.   However, perhaps, it
ultimately turned out for the best.   One must feel more than
usual for the sore places of humanity, even to fight properly
in their behalf.   Never shall I forget her face, as it used to
appear to me coming up the cloisters, with that weary hang
of the head on one side, and that melancholy smile!

One holiday, in a severe winter, as she was taking me home,
she was petitioned for charity by a woman sick and ill-cloth-
ed.   It was in Blackfriars' Road, I think about midway.
My mother, with the tears in her eyes, turned up a gateway, or
some such place, and beckoning the woman to follow, took
off her flannel petticoat and gave it her.   It is supposed that
a cold which ensued, fixed the rheumatism upon her for life.
Actions like these have doubtless been often performed, and
do not of necessity imply any great virtue in the performer:
but they do if they are of a piece with the rest of the character.   Saints have been made for charities no greater.

The reader will allow me to quote a passage out of a poem
of mine, because it was suggested by a recollection I had
upon me of this excellent woman.   It is almost the only
passage in that poem worth repeating ; which I mention, in
order that he may lay the quotation to its right account,
and not suppose I am anxious to repeat my verses because
I fancy they must be good.   In every thing but the word
"happy," the picture is from life.   The bird spoken of is
the nightingale : the

> " Bird of wakeful glow,
> Whose louder song is like the voice of life,
> Triumphant o'er death's image ; but whose deep,
> Low, lovelier note is like a gentle wife,
> A poor, a pensive, yet a happy one,
> Stealing when daylight's common tasks are done,
> An hour for mother's work ; and singing low,
> While her tired husband and her children sleep."

I have spoken of my mother during my father's troubles

in England. She stood by him through them all; and in every thing did more honor to marriage, than marriage did good to either of them : for it brought little happiness to her, and too many children to both. Of his changes of opinion, as well as of fortune, she partook also. She became a Unitarian, a Universalist, perhaps a Republican ; and in her new opinions, as in her old, was apt, I suspect, to be a little too peremptory, and to wonder at those who could be of the other side. It was her only fault. She would have mended it, had she lived till now. Though not a republican myself, I have been thought, in my time, to speak too severely of kings and princes. I think I did, and that society is no longer to be bettered in that manner, but in a much calmer and nobler way. But I was a witness, in my childhood, to a great deal of suffering ; I heard of more all over the world ; and kings and princes bore a great share in the causes to which they were traced. Some of those causes were not to be denied.

It is now understood, on all hands, that the continuation of the American war was owing to the personal stubbornness of the king. My mother, in her indignation at him, for being the cause of so much unnecessary bloodshed, thought that the unfortunate malady into which he fell was a judgment of Providence. The truth is, it was owing to mal-organization, and to the diseases of his father and mother. A healthy consort restored reason to the family ; and the politics of Queen Victoria have been as remarkable for good sense, as those of her grandfather were too frequently otherwise.

My mother's intolerance, after all, was only in theory. When any thing was to be done, charity in her always ran before faith. If she could have served and benefited the king himself personally, indignation would soon have given way to humanity. She had a high opinion of every thing that was decorous and feminine on the part of a wife ; yet when a poor, violent woman, the wife of an amiable and eloquent preacher, went so far on one occasion as to bite his hand in a fit of jealous rage as he was going to ascend his pulpit (and he preached with it in great pain), she was the only female of her acquaintance that continued to visit her ; al-

leging that she wanted society and comfort so much the more.
She had the highest notions of chastity; yet when a servant
came to her, who could get no place because she had had
an illegitimate child, my mother took her into her family,
upon the strength of her candor and her destitute condition,
and was served with an affectionate gratitude.

My mother's favorite books were Dr. Young's *Night
Thoughts* (which was a pity), and Mrs. Rowe's *Devout
Exercises of the Heart.* I remember also her expressing
great admiration of the novels of Mrs. Inchbald, especially
the *Simple Story.* She was very fond of poetry, and used
to hoard my verses in her pocket-book, and encourage me to
write, by showing them to the Wests and the Thorntons.
Her friends loved and honored her to the last : and, I believe,
they retained their regard for the family.

My mother's last illness was long, and was tormented with
rheumatism. I envy my brother Robert the recollection of
the filial attentions he paid her ; but they shall be as much
known as I can make them, not because he was my brother
(which is nothing), but because he was a good son, which is
much ; and every good son and mother will be my warrant.
My other brothers, who were married, were away with their
families ; and I, who ought to have attended more, was as
giddy as I was young, or rather a great deal more so. I attended, but not enough. How often have we occasion to
wish that we could be older or younger than we are, according as we desire to have the benefit of gayety or experience !
Her greatest pleasure during her decay was to lie on a sofa,
looking at the setting sun. She used to liken it to the door of
heaven ; and fancy her lost children there, waiting for her. She
died in the fifty-third year of her age, in a little miniature
house which stands in a row behind the church that has
been since built in Somers Town ; and she was buried, as
the had always wished to be, in the church-yard of Hampstead.

CHAPTER II.

I HAVE spoken of the Duke of Chandos, to whose nephew,
Mr. Leigh, my father became tutor. Mr. Leigh, who gave
me his name, was son of the duke's sister, Lady Caroline,
and died a member of Parliament for Addlestrope. He was
one of the kindest and gentlest of men, addicted to those
tastes for poetry and sequestered pleasure, which have been
conspicuous in his son, Lord Leigh ; for all which reasons it
would seem, and contrary to the usurping qualities in such
cases made and provided, he and his family were subjected
the other day to one of the most extraordinary charges that
a defeated claim ever brought drunken witnesses to set up ;
no less than the murder and burial of a set of masons, who
were employed in building a bridge, and whose destruction
in the act of so doing was to bury both them and a menument which they knew of, for ever ! To complete the romance of the tragedy, a lady, the wife of the usurper, presides over the catastrophe. She cries, " Let go," while the
poor wretches are raising a stone at night-time, amidst a
scene of torches and seclusion ; and down goes the stone aided by this tremendous father and son, and crushes the victims of her ambition ! She meant, as Cowley says Goliah
did of David,

> " At once their murder and their monument."

If a charge of the most awful crimes could be dug up

against the memories of such men as Thomson and Shen-stone, or of Cowley, or Cowper, or the " Man of Ross," it could not have created more laughing astonishment in the minds of those who knew them, than such a charge against the family of the Leighs.   Its present representative in the notes to his volume of poems, printed some years ago, quotes the " following beautiful passage" out of Fielding :

" It was the middle of May, and the morning was re-markably serene, when Mr. Allworthy walked forth on the terrace, where the dawn opened every minute that lovely prospect we have before described, to his eye.   And now having sent forth streams of light which ascended to the firmament before him, as harbingers preceding his pomp, in the full blaze of his majesty up rose the sun ; than which one object alone in this lower creation could be more glorious, and that Mr. Allworthy himself presented : a human being replete with benevolence, meditating in what manner he might render himself most acceptable to his Creator by doing most good to his creatures."

" This," adds the quoter, " is the portrait of a fictitious personage ; but I see in it a close resemblance to one whose memory I shall never cease to venerate."

The allusion is to his father, Mr. Leigh.

But I must not anticipate the verdict of a court of justice,* Indeed, I should have begged pardon of my noble friend for speaking of this preposterous accusation, did not the very ex-cess of it force the words from my pen, and were I not sure that my own father would have expected them from me, had he been alive to hear it.   His lordship must accept them as an effusion of grateful sympathy from one father and son to another.

Lord Leigh has written many a tender and thoughtful verse, in which, next to the domestic affections and the pro-gress of human kind, he shows that he loves above all things the beauties of external nature, and the tranquil pleasures they suggest.

---

* The verdict has since been given.   It almost seemed ridiculous, it was so unnecessary ; except, indeed, as a caution to the like of those whom it punished.

So much do I agree with him, that it is a pleasure to me to know that I was even born in so sweet a village as South-gate. I first saw the light there on the 19th of October 1784. It found me cradled, not only in the lap of the nature which I love, but in the midst of the truly English scenery which I love beyond all other. Middlesex in general, like my noble friend's county of Warwickshire, is a scene of trees and meadows, of "greenery" and nestling cottages; and Southgate is a prime specimen of Middlesex. It is a place lying out of the way of innovation, therefore it has the pure, sweet air of antiquity about it; and as I am fond of local researches in any quarter, it may be pardoned me if in this instance I would fain know even the meaning of its name. There is no Northgate, Eastgate, or Westgate in Middlesex: what, then, is Southgate? No topographer tells us; but an old map of the country twenty-five miles round London, drawn up some years previous to my childhood, is now before me; and on looking at the boundaries of Enfield Chase, I see that the "Chase-gate," the name most likely of the principal entrance, is on the north side of it, by North-Hall and Potter's Bar: while Southgate, which has also the name of "South-street," is on the Chase's opposite border; so that it seems evident, that Southgate meant the southern entrance into the Chase, and that the name became that of a village from the growth of a street. The street, in all probability, was the consequence of a fair held in a wood which ran on the western side of it, and which, in the map, is designated "Bush Fair." *Bush*, in old English, meant not only a hedge, but a wood; as *Bois* and *Bosco* do in French and Italian. Moses and the "burning bush" is Moses and the "burning wood;" which, by the way, presents a much grander idea than the modicum of hedge, commonly assigned to the celestial apparition. There is a good deal more wood in the map than is now to be found. I wander in imagination through the spots marked in the neighborhood, with their pleasant names—Woodside, Wood-green, Palmer-green Nightingale-hall, &c., and fancy my father and mother listening to the nightingales, and loving the new little baby, who has now lived to see more years than they did.

Southgate lies in a cross-country road, running from Edmonton through Enfield Chase into Hertfordshire. It is in the parish of Edmonton; so that we may fancy the *Merry Devil* of that place still playing his pranks hereabouts, and helping innocent lovers to a wedding, as in the sweet little play attributed to Drayton. For as to any such devils going to a place less harmonious, it is not to be thought possible by good Christians. Furthermore, to show what classical ground is round about Southgate, and how it is associated with the best days of English genius, both old and new, Edmonton is the birth-place of Marlowe, the father of our drama, and of my friend Horne, his congenial celebrator. In Edmonton church-yard lies Charles Lamb; in Highgate church-yard, Coleridge: and in Hampstead have resided Shelley and Keats, to say nothing of Akenside before them, and of Steele and Arbuthnot before Akenside.

But the neighborhood is dear to me on every account; for near Southgate is Colney Hatch, where my mother became acquainted with some of her dearest friends, whom I shall mention by-and-by. Near Colney Hatch is Finchley, where our family resided on quitting Southgate; and at no great distance from Finchley is Mill Hill, where lived excellent Dr. Trinder, who presented in his person the rare combination of clergyman and physician. He boasted that he had cured a little child (to-wit, myself) of a dropsy in the head. The fact was contested, I believe, by the lay part of the profession; but it was believed in the family, and their love of the good doctor was boundless. He deserved it for his amiable qualities, as I shall presently show.

I may call myself, in every sense of the word, etymological not excepted, a son of mirth and melancholy; for my father's Christian name (as old students of onomancy would have heard with serious faces) was Isaac, which is Hebrew for "laughter," and my mother's was Mary, which comes from a word in the same language signifying "bitterness." And, indeed, as I do not remember to have ever seen my mother smile, except in sorrowful tenderness, so my father's shouts of laughter are now ringing in my ears. Not at any expense to her gravity, for he loved her, and thought her an angel on earth ; but because his animal spirits were invincible. I inherit from my mother a tendency to jaundice, which at times has made me melancholy enough. I doubt, indeed, whether I have passed a day during half my life, without reflections, the first germs of which are traceable to sufferings which this tendency once cost me. My prevailing temperament, nevertheless, is my father's ; and it has not only enabled me to turn those reflections into sources of tranquillity and exaltation, but helped my love of my mother's memory to take a sort of pride in the infirmity which she bequeathed me. The energetic influence of this temperament must have been wonderful ; for in childhood I had all the diseases (so to speak) which the infant " spitals know." The first of them was the real or supposed dropsy in the head, for which the reverend physician was called in.

Let the reader indulge me with fancying that I discharge a filial duty in speaking of this gentleman, and in saying something of his efforts in the cause of humanity in general. I had the pleasure of picking up, the other day, at a bookstall, "Practical Sermons, preached at Hendon, in Middlesex, by W. M. Trinder, LL.B., and M.D., Rivingtons, 1786 ;" so that, supposing LL.B. (bachelor of laws) to mean any thing but a courtesy, the good doctor combined in his person not only the two, but the three professions. He was clergyman, physician and lawyer, at once. How this singular triplicity came to take place, I can not say. Probably his philanthropy induced him to study the law, as that of Shelley induced my friend to walk the hospitals, for the purpose of doing good among the poor. The doctor may, indeed, have studied medicine for the like reason ; for divinity appears to have been his profession paramount. I suspect that he was physician first, and clergyman afterward. Perhaps he must have been so ; for I am not aware that clergymen would be suffered to take medical degrees. It might be supposed that he was a dissenter ; but he was emphatically otherwise, very orthodox and loyal. Among the subscribers' names to his sermons, besides that of my father, who was a Church-of-England clergyman, are those

of several others, including the Hendon vicar ; and in the
list is Garrick, who was lord of the manor. The sermons
are not profound, but they are replete with feeling and good
sense ; and they mix up the physician with the divine to so
much purpose as to make a reader wish that the offices
could be more frequently combined. One of them, " On
Education," threatens the Divine displeasure against mothers
who do not suckle their children ; and it enters into medical
reasons why the failure to do so is injurious to both parties.
Another, " On Cruelty," does not hesitate to condemn the
" gentle craft " of anglers ; and it is particularly severe, and
probably did great good, on the subject of cock-throwing——a
brutality now extinguished ; for cocks scream, but fish
only gasp and are stifled ; so that the latter must probably
wait another century before the Trinders can procure them
justice.

Many brave and good men have been anglers, as well as
many men of a different description ; but their goodness
would have been complete, and their bravery of a more
generous sort, had they possessed self-denial enough to look
the argument in the face, and abstained from procuring themselves pleasure at the expense of a needless infliction. The
charge is not answered by the favorite retorts about effeminacy, God's providence, neighbors' faults, and doing " no
worse." They are simple beggings of the question. I am
not aware that anglers, or sportsmen in general, are braver
than the ordinary run of mankind. Sure I am that a great
fuss is made if they hurt their fingers ; much more if they
lie gasping, like fish, on the ground. I am equally sure
that many a man who would not hurt a fly is as brave as
they are ; and as to the reference to God's providence, it is
an edge-tool that might have been turned against themselves
by any body who chose to pitch them into the river, or knock
out their brains. They may lament, if they please, that
they should be forced to think of pain and evil at all; but
the lamentation would not be very magnanimous under any
circumstances ; and it is idle, considering that the manifest
ordination and progress of things demand that such thoughts
be encountered. The question still returns—Why do they

seek amusement in sufferings which are unnecessary and avoidable ? and till they honestly and thoroughly answer this question, they must be content to be looked upon as disingenuous reasoners, who are determined to retain a selfish pleasure.

As to old Izaak Walton, who is put forward as a substitute for argument on this question, and whose sole merits consisted in his having a taste for nature and his being a respectable citizen, the trumping him up into an authority and a kind of saint is a burlesque. He was a writer of conventionalities ; who having comfortably feathered his nest, as he thought, both in this world and in the world to come, concluded he had nothing more to do than to amuse himself by putting worms on a hook and fish into his stomach, and so go to heaven, chuckling and singing psalms. There would be something in such a man and in his book offensive to a real piety, if that piety did not regard whatever has happened in the world, great and small, with an eye that makes the best of what is perplexing, and trusts to eventual good out of the worst. Walton was not the hearty and thorough advocate of nature he is supposed to have been. There would have been something to say for him on that score, had he looked upon the sum of evil as a thing not to be diminished. But he shared the opinions of the most commonplace believers in sin and trouble, and only congratulated himself on being exempt from their consequences. The overweening old man found himself comfortably off somehow ; and it is good that he did. It is a comfort to all of us, wise or foolish. But to reverence him is a jest. You might as well make a god of an otter. Mr. Wordsworth, because of the servitor manners of Walton and his biographies of divines (all *anglers*), wrote an idle line about his " meekness" and his " heavenly memory." When this is quoted by the gentle brethren, it will be as well if they add to it another passage from the same poet, which returns to the only point at issue, and upsets the old gentleman altogether. Mr. Wordsworth's admonition to us is,

> " Never to link our pastime, or our pride,
> With suffering to the meanest thing that lives."

It was formerly thought effeminate not to hunt Jews;
then not to roast heretics ; then not to bait bears and bulls;
then not to fight cocks, and to throw sticks at them.   All
these evidences of manhood became gradually looked upon
as no such evidences at all, but things fit only for manhood
to renounce ; yet the battles of Waterloo and of Sobraon
have been won, and Englishmen are not a jot the less brave
all over the world. Probably they are braver, that is to
say, more deliberately brave, more serenely valiant ; also
more merciful to the helpless, and that is the crown of valor.

It was during my infancy, if I am not mistaken, that
there lived at Hampstead (a very unfit place for such a
resident), a man whose name I suppress lest there should be
possessors of it surviving, and who was a famous cock-fighter.
He was rich and idle, and therefore had no bounds to set to
the unhappy passions that raged within him.   It is related of
this man, that, having lost a bet on a favorite bird, he tied
the noble animal to a spit in his kitchen before the fire, and
notwithstanding the screams of the sufferer and the indignant
cries of the beholders, whose interference he wildly resisted
with the poker, actually persisted in keeping it there burning,
till he fell down in his fury and died.

Let us hope he was mad.   What, indeed, is more probable ?   It is always a great good, when the crimes of a fellow-creature can be traced to madness ; to some fault of the
temperament or organization ; some " jangle of the sweet
bells ;" some overbalance in the desired equipoise of the
faculties, originating, perhaps, in accident or misfortune.   It
does not subject us the more to their results.   On the contrary, it sets us on our guard against them.   And, meantime,
it diminishes one of the saddest, most injurious, and most
preposterous notions of human ignorance—the belief in the
wickedness of our kind.

But I have said enough of these barbarous customs, and
must take care that my reflections do not carry me too far
from my reminiscences

I forget whether it was Dr. Trinder—for some purpose
of care and caution—but somebody told my mother (and she
believed it, that if I survived to the age of fifteen I might

turn out to possess a more than average amount of intellect;
but that otherwise I stood a chance of dying an idiot. The
reader may imagine the anxiety which this information would
give to a tender mother. Not a syllable, of course, did she
breathe to me on the subject till the danger was long past,
and doubly did I then become sensible of all the marks of
affection which I called to mind; of the unusual things
which she had done for me; of the neglect, alas! which they
had too often experienced from me, though not to her knowledge; and of the mixture of tenderness and anxiety which I
had always noted in her face. I was the youngest and least
robust of her sons, and during early childhood I used hardly
to recover from one illness before I was seized with another.
The doctor said I must have gone through an extraordinary
amount of suffering. I have sometimes been led to consider
this as the first layer of that accumulated patience with which
in after life I had occasion to fortify myself; and the supposi-
tion has given rise to many consolatory reflections on the
subject of endurance in general.

To assist my recovery from one of these illnesses, I was
taken to the coast of France, where, as usual, I fell into
another; and one of my earliest recollections is of a good-
natured French woman, the mistress of the lodging-house at
Calais, who cried over the "poore littel boy," because I was
a heretic. She thought I should go to the devil. Poor
soul! What torments must the good-hearted woman have
undergone; and what pleasant pastime it is for certain of
her loud and learned inferiors to preach such doctrines, careless of the injuries they inflict, or even hoping to inflict them
for the sake of some fine deity-degrading lesson, of which their
sordid imaginations and splenetic itch of dictation assume
the necessity. It was lucky for me that our hostess was a
gentle, not a violent bigot, and susceptible at her heart of
those better notions of God which are instinctive in the best
natures. She might otherwise have treated me, as a late
traveler says, infants have been treated by Catholic nurses,
and murdered in order to save me.*

* *Letters from the By-ways of Italy:* By Mrs. HENRY STISTED.
As the passage is very curious, and the book, though otherwise inte-

In returning from the coast of France, we stopped at Deal,
and I found myself, one evening, standing with an elder
brother on the beach, looking at a shoal of porpoises, creatures
of which he had given me some tremendous, mysterious notion.
I remember, as if it was yesterday, feeling the shades of

resting, not likely to be found on the highways of the reading public,
it shall be here repeated.

"Among the followers of the house of Stuart," says the authoress,
"there was a faithful follower of the name of Hadfield. The fallen
line, having no better return to make him for years of service, established him in an hotel on the Arno, at Florence, now the *Quatre-Na-
tions ;* to which the partisans of the royal exiles, in consequence, re-
sorted. Mr. Hadfield had recently married : the birth of a son soon
completed his domestic happiness. There could not be a finer, healthier boy. After a few months, the child fell asleep one day and awoke
no more—his death was in no way to be accounted for! The grief
and disappointment of his parents only gave way to the birth of another infant the following year; it was also a boy, blooming, and full
of life. He also slept the sleep of death, to awake no more! A third
was born, and the same mysterious fate awaited him : the horror of the
heart-stricken parents can only be imagined—

"'The shaft flew thrice, and thrice their peace was slain.'

"The following year, the olive branch was again held forth in
mercy. A fourth child was vouchsafed—it was a girl. The parents
watched and prayed, but trembled! Only a few weeks had passed
over, when the nurse, to whom the infant had been intrusted, ran to
them one day, her countenance full of horror, her lips livid; she could
not articulate, but held out the babe to its mother. After some re-
storatives had been given, the poor creature recovered sufficiently to
tell, that, having left the nursery for a moment, while the child slept,
and without her shoes for fear of awaking her, she was amazed, on her
return with noiseless step, to find old Brigida, the laundress of the
hotel, leaning over the cradle with a vial in her hand. The crone,
unconscious of her presence, was talking to herself. The nurse could
distinctly hear her words to this effect : 'I must snatch another heretic
from hell! Drink my child, and join your brothers : they are angels
in paradise. The Blessed Virgin waits for you.' The wretch was in
the act of applying the vial to the infant's lips, when the nurse darted
forward, snatched up the child, and fled! Old Brigida fled, too—but
it was to a convent, a sanctuary! where her guilt was deemed meri-
torious and her redemption secure. She died soon after, in the odor
of sanctity.

"The child was saved," concludes Mrs. Stisted; "but the af-
frighted parents, obliged to live abroad, baptized her according to the
rites of the Roman church. Their daughter proved of precocious

evening, and the solemnity of the spectacle, with an awful
intensity. There they were tumbling along in the foam
what exactly I knew not, but fearful creatures of some sort.
My brother spoke to me of them in an under tone of voice,
and I held my breath as I looked. The very word "porpoise," had an awful mouth-filling sound.

Perhaps they were dolphins. The dolphin is found on the
English coast, and, indeed, the porpoise is a species of dolphin.
Certainly, no Greek could have held him in more respect
than I did at that moment. I did not know that his name,
porpoise, meant hog-fish; and as little was I aware that he
was no fish at all, but an animal of the "cetaceous" order,
boned and warm-blooded like myself, and forced to breathe
air. This might have added to my notions of him, had my
brother possessed the information, and they would have been
aggravated, had I learned that he went by the name of
Goblin (Nisack) among the Zetlanders. "Certainly," says
the gentleman who informs us of this circumstance, "a porpoise in the act of tumbling in the sea is no bad personifica-
tion of a goblin."* But that was pretty much my feeling
about him, as it was. I looked on him as something between
fish and ogre; and I never thought of the sea long afterward, without picturing him and his fellows in my imagination going monstrously along.

In subsequent years, poetry and mythology taught me to

mind. Her talents and beauty rendered her well known in after years
in England: she was the celebrated Maria Cosway."—p. 479.

This story is related on the authority of a sister of Mrs. Cosway,
with whom Mrs. Stisted was intimate; and she adds, that it is still
remembered in Italy, but alluded to with horror.

The fair author, however, who is herself zealous for the making of
proselytes and the salvation of souls, does not see that she is playing
with a tremendous two-edged weapon in calling old Brigida a wretch,
and that the first germ of the horror lay in those opinions, common to
both, which associate the Divine Being himself with horrors infinitely
more shocking.

It is not Mrs. Stisted's creed that will have saved the world from
the continuance of such melancholy absurdities, but those better opinions of God and man which the progress of knowledge and loving-
kindness is gradually introducing into all creeds.

* Bell's *British Quadrupeds and Cetacea*, p. 475.

love the porpoise.   Who does not learn to love every thing
in the all-embracing sweetness of poetry ?   The porpoise was
the cousin of Arion's dolphin, if not the musician's actual
bearer.   I therefore discovered that he was a very pleasant,
gamboling fellow, full of sociality, and classical withal ; a
reputation old as the seas, yet fresh as the gale of yesterday.   And he, or his kind, were the horses of the sea-
nymphs.

> A team of dolphins, rangèd in array.
>   Drew the smooth chariot of sad Cymoënt :
> They were all taught by Triton to obey
>   To the long reins at her commandèment :
>   As swift as swallows on the waves they went,
> That their broad, flaggy fins no foam did rear,
>   Nor bubbling roundel they behind them sent :
> The rest, of other fishes, drawen were,
> Which with their finny oars the swelling sea did shear.
>
> Soon as they been arriv'd upon the brim
>   Of the Rich Strand, their chariots they forlore,

(These ladies of the sea were on a visit)

> And let their teamèd fishes softly swim
>   Along the margent of the foamy shore ;
>   Lest they their fins should bruise, and surbeat sore
> Their tender feet upon the stony ground.
>   *Faerie Queene, Book III, Canto* iv

Who would not think that Spenser had kept a dolphin-
chariot and pair ?   Cymoënt is a sea-nymph, coming, with
her sisters of the ocean, to visit her son Marinell, Lord of
the Precious Shore.

It is thus that dreams of goblins vanish in the light of
knowledge and beauty.

This brother of mine, who is now no more, and who
might have been a Marinell himself, for his notions of wealth
and grandeur (to say nothing of his marrying, in succession,
two ladies with dowries, from islands, whom ancient imagination could easily have exalted into sea-nymphs), was then
a fine, tall lad of intrepid spirit, a little too much given to
playing tricks on those who had less.   My other brothers
were all as bold as himself ; but he had discovered that the

latest born was more "nervous," and that a new field lay
open for his amusement in the little one's imagination. He
was a dozen years older than I was, and as he had a good
deal of the despot in a nature otherwise generous, and had
succeeded even in lording it over such of his brothers as chose
to let him (for disputes frightened my mother), his ascendency
threatened to enslave their junior altogether. I had acquired
however, an art of evading his tyranny, by the help of my
very childhood, which enabled me to keep out of his way;
and in addition to this resource, I had a certain resentment
of my own weakness, which came in aid of the family spirit.

To give an instance of the lengths to which my brother S.
carried his claims of ascendency, he used to astonish the
boys, at a day-school to which he went in Finchley, by appearing among them with clean shoes, when the bad state of
the lanes rendered the phenomenon unaccountable. Reserve
on one side, and shame on another, kept the mystery a secret
for some time. At length it turned out, that he was in the
habit, on muddy days, of making one of his brothers carry
him to school on his shoulders.

This brother (Robert), who is still living to laugh at the
recollection, and who, as I have intimated, was quite as
brave as himself, was at a disadvantage on such occasions,
from his very bravery; since he knew what a horror my
mother would have felt, had there been any collision between
them; so he used to content himself with an oratorical protest, and acquiesce. Being a brave, or at all events irritable
little fellow enough myself, till illness, imagination, and an
ultra tender and anxious rearing, conspired to render me
fearful and patient, I had no such consequences to think of.
When S. took me bodily in hand, I was only exasperated.
I remember the furious struggles I used to make, and my
endeavors to get at his shins, when he would hold me at
arm's length, "aggravating" me (as the phrase is) by taunt-
ing speeches, and laughing like a goblin.

But on the "night-side of human nature," as Mrs. Crowe
calls it, he "had me." I might confront him and endeavor
to kick his shins by day-light, but with respect to ghosts, as
the sailor said, I did not "understand their tackle." I had

unfortunately let him see that I did not like to be in the dark,
and that I had a horror of dreadful faces ; even in books. I
had found something particularly ghastly in the figure of an
old man crawling on the ground, in some frontispiece—I
think to a book called the *Looking-Glass;* and there was
a fabulous wild-beast, a portrait of which, in some picture-
book, unspeakably shocked me. It was called the Mantichora. It had the head of a man, grinning with rows of
teeth, and the body of a wild-beast, brandishing a tail armed
with stings. It was sometimes called by the ancients *Mar-*
tichora. But I did not know that. I took the word to be
a horrible compound of *man* and *tiger.* The beast figures
in Pliny and the old travelers. Apollonius had heard of him.
He takes a fearful joy in describing him, even from report :

" Apollonius asked " if they had among them the Marti-
chora." " What !" said Iarchas, " have you heard of that
animal ; for if you have, you have probably heard something
extraordinary of its figure." " Great and wonderful things
have I heard of it," replied Apollonius. " It is of the number of quadrupeds, has a head like a man's, is as large as a
lion, with a tail from which bristles grow, of the length of
a cubit, all as sharp as prickles, which it shoots forth like
so many arrows against its pursuers."*

That sentence, beginning " Great and wonderful things,"
proves to me, that Apollonius must once have been a little
boy, looking at picture-books. The possibility of such " creatures" being " pursued" never occurred to me. Alexander, I
thought, might have been encountered while crossing the
Granicus, and elephants might be driven into the sea ; but
how could any one face a beast with a man's head ? One
look of its horrid countenance (which it always carried fronting you, as it went by—I never imagined it seen in profile)
would have been enough, I concluded, to scare an army.
Even full-grown dictionary-makers had been frightened out
of their propriety at the thought of him. " Mantichora,"
says old Morell—" *bestia horrenda*"—(a brute fit to give
one the horrors).

In vain my brother played me repeated tricks with this

* Berwick's Translation, p. 176.

frightful anomaly. I was always ready to be frightened again. At one time he would grin like the Mantichora; then he would roar like him; then call about him in the dark. I remember his asking me to come up to him one night at the top of the house. I ascended, and found the door shut. Suddenly a voice came through the key-hole, saying, in its hollowest tones, " The Mantichora's coming." Down I rushed to the parlor, fancying the terror at my heels.

I dwell the more on this seemingly petty circumstance, because such things are no petty ones to a sensitive child. My brother had no idea of the mischief they did me. Perhaps the mention of them will save mischief to others. They helped to morbidize all that was weak in my temperament, and cost me many a bitter night.

Another time I was reading to him, while he was recovering in bed from an accident. He was reckless in his play; had once broken his leg on Hampstead Heath; and was now getting well from a broken collar bone. He gave me a volume, either of " Elegant Extracts," or " Aikin's Miscellanies," to read (I think the former), and selected the story of *Sir Bertrand*. He did not betray by his face what was coming. I was enchanted with the commencement about the "dreary moors" and the " curfew ;" and I was reading on with breathless interest, when, at one of the most striking passages— probably some analogous one about a noise—he contrived, with some instrument or other, to give a tremendous knock on the wall. Up I jumped, aghast; and the invalid lay rolling with laughter.

It was lucky for me that I inherited a check to this sensibility, in the animal spirits of my father : and unceasing, above all, has been my gratitude, both to father and mother, for the cheerful opinions which they took care to give me in religion. What the reverse might have done for me, I shudder to think. I hope good sense would have predominated, and moral courage enough been left me to go to a physician and cultivate my bodily strength ; but among the strange compliments which superstition pays to the Creator, is a scorn and contempt for the fleshly investiture which he has bestowed on us, at least among Christians ; for the

Pagans were far more pious in this respect; and Mohammed agreed with them in doing justice to the beauty and dignity of the human frame. It is quite edifying, in the Arabian nights, to read the thanks that are so often and so rapturously given to the Supreme Being for his bestowal of such charms on his creatures. Nor was a greater than Mohammed of a nature to undervalue the earthly temples of gentle and loving spirits. Ascetic mistakes have ever originated in want of heartiness or of heart ; in consciousness of defect, or vulgarity of nature, or in spiritual pride. A well-balanced body and soul never, we may be sure, gave way to it. What an extraordinary flattery of the Deity to say, " Lord ! I thank thee for this jewel of a soul which I possess ; but what a miserable casket thou hast given me to put it in !"

So healthily had I the good fortune to be brought up in point of religion, that (to anticipate a remark which might have come in at a less effective place), I remember kneeling one day at the school-church during the Litany, when the thought fell upon me, " Suppose eternal punishment should be true." An unusual sense of darkness and anxiety crossed me—but only for a moment. The next instant the extreme absurdity and impiety of the notion restored me to my ordinary feelings ; and from that moment to this—respect the mystery of the past as I do, and attribute to it what final good out of fugitive evil I may—I have never for one instant doubted the transitoriness of the doctrine, and the unexclusive goodness of futurity. All those question-begging argumentations of the churches and schools, which are employed to reconcile the inflictions of the nursery to the gift of reason, and which would do quite as well for the absurdities of any one creed as another (indeed they would be found to have done so, were we as deeply read in the religions of East as of West), come to nothing before the very modesty to which they appeal, provided it is a modesty healthy and loving. The more even of fugitive evil which it sees (and no ascertained evil suffered by any individual creature is otherwise), nay, the more which is disclosed to it in the very depths and concealments of nature, only the more convinces it that the great mystery of all things will allow of no lasting evil, visi-

ble or invisible ; and therefore it concludes that the evil
which does exist is for some good purpose, and for the final
blessing of all sentient beings, of whom it takes a care so
remarkable.

I know not whether it was fortunate or unfortunate for
me, humanly speaking, that my mother did not see as far
into healthiness of training in other respects as in this.
Some of the bad consequences to myself were indeed óbvious,
as the reader has seen ; but it may have enabled me to save
worse to others. If I could find any fault with her memory
(speaking after an ordinary fashion), it would be that I was
too delicately bred, except as to what is called good living.
My parents were too poor for luxury. But she set me an
example of such excessive care and anxiety for those about
us, that I remember I could not see her bite off the ends of
her thread while at work without being in pain till I was
sure she would not swallow them. She used to be so
agitated at the sight of discord and quarreling, particularly
when it came to blows, and between the rudest or gayest
combatants in the street, that although it did not deprive
her of courage and activity enough to interfere (which she
would do if there was the slightest chance of effect, and
which produced in myself a corresponding discrimination
between sensibility and endeavor), it gave me an ultra-
sympathy with the least show of pain and suffering ; and
she had produced in me such a horror, or rather such an
intense idea of even violent words, and of the commonest
trivial oath, that being led one day, perhaps by the very
excess of it, to snatch a " fearful joy" in its utterance, it
gave me so much remorse that for some time afterward I
could not receive a bit of praise, or a pat of encouragement
on the head, without thinking to myself, "Ah, they little
suspect that I am the boy who said, 'd——n it.'"

Dear mother ! No one could surpass her in generosity :
none be more willing to share, or to take the greatest portion
of blame to themselves, of any evil consequences of mistake
to a son ; but if I have not swallowed very many camels in
the course of my life, it has not been owing perhaps to this too
great a straining at gnats. How happy shall I be (if I may)

to laugh and compare notes with her on the subject in any humble corner of heaven; to recall to her the filial tenderness with which she was accustomed to speak of the mistakes of one of her own parents, and to think that her grandchildren will be as kind to the memory of their father.

I may here mention, as a ludicrous counterpart to this story, and a sample of the fantastical nature of scandal, that somebody having volunteered a defense of my character on some occasion to a distinguished living poet, as though the character had been questioned by him—the latter said he had never heard any thing against it, except that I was "given to swearing."

I certainly think little of the habit of swearing, however idle, if it be carried no further than is done by many gallant and very good men, wise and great ones not excepted. I wish I had no worse faults to answer for. But the fact is, that however I may laugh at the puerile conscience of the anecdote just mentioned, an oath has not escaped my lips from that day to this.

I hope no "good fellow" will think ill of me for it. If he did, I should certainly be tempted to begin swearing immediately, purely to *vindicate* my character. But there was no swearing in our family; there was none in our school (Christ-Hospital); and I seldom ever fell in the way of it any where except in books; so that the practice was not put into my head. I look upon Tom Jones, who swore, as an angel of light compared with Blifil, who, I am afraid, swore no more than myself. Steele, I suspect, occasionally rapped out an oath; which is not to be supposed of Addison. And this, again, might tempt me into a grudge against my nonjuring turn of colloquy; for I must own that I prefer open-hearted Steele with all his faults, to Addison with all his essays. But habit is habit, negative as well as positive. Let him that is without one, cast the first sarcasm.

After all, swearing was once seriously objected to me, and I had given cause for it. I must own, that I even begged hard to be allowed a few oaths. It was for an article in a magazine, where I had to describe a fictitious person, whose character I thought required it; and I pleaded truth to nature, and the practice of the good old novelists ; but in vain. The editor was not to be entreated. He was Mr. Theodore Hook.

Perhaps this was what gave rise to the poet's impression.

But to return to my reminiscences. It may appear surprising to some, that a child brought up in such scruples of conscience, and particularly in such objections to pugnacity, should have ever found himself in possession of such toys as a drum and a sword. A distinguished economist, who was pleased the other day to call me the " spoiled child of the public" (a title which I should be proud to possess), expressed his astonishment, that a person so "gentle" should have been a fighter in the thick of politics. But the "gentleness" was the reason. I mean, that under certain circumstances of training, the very love of peace and comfort, in begetting a desire to see those benefits partaken by others, begets a corresponding indignation at seeing them withheld.

I am aware of the perils of reaction to which this feeling tends ; of the indulgence in bad passions which it may disguise; of the desirableness of quietly advocating whatever is quietly to be secured ; of the perplexity occasioned to all these considerations by the example which appears to be set by nature herself in her employment of storm and tempest ; and of the answer to be given to that perplexity by the modesty of human ignorance and its want of certainty of foresight. Nevertheless, till this question be settled (and the sooner the justice of the world can settle it the better), it renders the best natures liable to inconsistencies between theory and practice, and forces them into self-reconcilements of conscience, neither quite so easy in the result, nor so deducible from perfect reason as they would suppose. My mother, whose fortunes had been blighted, and feelings agonized, by the revolution in America, and who had conceived such a horror of war, that when we resided once near the Park, she would take a long circuit (as I have before mentioned), rather than go through it, in order to avoid seeing the soldiers, permitted me, nevertheless, to have the drum nd the sword. Why ? Because if the sad necessity were to come, it would be her son's duty to war against war itself—to fight against those who oppressed the anti-fighters.

My father, entertaining these latter opinions without any misgiving (enforced, too, as they were by his classical education), and both my parents being great lovers of sermons, which he was in the habit of reading to us of an evening, I found myself at one time cultivating a perplexed ultra-conscientiousness with my mother ; at another, laughing and being jovial with my father ; and at a third, hearing from both of them stories of the Greek and Roman heroes, some of whom she admired as much as he did. The consequence was, that I one day, presented to the astonished eyes of the maid-servant a combination that would have startled Dr. Trinder, and delighted the eyes of an old Puritan. To clap a sword by my side, and get the servant to pin up my hat into the likeness of the hat military, were symptoms of an ambition which she understood and applauded ; but when I proceeded to append to this martial attire one of my father's bands, and, combining the military with the ecclesiastical authority, got upon a chair to preach to an imaginary audience over the back of it, she seemed to think the image realized of "heaven and earth coming together." However, she ended with enjoying, and even abetting, this new avatar of the church militant. Had I been a Mohammed, she would have been my first proselyte, and I should have called her the Maid-servant of the Faithful. She was a good, simple-hearted creature, who from not having been fortunate with the first orator in whom she believed, had stood a chance of ruin for life, till received into the only family that would admit her ; and she lived and died in its service.

The desire thus childishly exhibited, of impressing some religious doctrine, never afterward quitted me ; though, in consequence of the temperament which I inherited from one parent, and the opinions which I derived from both, it took a direction singularly cheerful. For a man is but his parents, or some other of his ancestors, drawn out. My father, though a clergyman of the Established Church, had settled, as well as my mother, into a Christian of the Universalist persuasion, which believes in the final restoration of all things. It was hence that I learned the impiety (as I have expressed it) of the doctrine of eternal punishment.   In the present day, a sense of that impiety, in some way or other, whether of doubt or sophistication, is the secret feeling of nine-tenths of all churches : and every church will discover, before long, that it must rid itself of the doctrine, if it would not cease to exist.   Love is the only creed destined to survive all others. They who think that no church can exist without a strong spice of terror, should watch the growth of education, and see which system of it is the most beloved.   They should see also which system in the very nursery is growing the most ridiculous.   The threat of the " black man and the coal-hole " has vanished from all decent infant training. What, answer, is the father, who would uphold the worst form of. it, to give to the child whom he has spared the best ?

How pleasant it is, in reviewing one's life, to look back on the circumstances that originated or encouraged any kindly tendency.   I behold, at this moment, with lively distinctness, the handsome face of Miss C., who was the first person I remember seeing at a piano-forte ; and I have something of a like impression of that of Miss M., mother, if I mistake not, or, at all events, near relation, of my distinguished friend Sheridan Knowles.   My parents and his were acquainted. My mother, though fond of music, and a gentle singer in her way, had missed the advantage of a musical education, partly from her coming of a half-quaker stock, partly (as I have said before) from her having been too diffident to avail herself of the kindness of Dr. Franklin, who offered to teach her the guitar.

The reigning English composer at that time was " Mr. Hook," as he was styled at the head of his songs.   He was the father of my punctilious editor of the magazine ; and had a real though small vein of genius, which was none the better for its being called upon to flow profusely for Ranelagh and Vauxhall.   He was composer of the *Lass of Richmond Hill* (an allusion to a penchant of George III.), and of another popular song more lately remembered, *'Twas within a mile of. Edinborough town*.   The songs of that day abounded in Strephons and Delias, and the music partook of the gentle inspiration. The association of early ideas with that kind of commonplace, has given me more than a toleration for it. I find something even touching in the endeavors of an innocent set of ladies and gentlemen, my fathers and mothers, to identify themselves with shepherds and shepherdesses, even in the most impossible hats and crooks. I think of the many heartfelt smiles that must have welcomed love-letters and verses containing that sophisticate imagery, and of the no less genuine tears that were shed over the documents when faded; and criticism is swallowed up in those human drops. This is one of the reasons why I can read even the most faded part of the works of Shenstone, and why I can dip again and again into such correspondence as that of the Countesses of Hertford and Pomfret, and of my Lady Luxborough, who raises monuments in her garden to the united merits of Mr. Somerville and the god Pan. The feeling was true, though the expression was sophisticate and a fashion; and they who can not see the feeling for the mode do the very thing which they think they scorn; that is, sacrifice the greater consideration to the less.

But Hook was not the only, far less the most fashionable composer. There was (if not all personally, yet popularly contemporaneous) Mr. Lampe, and Mr. Oswald, and Dr. Boyce, and Linley, and Jackson, and Shield, and Storace, with Paesiello, Sacchini, and others at the King's Theatre, whose delightful airs wandered into the streets out of the English operas that borrowed them, and became confounded with English property. I have often, in the course of my life, heard *Whither, my love?* and *For tenderness formed*, boasted of as specimens of English melody. For many years I took them for such myself, in common with the rest of our family, with whom they were great favorites. The first, which Stephen Storace adapted to some words in the " Haunted Tower," is the air of *La Rachelina* in Paesiello's opera, " La Molinara." The second, which was put by General Burgoyne to a song in his comedy of the " Heiress," is *Io sono Lindoro*, in the same enchanting composer's " Barbiere di Seviglia." The once popular English songs and duets, &c., *How imperfect is expression; For me, my fair a wreath has wove; Henry cull'd the flow'ret's bloom; O, thou wert born to please me; Here's a health to all good lasses; Youth's the season made for joys; Gently touch the warbling lyre; No, 'twas neither shape or feature; Pray, Goody, please to moderate; Hope told a flattering tale*, and a hundred others, were all foreign compositions, chiefly Italian. Every burlesque or *buffo* song, of any pretension, was pretty sure to be Italian.

When Edwin, Fawcett, and others, were rattling away in the happy comic songs of O'Keeffe, with his triple rhymes and illustrative jargon, the audience little suspected that they were listening to some of the finest animal spirits of the south—to Piccini, Paesiello, and Cimarosa. Even the wild Irishman thought himself bound to go to Naples, before he could get a proper dance for his gayety. The only genuine English compositions worth any thing at that time, were almost confined to Shield, Dibdin, and Storace, the last of whom, the author of *Lullaby*, who was an Italian born in England, formed the golden link between the music of the two countries, the only one, perhaps, in which English accentuation and Italian flow were ever truly amalgamated; though I must own that I am heretic enough (if present fashion is orthodoxy) to believe, that Arne was a real musical genius, of a very pure, albeit not of the very first water. He has set, indeed, two songs of Shakspeare's (the *Cuckoo song*, and *Where the bee sucks*) in a spirit of perfect analogy to the words, as well as of the liveliest musical invention; and his air of *Water parted*, in "Artaxerxes," winds about the feelings with an earnest and graceful tenderness of regret, worthy in the highest degree of the affecting beauty of the sentiment.

All the favorite poetry of the day, however, was of one cast. I have now before me a "Select Collection of English Songs," by Ritson, published in the year 1783, in three volumes octavo, the last of which contains the musical airs The style is of the following description :

> Almeria's face, her shape, her air,
> *With charms resistless wound the heart*, &c. p. 2.

(I should not wonder if dear Almeria T., whose tender affection for my mother will appear in another chapter, was christened out of this song).

> Say, Myra, why is gentle love, &c.
> *Which racks the amorous breast,*

by Lord Lyttelton, the most admired poet, perhaps, of the age.

> *When Delia on the plain appears,*

also by his lordship.

> In vain, *Philander,* at my feet.
>
> Ah, *Damon, dear shepherd,* adieu.
>
> Come, thou rosy dimpled boy,
> Source of every heartfelt joy,
> Leave the blissful bowers a while,
> *Paphos and the Cyprian isle.*

This was a favorite song in our house. So was *Come, now, all ye social powers,* and

> Come let us dance and sing,
> While all Barbados bells shall ring ;

probably on account of its mention of my father's native place. The latter song is not in Ritson. It was the finale in Colman's "Inkle and Yarico," a play founded on a Barbadian story, which our family must have gone with delight to see. Another favorite, which used to make my mother shed tears, on account of my sister Eliza, who died early, was Jackson of Exeter's song,

> Encompass'd in an angel's frame.

It is, indeed, a touching specimen of that master. The *Hardy tar,* also, and *The topsails shiver in the wind,* used to charm yet sadden her, on account of my eldest brother then living, who was at sea. The latter, written by the good-natured and gallant Captain Thompson, was set to music, I think, by Arne's son, Michael, who had a fine musical sea-vein, simple and strong. He was the composer of *Fresh and strong the breeze is blowing.*

The other day I found two songs of that period on a music-stall, one by Mr. Hook, entitled *Alone by the light of the moon :* the other, a song with a French burden, called

Dans votre lit; an innocent production, notwithstanding its title. They were the only songs I recollect singing when a child, and I looked on them with the accumulated tenderness of sixty-three years of age. I do not remember to have set eyes on them in the interval. What a difference between the little, smooth-faced boy at his mother's knee, encouraged to lift up his voice to the pianoforte, and the battered grey-headed senior, looking again, for the first time, on what he had sung at the distance of more than half a century. Life often seems a dream; but there are occasions when the sudden re-appearance of early objects, by the intensity of their presence, not only renders the interval less present to the consciousness than a very dream, but makes the portion of life which preceded it seem to have been the most real of all things, and our only undreaming time.

Alone, by the light of the moon, and *Dans votre lit!* how had they not been thumbed and thrown aside by all the piano-forte young ladies—our mothers and grandmothers— fifty years ago, never to be brought forth again, except by an explorer of old stalls, and to meet, perhaps, with no sympathy but in his single imagination! Yet there I stood; and Wardour-street, every street, all London, as it now exists, became to me as if it had never been. The universe itself was nothing but a poor sitting-room in the year '89 or '90, with my mother in it bidding me sing, Miss C. at the piano-forte, harpsichord more likely, and my little sister, Mary, with her round cheeks and blue eyes, wishing me to begin. What a great singer is that little boy to those loving relations, and how Miss C., with all her good nature, must be smiling at the importance of little boys to their mothers! *Alone, by the light of the moon,* was the "show-song," but *Dans votre lit* was the favorite with my sister, because, in her ignorance of the French language, she had associated the name of her brother with the sound of the last word.

The song was a somewhat gallant, but very decorous song, apostrophizing a lady as a lily in the flower-bed. It was "silly, sooth," and "dallied with the innocence of love" in those days, after a fashion which might have excited livelier ideas in the more restricted imaginations of the present.

The reader has seen, that my mother, notwithstanding her charitableness to the poor maid-servant, was a woman of strict morals; the tone of the family conversation was scrupulously correct, though, perhaps, a little flowery and Thomson-like (Thomson was our favorite poet); yet the songs that were sung at that time by the most fastidious, might be thought. a shade freer than would suit the like kind of society at present. Whether we are more innocent in having become more ashamed, I shall not judge. Assuredly, the singer of those songs was as innocent, as the mother that bade him sing them.

My little sister, Mary, died not long after. She was so young, that my only recollection of her, besides her blue eyes, is her love of her brother, and her custom of leading me by the hand to some stool, or seat on the staircase, and making me sing the song with her favorite burden. We were the two youngest children, and about of an age.

I please myself with picturing to my imagination what was going forward during my childhood in the world of politics, literature, and public amusements; how far they interested my parents; and what amount of impression they may have left on my own mind. The American Revolution, which had driven my father from Philadelphia, was not long over, and the French Revolution was approaching. My father, for reasons which have already been mentioned, listened more and more to the new opinions, and my mother listened, not only from love to her husband, but because she was still more deeply impressed by speculations regarding the welfare of human kind. The public mind, after a long and comparatively insipid tranquillity, had begun to be stirred by the eloquence of Burke; by the rivalries of Pitt and Fox; by the thanks which the king gave to Heaven for his recovery from his first illness; by the warlike and licentious energies of the Russian Empress, Catherine II., who partly shocked and partly amused them; and by the gentler gallantries and showy luxury of the handsome young Prince of Wales, afterward George IV.

In the world of literature and art, Goldsmith and Johnson had gone; Cowper was not yet much known; the most prominent poets were Hayley and Darwin ; the most distinguished prose-writer, Gibbon. Sir Joshua Reynolds was in his decline, so was Horace Walpole. The Kembles had come up in the place of Garrick. There were excellent comic actors in the persons of Edwin, Lewis, young Bannister, &c. They had O'Keefe, an original humorist, to write for them. I have already noticed the vocal portion of the theatres. Miss Burney, afterward Madam d'Arblay, surprised the reading world with her entertaining, but somewhat vulgar novels ; and Mrs. Inchbald, Mrs. Charlotte Smith, and a then anonymous author, Robert Bage (who wrote " Hermsprong," and " Man as He Is"), delighted liberal politicians with theirs. Mrs. Inchbald was also a successful dramatist ; but her novels, which were written in a style to endure, were her chief merits.

My mother was one of their greatest admirers. I have, heard her expatiate with delight on the characters in " Nature and Art," which, though not so masterly a novel as the " Simple Story," and a little willful in the treatment, was full of matter for reflection, especially on conventional, and what are now called "class" points. Dr. Philpotts would have accused her of disaffection to the church ; and she would not have mended the matter by retreating on her admiration of Bishops Hoadley and Shipley. Her regard for the reverend author of " Meditations in a Flower Garden" would have made the doctor smile, though she would have recovered, perhaps, something of his good opinion by her admiration of Dr. Young and his " Night Thoughts." But Young deluded her with his groans against the world, and his lamentations for his daughter. She did not know that he was a preferment-hunter, who was prosperous enough to indulge in the " luxury of woe," and to groan because his toast was not thrice buttered.

Ranelagh and Vauxhall, as painted in Miss Burney's novels, were among the fashionable amusements of those days. My mother was neither rich nor gay enough to see much of them ; but she was no ascetic, and she went where others did, as occasion served. My father, whose manners were at once high-bred and lively, had some great acquaintauces ; but I recollect none of them personally, except an old lady of quality, who (if memory does not strangely deceive me, and give me a personal share in what I only heard talked of ; for old autobiographers of childhood must own themselves liable to such confusions) astounded me one day, by letting her false teeth slip out, and clapping them in again.

I had no idea of the existence of such phenomena, and could almost as soon have expected her to take off her head and re-adjust it.   She lived in Red Lion Square, a quarter in different estimation from what it is now.   It was at her house, I believe, that my father one evening met Wilkes. He did not know him by sight, and happening to fall into conversation with him, while the latter sat looking down, he said something in Wilkes's disparagement ; on which the jovial demagogue looked up in his face and burst out a laughing.

I do not exactly know how people dressed at that time ; but I believe that sacks, and negligées, and toupees were going out, and the pigtail and the simpler modern style of dress coming in.   I recollect hearing my mother describe the misery of having her hair dressed two or three stories high, and of lying in it all night ready for some visit or spectacle next day.   I think I also recollect seeing Wilkes himself in an old-fashioned flap-waistcoated suit of scarlet and gold ; and I am sure I have seen Murphy, the dramatist, a good deal later, in a suit of a like fashion, though soberer, and a large cocked-hat.   The cocked-hat in general survived till nearly the present century.   It was superseded by the round one during the French Revolution.   I remember our steward at school, a very solemn personage, making his appearance in one to our astonishment, and not a little to the diminution of his dignity.   Some years later, I saw Mr. Pitt in a blue coat, buckskin breeches and boots, and a round hat, with powder and pigtail.   He was thin and gaunt, with his hat off his forehead, and his nose in the air.   Much about the same time I saw his friend, the first Lord Liverpool, a respectable looking old gentleman, in a brown wig.   Later still, I saw Mr. Fox, fat and jovial, though he was then declining.   He, who had been a "beau" in his youth, then looked something Quaker-like as to dress, with plain colored clothes, a broad round hat, white waistcoat, and, if I am not mistaken, white stockings. He was standing in Parliament-street, just where the street commences as you leave White-hall ; and was making two young gentlemen laugh heartily at something which he seemed to be relating.

My father once took me—but I can not say at what period of my juvenility—into both houses of Parliament. In the Commons, I saw Mr. Pitt sawing the air, and occasion-ally turning to appeal to those about him, while he spoke in a loud, important, and hollow voice. When the persons he appealed to, said " Hear ! hear !" I thought they said " Dear ! dear !" in objection ; and I wondered that he did not seem in the least degree disconcerted. The house of Lords, I must say (without meaning disrespect to an assembly which must always have contained some of the most accomplished men in the country), surprised me with the personally in-significant look of its members. I had, to be sure, conceived exaggerated notions of the magnates of all countries ; and perhaps might have expected to behold a set of conscript fa-thers ; but in no respect, real or ideal, did they appear to me in their corporate aspect, like any thing which is understood by the word " noble." The Commons seemed to me to have the advantage ; though they surprised me with lounging on the benches and retaining their hats. I was not then in-formed enough to know the difference between apparent and substantial importance ; much less aware of the positive ex-altation, which that very simplicity, and that absence of pretension, gave to the most potent assembly in Europe.

CHAPTER III.

Children's books.—Hogarth.—Christ-Hospital.—Moral and personal
courage.—Anecdote of a racket-ball.—Fagging.—Visits of Queen
Victoria to the school.—Details respecting that foundation, its manners and customs, modes of training, distinguished scholars, preachers, and schoolmasters, &c.—Tooke's Pantheon and the British
Poets.—Scalded legs and the luxuries of a sick ward.

BOOKS for children during the latter part of the eighteenth
century had been in a bad way, with sordid and merely
plodding morals—ethics that were necessary perhaps for a
certain stage in the progress of commerce and for its greatest
ultimate purposes (undreamt of by itself), but which thwarted
healthy and large views of society for the time being. They
were the consequences of an altogether unintellectual state
of trade, aided and abetted by such helps to morality as
Hogarth's pictures of the Good and Bad Apprentice, which
identified virtue with prosperity.

Hogarth, in most of his pictures, was as healthy a moralist
as he supposed himself, but not for the reasons which he
supposed. The gods he worshiped were Truth and Prudence ; but he saw more of the carnal than spiritual beauties
of either. He was somewhat of a vulgarian in intention as
well as mode. But wherever there is genius, there is a genial
something greater than the accident of breeding, than the
prevailing disposition, or even than the conscious design ; and
this portion of divinity within the painter, saw fair-play between his conventional and immortal part. It put the
beauty of color into his mirth, the counteraction of mirth
into his melancholy, and a lesson beyond his intention into
all : that is to say, it suggested redemptions and first causes
for the objects of his satire ; and thus vindicated the justice
of nature, at the moment when he was thinking of little but
the pragmaticalness of art.

The children's books in those days were Hogarth's pictures

taken in their most literal acceptation. Every good boy was to ride in his coach, and be a lord mayor ; and every bad boy was to be hung, or eaten by lions. The gingerbread was gilt, and the books were gilt like the gingerbread ; a "take in" the more gross, inasmuch as nothing could be plainer or less dazzling than the books of the same boys when they grew a little older. There was a lingering old ballad or so in favor of the gallanter apprentices who tore out lion's hearts and astonished gazing sultans ; and in antiquarian corners, Percy's " Reliques" were preparing a nobler age, both in poetry and prose. But the first counteraction came, as it ought, in the shape of a new book for children. The pool of mercenary and time-serving ethics was first blown over by the fresh country breeze of Mr. Day's " Sandford and Merton"—a production that I well remember, and shall ever be grateful to. It came in aid of my mother's perplexities between delicacy and hardihood, between courage and conscientiousness. It assisted the cheerfulness I inherited from my father ; showed me that circumstances were not to crush a healthy gayety, or the most masculine self-respect ; and helped to supply me with the resolution of standing by a principle, not merely as a point of lowly or lofty sacrifice, but as a matter of common sense and duty, and a simple co-operation with the elements of natural welfare.

I went, nevertheless, to school at Christ-Hospital, an ultrasympathizing and timid boy. The sight of boys fighting, from which I had been so anxiously withheld, frightened me as something devilish ; and the least threat of corporal chastisement to a school-fellow (for the lesson I had learned would have enabled me to bear it myself) affected me to tears. I remember to this day, merely on that account, the name of a boy who was to receive punishment for some offense about a task. It was Lemoine. (I hereby present him with my respects, if he is an existing old gentleman, and hope he has not lost a pleasing countenance.) He had a cold and hoarseness ; and his voice, while pleading in mitigation, sounded to me so pathetic, that I wondered how the master could have the heart to strike him.

Readers, who have been at a public school, may guess the
consequence.   I was not of a disposition to give offense, but
neither was I quick to take it; and this, to the rude, energy-
cultivating spirit of boys in general (not the worst thing in
the world, till the pain in preparation for them can be
diminished), was itself an offense.   I therefore " went to
the wall," till address, and the rousing of my own spirit,
tended to right me; but I went through a great deal of fear
in the process.   I became convinced, that if I did not put
moral courage in the place of personal, or, in other words,
undergo any stubborn amount of pain and wretchedness,
rather than submit to what I thought wrong, there was an
end for ever, as far as I was concerned, of all those fine
things that had been taught me, in vindication of right and
justice.

Whether it was, however, that by the help of animal
spirits I possessed some portion of the courage for which the
rest of the family was remarkable, or whether I was a veritable coward, born or bred, destined to show, in my person,
how far a spirit of love and freedom could supersede the
necessity of gall, and procure me the respect of those about
me, certain it is, that although, except in one instance, I
did my best to avoid, and succeeded honorably in avoiding,
those personal encounters with my school-fellows, which, in
confronting me on my own account with the face of a fellow-creature, threw me upon a sense of something devilish,
and overwhelmed me with a sort of terror for both parties,
yet I gained at an early period of boyhood the reputation
of a romantic enthusiast, whose daring in behalf of a
friend or a good cause nothing could put down.   I was
obliged to call in the aid of a feeling apart from my own
sense of personal antagonism, and so merge the diabolical,
as it were, into the human.   In other words, I had not
self-respect or gall enough to be angry on my own account,
unless there was something at stake which, by concerning
others, gave me a sense of support, and so pieced out my
want with their abundance.   The moment, however, that
I felt thus supported, not only did all misgiving vanish from
my mind, but contempt of pain took possession of my body.

and my poor mother might have gloried through her tears in the loving courage of her son.

I state the case thus proudly, both in justice to the manner in which she trained me, and because I conceive it may do good. I never fought with a boy but once, and then it was on my own account; but though I beat him, I was frightened and eagerly sought his good will. I dared every thing, however, from the biggest and strongest boys on other accounts, and was sometimes afforded an opportunity of showing my spirit of martyrdom. The truth is, I could suffer better than act; for the utmost activity of martyrdom is supported by a certain sense of passiveness. We are not bold from ourselves, but from something which compels us to be so, and which supports us by a sense of the necessity.

I had not been long in the school, when this spirit within me broke out in a manner that procured me great esteem. There was a monitor or " big boy" in office, who had a trick of entertaining himself by pelting lesser boys' heads with a hard ball. He used to throw it at this boy and that; make the *throwee* bring it back to him; and then send a rap with it on his cerebellum, as he was going off.

I had borne this spectacle one day for some time, when the family precepts rising within me, I said to myself, " I must go up to the monitor, and speak to him about this." I issued forth accordingly and to the astonishment of all present, who had never witnessed such an act of insubordination, I said, " You have no right to do this." The monitor, more astounded than any one, exclaimed " What ?" I repeated my remonstrance. He treated me with the greatest contempt, as if disdaining even to strike me; and finished, by ordering me to " stand out." " Standing out" meant going to a particular spot in the hall where we dined. I did so; but just as the steward (the master in that place) was entering it, the monitor called to me to come away; and I neither heard any more of standing out, nor saw any more of the ball. I do not recollect that he even " spited" me afterward, which must have been thought very remarkable. I seemed fairly to have taken away the breath of his calculations. The probability is, that he was a good lad, who

had got a bad habit.   Boys often become tyrants from a
notion of its being grand and manly.

Another monitor, a year or two afterward, took it into his
head to force me to be his fag.   Fag was not the term at
our school, though it was in our vocabulary.   Fag, with us,
meant eatables.   The learned derived the word from the
Greek *phago*, to eat.   I had so little objection to serve out
of love, that there is no office I could not have performed
for good-will; but it had been given out that I had determined not to be a menial on any other terms, and the monitor in question undertook to bring me to reason.   He was a
mild, good-looking boy about fourteen, remarkable for the
neatness, and even elegance of his appearance.

Receiving the refusal, for which he had been prepared,
he showed me a knot in a long handkerchief, and told me I
should receive a lesson from that handkerchief every day,
with the addition of a fresh knot every time, unless I chose
to alter my mind.   I did not choose.   I received the daily
or rather nightly lesson, for it was then most convenient to
strip me, and I came out of the ordeal in triumph.   I never
was fag to any body; never made any body's bed, or cleaned
his shoes, or was the boy to get his tea, much less expected
to stand as a screen for him before the fire; which I have
seen done, though upon the whole the boys were very mild
governors.

Lamb has noticed the character of the school for good
manners, which he truly describes as being equally removed
from the pride of aristocratic foundations and the servility of
the charity-schools.   I believe it retains this character still;
though the changes which its system underwent not long
ago, fusing all the schools into one another, and introducing
a more generous diet, is thought by some not to have been
followed by an advance in other respects.   I have heard the
school charged, more lately, with having been suffered, in
the intervals between the school hours, to fall out of the
liberal and gentlemanly supervision of its best teachers, into
the hands of an officious and ignorant sectarianism.   But
this may only have been a passing abuse.

I love and honor the school on private accounts: and I

feel a public interest in its welfare, inasmuch as it is one of those judicious links with all classes, the importance of which, especially at a time like the present, can not be too highly estimated ; otherwise I should have said nothing to its possible, and I hope transient disadvantage.   Queen Victoria recognized its importance, by visits and other personal condescensions, long before the late changes in Europe could have diminished the grace of their bestowal; and I will venture to say, that every one of those ·attentions will have sown for her generous nature a crop of loyalty worth having.

But for the benefit of such as are unacquainted with the city, or with a certain track of reading, I must give a more particular account of a school which, in truth is a curiosity. Thousands of inhabitants of the metropolis have gone from west-end to east-end, and till the new hall was laid open to view by the alterations in Newgate-street, never suspected that in the heart of it lies an old cloistered foundation, where a boy may grow up, as I did, among seven hundred others, and know as little of the very neighborhood as the world does of him.

Perhaps there is not a foundation in the country so truly English, taking that word to mean what Englishmen wish it to mean ; something solid, unpretending, of good character, and free to all.   More boys are to be found in it who issue from a greater variety of ranks, than in any other school in the kingdom : and as it is the most various, so it is the largest, of all the free schools.   Nobility do not go there except as boarders.   Now and then a boy of a noble family may be met with, and he is reckoned an interloper, and against the charter ; but the sons of poor gentry and London citizens abound ; and with them an equal share is given to the sons of tradesman of the very humblest description, not omitting servants.   I would not take my oath, but I have a strong recollection, that in my time there were two boys, one of whom went up into the drawing-room to his father, the master of the house ; and the other down into the kitchen to *his* father, the coachman.   One thing, however, I know to be certain, and it is the noblest of all ; namely, that the boys themselves (at least it was so in my time), had no sort of feeling of the difference of one another's ranks out of doors. The clever-est boy was the noblest, let his father be who he might.

CHRIST-HOSPITAL is a nursery of tradesmen, of merchants, of naval officers, of scholars ; it has produced some of the greatest ornaments of their time ; and the feeling among the boys themselves is, that it is a medium, between the patrician pretension of such schools as Eton and Westminster, and the plebeian submission of the charity schools. In point of Uni-versity honors, it claims to be equal with the best; and though other schools can show a greater abundance of emi-nent names, I know not where many will be found who are a greater host in themselves. One original author is worth a hundred transmitters of elegance ; and such a one is to be found in Richardson, who here received what education he possessed. Here Camden also received the rudiments of his, Bishop Stillingfleet, according to the memoirs of Pepys, lately published, was brought up in this school. We have had many eminent scholars, two of them Greek professors, to-wit, Barnes, and the present Mr. Scholefield, the latter of whom attained an extraordinary succession of University honors. The rest are Markland ; Middleton, late Bishop of Calcutta ; and Mitchell the translator of "Aristophanes." Christ-Hos-pital, I believe, toward the close of the last century, and the beginning of the present, sent out more living writers, in its proportion than any other school. There was Dr. Richards, author of the "Aboriginal Britons ;" Dyer, whose life was one unbroken dream of learning and goodness, and who used to make us wonder with passing through the school-room (where no other person in "town-clothes" ever appeared) to consult books in the library ; Le Grice, the translator of "Longus ;" Horne, author of some well-known productions in controversial divinity ; Surr, the novelist (not in the Grammar school) ; James White, the friend of Charles Lamb, and not unworthy of him, author of "Falstaff's letters," (this was he who used to give an anniversary dinner to the chimney-sweepers, merrier than, though not so magnificent as Mrs. Montague's) ; Pitman, a celebrated preacher, editor of some school-books, and religious classics ; Mitchell, before mentioned; myself, who stood next him; Barnes, who came next, the editor of the "Times," than whom no man (if he had cared for it) could have been more certain of attaining celebrity for wit and literature;. Townsend, a prebendary of Durham, author of "Armageddon," and several theological works; Gilly another of the Durham prebendaries, who wrote the "Narrative of the Waldenses;" Scargill, a Unitarian minister, author of some tracts on Peace and War, &c.; and lastly, whom I have kept by way of climax, Coleridge and Charles Lamb, two of the most original geniuses, not only of the day, but of the country. We have had an embassador among us; but, as he, I understand, is ashamed of us, we are hereby more ashamed of him, and accordingly omit him.

In the time of Henry the Eighth, Christ-Hospital was a monastery of Franciscan friars. Being dissolved among the others, Edward the Sixth, moved by a sermon of Bishop Ridley's, assigned the revenues of it to the maintenance and education of a certain number of poor orphan children, born of citizens of London. I believe there has been no law passed to alter the letter of this intention; which is a pity, since the alteration has taken place. An extension of it was probably very good, and even demanded by circumstances. I have reason, for one, to be grateful for it. But tampering with matters-of-fact among children is dangerous. They soon learn to distinguish between allowed poetical fiction and that which they are told, under severe penalties, never to be guilty of; and this early sample of contradiction between the thing asserted and the obvious fact, can do no good even in an establishment so plain-dealing in other respects as Christ-Hospital. The place is not only designated as an Orphan-house in its Latin title, but the boys, in the prayers which they repeat every day, implore the pity of Heaven upon "us poor orphans." I remember the perplexity this caused me at a very early period. It is true, the word orphan may be used in a sense implying destitution of any sort; but this was not its Christ-Hospital intention; nor do the younger boys give it the benefit of that scholarly interpretation. There was another thing (now, I believe, done away) which existed in my time, and perplexed me still more. It seemed a glaring instance of the practice likely to result from the other assumption, and made me prepare for a hundred falsehoods and deceptions, which, mixed up with contradiction, as most things in society are, I sometimes did find, and oftener dreaded. I allude to a foolish custom they had in the ward which I first entered, and which was the only one that the company at the public suppers were in the habit of going into, of hanging up, by the side of each bed, a clean white napkin, which was supposed to be the one used by the occupiers. Now these napkins were only for show, the real towels being of the largest and coarsest kind. If the masters had been asked about them, they would doubtless have told the truth ; perhaps the nurses would have done so. But the boys were not aware of this. There they saw these " white lies" hanging before them, a conscious imposition ; and I well remember how alarmed I used to feel, lest any of the company should direct their inquiries to me.

Christ-Hospital (for this is its proper name, and not Christ's Hospital) occupies a considerable portion of ground between Newgate-street, Giltspur-street, St. Bartholomew's, and Little Britain. There is a quadrangle with cloisters ; and the square inside the cloisters is called the Garden, and most likely was the monastery garden. Its only delicious crop, for many years, has been pavement. Another large area, presenting the Grammer and Navigation schools, is also misnomered the Ditch : the town-ditch having formerly run that way. In Newgate-street is seen the hall, or eating-room, one of the noblest in England, adorned with enormously long paintings by Verrio and others, and with an organ. A portion of the old quadrangle once contained the library of the monks, and was built or repaired by the famous Whittington, whose arms were to be seen outside ; but alterations of late years have done it away.

In the cloisters, a number of persons lie buried, besides the officers of the house. Among them is Isabella, wife of Edward the Second, the "she-wolf of France." I was not aware of this circumstance then; but many a time, with a recollection of some lines in " Blair's Grave" upon me, have I run as hard as I could at night-time from my ward to another, in order to borrow the next volume of some ghostly romance. In one of the cloisters was an impression resembling a gigantic foot, which was attributed by some to the angry stamping of the ghost of a beadle's wife! A beadle was a higher sound to us than to most, as it involved ideas of detected apples in church-time, "skulking" (as it was called) out of bounds, and a power of reporting us to the masters. But fear does not stand upon rank and ceremony.

The wards, or sleeping-rooms, are twelve, and contained, in my time, rows of beds on each side, partitioned off, but connected with one another, and each having two boys to sleep in it. Down the middle ran the bins for holding bread and other things, and serving for a table when the meal was not taken in the hall; and over the bins hung a great homely chandelier.

To each of these wards a nurse was assigned, who was the widow of some decent liveryman of London, and who had the charge of looking after us at night-time, seeing to our washing, &c. and carving for us at dinner : all of which gave her a good deal of power, more than her name warranted. The nurses, however, were almost invariably very decent people, and performed their duty; which was not always the case with the young ladies, their daughters. There were five schools; a grammar-school, a mathematical or navigation-school (added by Charles the Second), a writing, a drawing, and a reading school. Those who could not read when they came on the foundation, went into the last. There were few in the last-but-one, and I scarcely know what they did, or for what object. The writing-school was for those who were intended for trade and commerce; the mathematical, for boys who went as midshipmen into the naval and East India service; and the grammar-school for such as were designed for the Church, and to go to the University. The writing-school was by far the largest; and, what is very curious (which is not the case now), all these schools

were kept quite distinct so that a boy might arrive at the
age of fifteen in the grammar-school, and not know his mul-
tiplication-table ; which was the case with myself.   Nor do
I know it to this day !   Shades of Horace Walpole and of
Lord Lyttelton ! come to my assistance, and enable me to
bear the confession : but so it is.   The fault was not my
fault at the time ; but I ought to have repaired it when I
went out in the world ; and great is the mischief which it
has done me.

Most of these schools had several masters ; besides whom
there was a steward, who took care of our subsistence, and
who had a general superintendence over all hours and circumstances not connected with teaching.   The masters had
almost all been in the school, and might expect pensions
or livings in their old age.   Among those in my time, the
mathematical master was Mr. Wales, a man well known
for his science, who had been round the world with Captain
Cook : for which we highly venerated him.   He was a good
man, of plain, simple manners, with a heavy, large person and
a benign countenance.   When he was in Otaheite, the na-
tives played him a trick while bathing, and stole his small-
clothes ; which we used to think a liberty, scarcely credible
The name of the steward, a thin stiff man of invincible formality of demeanor, admirably fitted to render encroach-
ment impossible, was Hathaway.   We of the grammar-
school used to call him " the Yeoman," on account of Shakspeare having married the daughter of a man of that name,
designated as " a substantial yeoman."

Our dress was of the coarsest and quaintest kind, but was
respected out of doors, and is so.   It consisted of a blue drugget gown, or body, with ample coats to it ; a yellow vest
underneath in winter-time ; small-clothes of Russia duck ;
worsted yellow stockings ; a leathern girdle ; and a little
black worsted cap, usually carried in the hand.   I believe it
was the ordinary dress of children in humble life, during the
reign of the Tudors.   We used to flatter ourselves that it
was taken from the monks ; and there went a monstrous tradition, that at one period it consisted of blue velvet with silver buttons.   It was said also, that during the blissful era

of the blue velvet, we had roast mutton for supper, but that the small-clothes not being then in existence, and the mutton suppers too luxurious, the eatables were given up for the ineffables.

A malediction, at heart, always followed the memory of him who had taken upon himself to decide so preposterously To say the truth, we were not too well fed at that time, either in quantity or quality; and we could not enter with our hungry imaginations into these remote philosophies. Our breakfast was bread and water, for the beer was too bad to drink. The bread consisted of the half of a three-halfpenny loaf, according to the prices then current. I suppose it would now be a good twopenny one; certainly not a threepenny. This was not much for growing boys, who had had nothing to eat from six or seven o'clock the preceding evening. For dinner, we had the same quantity of bread, with meat only every other day, and that consisting of a small slice, such as would be given to an infant three or four years old. Yet even that, with all our hunger, we very often left half-eaten; the meat was so tough. On the other days, we had a milk-porridge, ludicrously thin; or rice-milk, which was better. There were no vegetables or puddings. Once a month we had roast beef; and twice a year (I blush to think of the eagerness with which it was looked for!) a dinner of pork. One was roast, and the other boiled; and on the latter occasion we had our only pudding, which was of pease. I blush to remember this, not on account of our poverty, but on account of the sordidness of the custom. There had much better have been none. For supper, we had a like piece of bread, with butter or cheese; and then to bed, " with what appetite we might."

Our routine of life was this. We rose to the call of a bell, at six in summer, and seven in winter; and after combing ourselves, and washing our hands and faces, went at the call of another bell to breakfast. All this took up about an hour.

From breakfast we proceeded to school, where we remained till eleven, winter and summer, and then had an hour's play. Dinner took place at twelve. Afterward was a little play till one, when we again went to school, and remained

till five in summer and four in winter.   At six was the supper.   We used to play after it in summer till eight.   In
winter, we proceeded from supper to bed.   On Sundays, the
school-time of the other days was occupied in church, both
morning and evening ; and as the Bible was read to us every
day before every meal, and on going to bed, besides prayers
and graces, we rivaled the monks in the religious part of our
duties.

The effect was certainly not what was intended.   The
Bible perhaps was read thus frequently, in the first instance,
out of contradiction to the papal spirit that had so long kept
it locked up ; but, in the eighteenth century, the repetition
was not so desirable among a parcel of hungry boys, anxious
to get their modicum to eat.   On Sunday, what with the
long service in the morning, the service again after dinner,
and the inaudible and indifferent tones of some of the
preachers, it was unequivocally tiresome.   I, for one, who
had been piously brought up, and continued to have religion
inculcated on me by father and mother, began secretly to
become as indifferent as I thought the preachers; and,
though the morals of the school were in the main excellent
and exemplary, we all felt, without knowing it, that it was
the orderliness and example of the general system that kept
us so, and not the religious part of it ; which seldom entered
our heads at all, and only tired us when it did.

I am not begging any question here, or speaking for or
against.   I am only stating a fact.   Others may argue, that,
however superfluous the readings and prayers might have,
been, a good general spirit of religion must have been inculcated, because a great deal of virtue and religious charity is
known to have issued out of that school, and no fanaticism.   I
shall not dispute the point.   The case is true; but not the less
true is what I speak of.   Latterly there came, as our parish
clergyman, Mr. Crowther, a nephew of our famous Richardson, and worthy of the talents and virtues of his kinsman,
though inclining to a mode of faith which is supposed to
produce more faith than charity.   But, till then, the persons
who were in the habit of getting up in our church pulpit
and reading-desk, might as well have hummed a tune to

their diaphragms. They inspired us with nothing but mim-
iory. The name of the morning-reader was Salt. He was
a worthy man, I believe, and might, for aught we knew,
have been a clever one; but he had it all to himself. He
spoke in his throat, with a sound as if he was weak and
corpulent; and was famous among us for saying "murra-
cles" instead of "miracles." When we imitated him, this
was the only word we drew upon: the rest was unintelligible suffocation. Our usual evening preacher was Mr. Sandiford, who had the reputation of learning and piety. It was
of no use to us, except to make us associate the ideas of
learning and piety in the pulpit with inaudible hum-drum.
Mr. Sandiford's voice was hollow and low; and he had a
habit of dipping up and down over his book, like a chicken
drinking. Mr. Salt was eminent for a single word. Mr.
Sandiford surpassed him, for he had two audible phrases.
There was, it is true, no great variety in them. One was
"the dispensation of Moses;" the other (with a due interval
of hum), "the Mosaic dispensation." These he used to repeat
so often, that in our caricatures of him they sufficed for an
entire portrait. The reader may conceive a large church
(it was Christ-Church, Newgate-street), with six hundred
boys, seated like charity-children up in the air, on each side
of the organ, Mr. Sandiford humming in the valley, and a
few maid-servants who formed his afternoon congregation.
We did not dare to go to sleep. We were not allowed to
read. The great boys used to get those that sat behind
them to play with their hair. Some whispered to their
neighbors, and the others thought of their lessons and tops.
I can safely say, that many of us would have been good
listeners, and most of us attentive ones, if the clergyman
could have been heard. As it was, I talked as well as the
rest, or thought of my exercise. Sometimes we could not
help joking and laughing over our weariness; and then the
fear was, lest the steward had seen us. It was part of the
business of the steward to preside over the boys in church-time.
He sat aloof, in a place where he could view the whole of
his flock. There was a ludicrous kind of revenge we had
of him, whenever a particular part of the Bible was read.

This was the parable of the Unjust Steward. The boys waited anxiously till the passage commenced; and then, as if by a general conspiracy, at the words " thou unjust steward," the whole school turned their eyes upon this unfortunate officer, who sat

" Like Teneriff or Atlas unremoved."

We persuaded ourselves, that the more unconscious he looked, the more he was acting.

By a singular chance, there were two clergymen, occasional preachers in our pulpit, who were as loud and startling, as the others were somniferous. One of them, with a sort of flat, high voice, had a remarkable way of making a ladder of it, climbing higher and higher to the end of the sentence. It ought to be described by the gamut, or written up-hill. Perhaps it was an association of ideas, that has made me recollect one particular passage. It is where Ahab consults the prophets, asking them whether he shall go up to Ramoth Gilead to battle. " Shall I go against Ramoth Gilead to battle, or shall I forbear ? and they said, Go up ; for the Lord shall deliver it into the hand of the king." He used to give this out in such a manner, that you might have fancied him climbing out of the pulpit sword in hand. The other was a tall, thin man, with a noble voice. He would commence a prayer in a most stately and imposing manner, full both of dignity and feeling ; and then, as if tired of it, would hurry over all the rest. Indeed, he began every prayer in this way, and was as sure to hurry it; for which reason, the boys hailed the sight of him, as they knew they should get sooner out of church. When he commenced in his noble style, the band seemed to tremble against his throat, as though it had been a sounding-board.

Being able to read, and knowing a little Latin, I was put at once into the Under Grammar School. How much time I wasted there in learning the accidence and syntax, I can not say ; but it seems to me a long while. My grammar seemed always to open at the same place. Things are managed differently now, I believe, in this as well as in many other respects. Great improvements have been made

in the whole establishment.   The boys feed better, learn
better, and have longer holidays in the country.   In my
time, they never slept out of the school, but on one occasion, during the whole of their stay ; this was for three
weeks in summer-time, which they were bound to pass
at a certain distance from London.   They now have these
holidays with a reasonable frequency ; and they all go to
the different schools, instead of being confined, as they
were then, some to nothing but writing and ciphering,
and some to the languages.   It has been doubted by some
of us elders, whether this system will beget such temperate,
proper students, with pale faces, as the other did.   I dare
say, our successors are not afraid of us.   I had the pleasure,
some years since, of dining in company with a Deputy Grecian, who, with a stout rosy-faced person, had not failed to
acquire the scholarly turn for joking ; which is common to
a classical education ; as well as those simple, becoming
manners, made up of modesty and proper confidence, which
have been often remarked as distinguishing the boys on this
foundation.

    " But what is a Deputy Grecian ?"   Ah, reader ! to ask
that question, and at the same time to know any thing at all
worth knowing, would at one time, according to our notion
of things, have been impossible.   When I entered the school,
I was shown three gigantic boys, young men rather (for the
eldest was between seventeen and eighteen), who, I was told,
were going to the University.   These were the Grecians.
They were the three head boys of the Grammar School, and
were understood to have their destiny fixed for the Church.
The next class to these, like a College of Cardinals to those
three Popes (for every Grecian was in our eyes infallible),
were the Deputy Grecians.   The former were supposed to
have completed their Greek studies, and were deep in
Sophocles and Euripides.   The latter were thought equally
competent to tell you any thing respecting Homer and Demosthenes.   These two classes, and the head boys of the
Navigation School, held a certain rank over the whole place,
both in school and out.   Indeed, the whole of the Navigation
School, upon the strength of cultivating their valor for the

navy, and being called King's Boys, had succeeded in estab·
lishing an extraordinary pretension to respect. This they
sustained in a manner as laughable to call to mind, as it
was grave in its reception. It was an etiquette among them
never to move out of a right line as they walked, whoever
stood in their way. I believe there was a secret understanding with Grecians and Deputy Grecians, the former of whom
were unquestionably lords paramount in point of fact, and
stood and walked aloof when all the rest of the school were
marshaled in bodies. I do not remember any clashing between these civil and naval powers; but I remember well
my astonishment when I first beheld some of my little
comrades overthrown by the progress of one of these very
straightforward marine personages, who walked on with as
tranquil and unconscious a face as if nothing had happened.
It was not a fierce-looking push; there seemed to be no intention in it. The insolence lay in the boy not appearing to
know that such inferior creatures existed. It was always
thus, wherever he came. If aware, the boys got out of his
way; if not, down they went, one or more; away rolled the
top or the marbles, and on walked the future captain,

In maiden navigation, frank and free.

These boys wore a badge on the shoulder, of which they
were very proud; though in the streets it must have helped
to confound them with charity boys. For charity boys, I
must own, we all had a great contempt, or thought so. We
did not dare to know that there might have been a little
jealousy of our own position in it, placed as we were midway between the homeliness of the common charity-school and
the dignity of the foundations. We called them "*chizzy-
wags*," and had a particular scorn and hatred of their nasal
tone in singing.

The under grammar-master, in my time, was the Reverend Mr. Field. He was a good-looking man, very gentlemanly, and always dressed at the neatest. I believe he once
wrote a play. He had the reputation of being admired by
the ladies. A man of a more handsome incompetence for
his situation perhaps did not exist. He came late of a morn-

ing ; went away soon in the afternoon ; and used to walk up and down, languidly bearing his cane, as if it was a lily, and hearing our eternal *Dominuses* and *As in præsenti's* with an air of ineffable endurance. Often he did not hear at all. It was a joke with us, when any of our friends came to the door, and we asked his permission to go to them to address him with some preposterous question wide of the mark ; to which he used to assent. We would say, for instance, "Are you not a great fool, sir ?" or "Isn't your daughter a pretty girl ?" To which he would reply, "Yes, child." When he condescended to hit us with the cane, he made a face as if he was taking physic. Miss Field, an agreeable-looking girl, was one of the goddesses of the school ; as far above us as if she had lived on Olympus. Another was Miss Patrick, daughter of the lamp-manufacturer in New-gate-street. I do not remember her face so well, not seeing it so often ; but she abounded in admirers. I write the names of these ladies at full length, because there is nothing that should hinder their being pleased at having caused us so many agreeable visions. We used to identify them with the picture of Venus in Tooke's Pantheon.

The other master, the upper one, Boyer——famous for the mention of him by Coleridge and Lamb——was a short, stout man, inclining to punchiness, with large face and hands, an aquiline nose, long upper lip, and a sharp mouth. His eye was close and cruel. The spectacles which he wore threw a balm over it. Being a clergyman, he dressed in black, with a powdered wig. His clothes were cut short ; his hands hung out of the sleeves, with tight wristbands, as if ready for execution ; and as he generally wore gray worsted stockings, very tight, with a little balustrade leg, his whole appearance presented something formidably succinct, hard, and mechan-ical. In fact, his weak side, and undoubtedly his natural destination, lay in carpentry ; and he accordingly carried, in a side-pocket made on purpose, a carpenter's rule.

The merits of Boyer consisted in his being a good verbal scholar, and conscientiously acting up to the letter of time and attention. I have seen him nod at the close of the long summer school-hours, wearied out ; and I should have pitied

him if he had taught us to do any thing but fear.   Though
a clergyman, very orthodox, and of rigid morals, he indulged
himself in an oath, which was " God's-my-life !"   When
you were out in your lesson, he turned upon you a round,
staring eye, like a fish ; and he had a trick of pinching you
under the chin, and by the lobes of the ears, till he would
make the blood come.   He has many times lifted a boy off
the ground in this way.   He was, indeed, a proper tyrant,
passionate and capricious ; would take violent likes and dislikes to the same boys ; fondle some without any apparent
reason, though he had a leaning to the servile, and, perhaps
to the sons of rich people ; and he would persecute others in
a manner truly frightful.   I have seen him beat a sickly-
looking, melancholy boy (C——n) about the head and ears, till
the poor fellow, hot, dry-eyed, and confused, seemed lost in
bewilderment.   C——n, not long after he took orders died
out of his senses.   I do not attribute that catastrophe to the
master ; and of course he could not wish to do him any lasting mischief.   He had no imagination of any sort.   But
there is no saying how far his treatment of the boy might
have contributed to prevent a cure.   Tyrannical schoolmasters nowadays are to be found, perhaps, exclusively in
such inferior schools as those described with such masterly
and indignant edification by my friend Charles Dickens ; but
they formerly seemed to have abounded in all ; and masters
as well as boys, have escaped the chance of many bitter reflections, since a wiser and more generous intercourse has
come up between them.

I have some stories of Boyer, that will completely show
his character, and at the same time relieve the reader's indignation by something ludicrous in their excess.   We had
a few boarders at the school ; boys, whose parents were too
rich to let them go on the foundation.   Among them, in my
time, was Carlton, a son of Lord Dorchester ; Macdonald, one
of the Lord Chief Baron's sons ; and R——, the son of a
rich merchant.   Carlton, who was a fine fellow, manly, and
full of good sense, took his new master and his caresses very
coolly, and did not want them.   Little Macdonald also could
dispense with them, and would put on his delicate gloves

after lesson, with an air as if he resumed his patrician plumage. R—— was meeker, and willing to be encouraged; and there would the master sit, with his arm round his tall waist, helping him to his Greek verbs, as a nurse does bread and milk to an infant; and repeating them, when he missed, with a fond patience; that astonished us criminals in drugget.

Very different was the treatment of a boy on the foundation, whose friends, by some means or other, had prevailed on the master to pay him an extra attention, and try to get him on. He had come into the school at an age later than usual, and could hardly read. There was a book used by the learners in reading, called " Dialogues between a Missionary and an Indian." It was a poor performance, full of inconclusive arguments and other commonplaces. The boy in question used to appear with this book in his hand in the middle of the school, the master standing behind him. The lesson was to begin. Poor ——, whose great fault lay in a deep-toned drawl of his syllables and the omission of his stops, stood half-looking at the book, and half-casting his eye toward the right of him, whence the blows were to proceed. The master looked over him; and his hand was ready. I am not exact in my quotation at this distance of time; but the *spirit* of one of the passages that I recollect was to the following purport, and thus did the teacher and his pupil proceed :

Master. " Now, young man, have a care; or I'll set you a *swinging* task." (A common phrase of his.)

Pupil. (Making a sort of heavy bolt at his calamity, and never remembering his stop at the word Missionary.) " *Missionary* Can you see the wind ?"

(Master gives him a slap on the cheek.)

Pupil. (Raising his voice to a cry, and still forgetting his stop.) " *Indian* No !"

Master. " God's-my-life, young man ! have a care how you provoke me."

Pupil. (Always forgetting the stop.) " *Missionary* How then do you know that there is such a thing ?"

(Here a terrible thump.)

Pupil   (With a shout of agony.)   "*Indian* Because I feel it."

One anecdote of his injustice will suffice for all.   It is of ludicrous enormity; nor do I believe any thing more flagrantly willful was ever done by himself.   I heard Mr. C——, the sufferer, now a most respectable person in a government office, relate it with a due relish, long after quitting the school.   The master was in the habit of "spiting" C——; that is to say, of taking every opportunity to be severe with him; nobody knew why.   One day he comes into the school, and finds him placed in the middle of it with three other boys.   He was not in one of his worst humors, and did not seem inclined to punish them, till he saw his antagonist.   "Oh, oh! sir," said he; "what, you are among them, are you?" and gave him an exclusive thump on the face.   He then turned to one of the Grecians, and said, "I have not time to flog all these boys : make them draw lots, and I'll punish one."   The lots were drawn, and C——'s was favorable.   "Oh, oh!" returned the master, when he saw them, "you have escaped, have you, sir?" and pulling out his watch, and turning again to the Grecian observed, that he found he *had* time to punish the whole three ; "and, sir," added he to C——, with another slap, "I'll begin with *you.*"   He then took the boy into the library and flogged him; and, on issuing forth again, had the face to say, with an air of indifference, "I have not time, after all, to punish these two other boys : let them take care how they provoke me another time."

Often did I wish that I was a fairy, in order to play him tricks like a Caliban.   We used to sit and fancy what we should do with his wig; how we would hamper and vex him; "put knives in his pillow, and halters in his pew."   To venture on a joke in our own mortal persons, was like playing with Polyphemus.   One afternoon, when he was nodding with sleep over a lesson, a boy of the name of Meader, who stood behind him, ventured to take a pin, and begin advancing with it up his wig.   The hollow, exhibited between the wig and the nape of the neck, invited him. The boys encouraged this daring act of gallantry.   Nods and becks, and then whispers of " Go it, M. !" gave more and more valor to his hand. On a sudden, the master's head falls back ; he starts, with eyes like a shark ; and seizing the unfortunate culprit, who stood helpless in the act of holding the pin, caught hold of him, fiery with passion.

A " swinging task" ensued, which kept him at home all the holidays. One of these tasks would consist of an impóssible quantity of Virgil, which the learner, unable to retain it at once, wasted his heart and soul out " to get up," till it was too late.

Sometimes, however, our despot got into a dilemma, and then he did not know how to get out of it. A boy, now and then, would be roused into open and fierce remonstrance. I recollect S., afterward one of the mildest of preachers, starting up in his place, and pouring forth on his astonished hearer a torrent of invectives and threats, which the other could only answer by looking pale, and uttering a few threats in return. Nothing came of it. He did not like such matters to go before the governors. Another time, Favell, a Grecian, a youth of high spirit, whom he had struck, went to the school-door, opened it, and, turning round with the handle in his grasp, told him he would never set foot again in the place, unless he promised to treat him with more delicacy. " Come back, child ; come back !" said the other, pale, and in a faint voice. There was a dead silence. Favell came back, and nothing more was done.

A sentiment, unaccompanied with something practical, would have been lost upon him. D——, who went afterward to the Military College at Woolwich, played him a trick, apparently between jest and earnest, which amused us exceedingly. He was to be flogged ; and the dreadful door of the library was approached. (They did not invest the books with flowers, as Montaigne recommends.) Down falls the criminal, and twisting himself about the master's legs, which he does the more when the other attempts to move, repeats without ceasing, " O, good God ! consider my father, sir ; my father, sir ; you know my father !" The point was felt to be getting ludicrous, and was given up. P——, now a popular preacher, was in the habit of entertaining the boys

that way. He was a regular wag ; and would snatch his
jokes out of the very flame and fury of the master, like snap-
dragon. Whenever the other struck him, P. would get up ;
and half to avoid the blows, and half render them ridiculous,
begin moving about the school-room, making all sorts of
antics. When he was struck in the face, he would clap his
hand with affected vehemence to the place, and cry as
rapidly, " *Oh*, Lord !" If the blow came on the arm, he
would grasp his arm, with a similar exclamation. The
master would then go, driving and kicking him ; while the
patient accompanied every blow with the same comments and
illustrations, making faces to us by way of index.

What a bit of a golden age was it, when the Rev. Mr.
Steevens, one of the under grammar-masters, took his place,
on some occasion, for a short time ! Steevens was short and
fat, with a handsome, cordial face. You loved him as you
looked at him ; and seemed as if you should love him the
more, the fatter he became. I stammered when I was at
that time of life : which was an infirmity, that used to get
me into terrible trouble with the master. Steevens used to
say, on the other hand, " Here comes our little black-haired
friend, who stammers so. Now, let us see what we can do
for him." The consequence was, I did, not hesitate half so
much as with the other. When I did, it was out of impatience to please him.

Such of us were not liked the better by the master as were
in favor with his wife. She was a sprightly, good-looking
woman, with black eyes ; and was beheld with transport by
the boys, whenever she appeared at the school-door. Her
husband's name, uttered in a mingled tone of good-nature
and imperativeness, brought him down from his seat with
smiling haste. Sometimes he did not return. On entering the school one day, he found a boy eating cherries.
" Where did you get those cherries ?" exclaimed he, thinking
the boy had nothing to say for himself. " Mrs. Boyer gave
them me, sir." He turned away, scowling with disappointment.

Speaking of fruit, reminds me of a pleasant trait on the
part of a Grecian of the name of Le Grice. He was the

maddest of all the great boys in my time ; clever, full of address, and not hampered with modesty. Remote rumors,
not lightly to be heard, fell on our ears, respecting pranks
of his among the nurses' daughters. He had a fair, handsome face, with delicate aquiline nose, and twinkling eyes.
I remember his astonishing me, when I was " a new boy,"
with sending me for a bottle of water, which he proceeded to
pour down the back of G. a grave Deputy Grecian. On the
master asking one day, why he, of all the boys, had given up
no exercise (it was a particular exercise that they were bound
to do in the course of a long set of holidays), he said he had
had " a lethargy." The extreme impudence of this puzzled
the master ; and I believe nothing came of it. But what I
alluded to about the fruit was this. Le Grice was in the
habit of eating apples in school-time, for which he had been
often rebuked. One day, having particularly pleased the
master, the latter who was eating apples himself, and who
would now and then with great ostentation present a boy
with some half-penny token of his mansuetude, called out to
his favorite of the moment ; " Le Grice, here is an apple for
you." Le Grice, who felt his dignity hurt as a Grecian, but
was more pleased at having this opportunity of mortifying
his reprover, replied, with an exquisite tranquillity of assur-
ance, " Sir, I never eat apples." For this, among other
things, the boys adored him. Poor fellow ! He and Favell
(who, though very generous, was said to be a little too sensible of an humble origin) wrote to the Duke of York, when
they were at College, for commissions in the army. The
Duke good-naturedly sent them. Le Grice died in the West
Indies. Favell was killed in one of the battles in Spain, but
not before he had distinguished himself as an officer and a
gentleman.

The Upper Grammar School was divided into four classes,
or forms. The two under ones were called Little and Great
Erasmus ; the two upper were occupied by the Grecians and
Deputy Grecians. We used to think the title of Erasmus
taken from the great scholar of that name ; but the sudden
appearance of a portrait among us, bearing to be the likeness
of a certain Erasmus Smith, Esq., shook us terribly in this

opinion, and was a hard trial of our gratitude.   We scarcely
relished this perpetual company of our benefactor, watching
us, as he seemed to do, with his omnipresent eyes.   I believe
he was a rich merchant, and that the forms of Little and
Great Erasmus were really named after him.   It was but
a poor consolation to think that he himself, or his great-uncle,
might have been named after Erasmus.   Little Erasmus
learned Ovid ; Great Erasmus, Virgil, Terence, and the
Greek Testament.   The Deputy Grecians, were in Homer,
Cicero, and Demosthenes ; the Grecians, in the Greek plays
and the mathematics.

When a boy entered the Upper School, he was understood
to be in the road to the University, provided he had inclination and talents for it ; but, as only one Grecian a year
went to College, the drafts out of Great and Little Erasmus
into the writing-school were numerous.   A few also became
Deputy Grecians without going farther, and entered the
world from that form.   Those who became Grecians, always
went to the University, though not always into the Church ;
which was reckoned a departure from the contract.   When
I first came to school, at seven years old, the names of the
Grecians were Allen, Favell, Thomson, and Le Grice, brother
of the Le Grice above-mentioned, and now a clergyman in
Cornwall.   Charles Lamb had lately been Deputy Grecian ;
and Coleridge had left for the University.

The master, inspired by his subject with an eloquence beyond himself, once called him, "that sensible fool, Cōlĕrĭdge ;"
pronouncing the word like a dactyl.   Coleridge must have
alternately delighted and bewildered him.   The compliment,
as to the bewildering, was returned, if not the delight.   The
pupil, I am told, said he dreamt of the master all his life,
and that his dreams were horrible.   A bonmot of his is recorded, very characteristic both of pupil and master.   Coleridge when he heard of his death, said, "It was lucky that
the cherubim who took him to heaven were nothing but faces,
and wings, or he would infallibly have flogged them by the
way."   This was his esoterical opinion of him.   His outward and subtler opinion, or opinion exoterical, he favored
the public with in his Literary Life.   He praised him, among

other things, for his good taste in poetry, and his not suffering
the boys to get into the commonplaces of Castalian Streams,
Invocations to the Muses, &c. Certainly there were no
such things in our days, at least, to the best of my remem
brance. But I do not think the master saw through them,
out of a perception of any thing farther. His objection to a
commonplace must have been itself commonplace.

I do not remember seeing Coleridge. when I was a child.
Lamb's visits to the school, after he left it, I remember well,
with his fine intelligent face. Little did I think I should
have the pleasure of sitting with it in after-times as an old
friend, and seeing it careworn and still finer. Allen, the
Grecian, was so handsome, though in another and more obvious way, that running one day against a barrow-woman in
the street, and turning round to appease her in the midst of
her abuse, she said, " Where are you driving to, you great
hulking, good-for-nothing, beautiful fellow, God bless you !"
Le G ice the elder was a wag, like his brother, but more
staid. He went into the Church, as he ought to do, and
married a rich widow. He published a translation, abridged,
of the celebrated pastoral of Longus ; and report at school
made him the author of a little anonymous tract on the *Art
of Poking the Fire.*

Few of us cared for any of the books that were taught :
and no pains were taken to make us do so. The boys had
no helps to information, bad or good, except what the master
afforded them respecting manufactures ; a branch of knowledge, to which, as I before observed, he had a great tendency,
and which was the only point on which he was enthusiastic
and gratuitous. I do not blame him for what he taught us
of this kind : there was a use in it, beyond what he was
aware of ; but it was the only one on which he volunteered
any assistance. In this he took evident delight. I remember, in explaining pigs of iron or lead to us, he made a point
of crossing one of his legs with the other, and cherishing it
up and down with great satisfaction, saying, " A pig, children, is about the thickness of my leg." Upon which, with
a slavish pretense of novelty, we all looked at it, as if he
had not told us so a hundred times. In every thing else we

had to hunt out our own knowledge. He would not help us with a word till he had ascertained that we had done all we could to learn the meaning of it ourselves. This discipline was useful; and, in this and every other respect, we had all the advantages which a mechanical sense of right, and a rigid exaction of duty, could afford us; but no farther. The only superfluous grace that he was guilty of, was the keeping a manuscript book, in which by a rare luck, the best exercise in English verse was occasionally copied out for immortality! To have verses in "the Book" was the rarest and highest honor conceivable to our imaginations.

How little did I care for any verses at that time, except English ones; I had no regard even for Ovid. I read and knew nothing of Horace; though I had got somehow a liking for his character. Cicero I disliked, as I can not help doing still. Demosthenes I was inclined to admire, but did not know why, and would very willingly have given up him and his difficulties together. Homer I regarded with horror, as a series of lessons, which I had to learn by heart before I understood him. When I had to conquer, in this way, lines which I had not construed, I had recourse to a sort of artificial memory, by which I associated the Greek words with sounds that had a meaning in English. Thus, a passage about Thetis I made to bear on some circumstance that had taken place in the school. An account of a battle was converted into a series of jokes; and the master, while I was saying my lesson to him in trepidation, little suspected what a figure he was often cutting in the text. The only classic I remember having any love for was Virgil; and that was for the episode of Nisus and Euryalus.

But there were three books which I read in whenever I could, and which often got me into trouble. These were Tooke's *Pantheon*, Lempriere's *Classical Dictionary*, and Spence's *Polymetis*, the great folio edition with plates. Tooke was a prodigious favorite with us. I see before me, as vividly now as ever, his Mars and Apollo, his Venus and Aurora, which I was continually trying to copy; the Mars, coming on furiously in his car; Apollo, with his radiant head, in the midst of shades and fountains; Aurora with hers, a golden dawn ; and Venus, very handsome, we thought, and not looking too modest, in "a slight cymar." It is curious how completely the graces of the pagan theology overcame with us the wise cautions and reproofs that were set against it in the pages of Mr. Tooke. Some years after my departure from school, happening to look at the work in question, I was surprised to find so much of that matter in him. When I came to reflect, I had a sort of recollection that we used occasionally to notice it, as something inconsistent with the rest of the text—strange, and odd, and like the interference of some pedantic old gentleman. This, indeed, is pretty nearly the case. The author has also made a strange mistake about Bacchus, whom he represents, both in his text and his print, as a mere belly-god; a corpulent child, like the Bacchus bestriding a tun. This is any thing but classical. The truth is, it was a sort of pious fraud, like many other things palmed upon antiquity. Tooke's *Pantheon* was written originally in Latin by the Jesuits.

Our Lempriere was a fund of entertainment. Spence's *Polymetis* was not so easily got at. There was also something in the text that did not invite us ; but we admired the fine large prints. However, Tooke was the favorite. I cannot divest myself of a notion, to this day, that there is something really clever in the picture of Apollo. The Minerva we "could not abide ;" Juno was no favorite, for all her throne and her peacock ; and we thought Diana too pretty. The instinct against these three godesses begins early. I used to wonder how Juno and Minerva could have the insolence to dispute the apple with Venus.

In those times, Cooke's edition of the British poets came up. I had got an odd volume of Spenser ; and I fell passionately in love with Collins and Gray. How I loved those little sixpenny numbers containing whole poets ! I doated on their size ; I doated on their type, on their ornaments, on their wrappers containing lists of other poets, and on the engravings from Kirk. I bought them over and over again, and used to get up select sets, which disappeared like butter-ed crumpets ; for I could resist neither giving them away, nor possessing them. When the master tormented me, when

I used to hate and loathe the sight of Homer, and Demosthenes, and Cicero, I would comfort myself with thinking of the sixpence in my pocket, with which I should go out to Paternoster-row, when the school was over, and buy another number of an English poet.

I was already fond of writing verses. The first I remember were in honor of the Duke of York's "Victory at Dunkirk;" which victory, to my great mortification, turned out to be a defeat. I compared him with Achilles and Alexander; or should rather say, trampled upon those heroes in the comparison. I fancied him riding through the field, and shooting right and left of him! Afterward, when in Great Erasmus, I wrote a poem called *Winter*, in consequence of reading Thomson; and when Deputy Grecian, I completed some hundred stanzas of another, called the *Fairy King*, which was to be in emulation of Spenser! I also wrote a long poem in irregular Latin verses (such as they were), entitled *Thor*; the consequence of reading Gray's Odes, and Mallett's *Northern Antiquities*. English verses were the only exercise I performed with satisfaction. Themes, or prose essays, I wrote so badly, that the master was in the habit of contemptuously crumpling them up in his hand, and calling out, "Here, children, there is something to amuse you." Upon which the servile part of the boys would jump up, seize the paper, and be amused accordingly.

The essays must have been very absurd, no doubt; but those who would have tasted the ridicule best, were the last to move. There was an absurdity in giving us such essays to write. They were upon a given subject, generally a moral one; such as ambition, or the love of money: and the regular process in the manufacture was this. You wrote out the subject very fairly at top, *Quid non mortalia*, &c. or *Crescit amor nummi*. Then the ingenious thing was to repeat this apophthegm in as many words and 'round-about phrases as possible; which took up a good bit of the paper. Then you attempted to give a reason or two, why *amor nummi* was bad; or on what accounts heroes ought to eschew ambition; after which naturally came a few examples, got out of Plutarch, or the *Selectæ e Profanis*; and

the happy moralist concluded with signing his name. Somebody speaks of schoolboys going about to one another on
these occasions, and asking for "a little sense." That was
not the phrase with us; it was "a thought." "P——,
can you give me a thought?" "C——, for God's sake,
help me to a thought, for it only wants ten minutes to
eleven." It was a joke with P——, who knew my hatred
of themes, and how I used to hurry over them, to come to
me at a quarter to eleven, and say, "Hunt, have you *begun*
your theme?"—"Yes, P——." He then, when the
quarter of an hour had expired and the bell tolled, came
again, and, with a sort of rhyming formula to the other
question, said, "Hunt, have you *done* your theme?"—
"Yes, P——."

How I dared to trespass in this way upon the patience
of the master, I can not conceive. ·I suspect that the themes
appeared to him more absurd than careless. Perhaps another thing perplexed him. The master was rigidly orthodox; the school-establishment also was orthodox and high
tory; and there was just then a little perplexity, arising
from the free doctrines inculcated by the books we learned,
and the new and alarming echo of them struck on the ears
of power by the French Revolution. My father was in the
habit of expressing his opinions. He did not conceal the
new tendency which he felt to modify those which he
entertained respecting both Church and State. His unconscious son at school, nothing doubting or suspecting, repeated
his eulogies of Timoleon and the Gracchi, with all a schoolboy's enthusiasm; and the master's mind was not of a pitch
to be superior to this unwitting annoyance. It was on these
occasions, I suspect, that he crumpled up my themes with
a double contempt, and with an equal degree of perplexity.

There was a better school exercise, consisting of an
abridgment of some paper in the *Spectator*. We made,
however, little of it, and thought it very difficult and perplexing. In fact, it was a hard task for boys, utterly unacquainted with the world, to seize the best points out of the writings
of masters in experience. It only gave the *Spectator* an
unnatural gravity in our eyes. A common paper for selec-

tion, because reckoned one of the easiest, was the one beginning, "I have always preferred cheerfulness to mirth." I
had heard this paper so often, and was so tired with it, that
it gave me a great inclination to prefer mirth to cheerfulness.

My books were a never-ceasing consolation to me, and
such they have ever continued. My favorites out of school-
hours, were Spenser, Collins, Gray, and the *Arabian Nights.*
Pope I admired more than loved; Milton was above me;
and the only play of Shakspeare's with which I was con-
versant was *Hamlet,* of which I had a delighted awe.
Neither-then, however, nor at any time, have I been as fond
of dramatic reading as of any other, though I have written
many dramas myself, and have even a special propensity for
so doing ; a contradiction, for which I have never been
able to account. Chaucer, who has since been one of my
best friends, I was not acquainted with at school, nor till
long afterward. *Hudibras* I remember reading through at
one desperate plunge, while I lay incapable of moving, with
two scalded legs. I did it as a sort of achievement, driving
on through the verses without understanding a twentieth
part of them, but now and then laughing immoderately at
the rhymes and similes, and catching a bit of knowledge
unawares. I had a schoolfellow of the name of Brooke,
afterward an officer in the East India service—a grave,
quiet boy, with a fund of manliness and good-humor. He
would pick out the ludicrous couplets, like plums ; such as
those on the astrologer.

> Who deals in destiny's dark counsels,
> And sage opinions of the moon sells ;

And on the apothecary's shop,

> With stores of deleterious med'cines,
> Which whosoever took is dead since.   .

He had the little thick duodecimo edition, with Hogarth's
plates, dirty, and well read, looking like Hudibras himself.

I read through, at the same time, and with little less
sense of it as a task, Milton's *Paradise Lost.* The divinity
of it was so much "Heathen Greek" to us. Unluckily, I
could not taste the beautiful "Heathen Greek" of the style.

Milton's heaven made no impression; not could I enter
even into the earthly catastrophe of his man and woman.
The only two things I thought of were their happiness in
Paradise, where (to me) they eternally remained; and the
strange malignity of the devil, who, instead of getting them
out of it, as the poet represents, only served to bind them
closer. He seemed an odd shade to the picture. The
figure he cut in the engravings was more in my thoughts,
than any thing said of him in the poem. He was a sort of
human wild beast, lurking about the garden in which they
lived; though, in consequence of the dress given him in
some of the plates, this man with a tail occasionally confused himself in my imagination with a Roman general. I
could make little of it. I believe, the plates impressed me
altogether much more than the poem. Perhaps they were
the reason why I thought of Adam and Eve as I did; the
pictures of them in their paradisaical state being more
numerous than those in which they appear exiled. Besides,
in their exile they were together; and this constituting the
best thing in their paradise, I suppose I could not so easily
get miserable with them when out of it.

The scald that I speak of, as confining me to bed was a bad
one. I will give an account of it, because it furthers the
elucidation of our school manners. I had then become a
monitor, or one of the chiefs of a ward; and I was sitting
before the fire one evening, after the boys had gone to bed,
wrapped up in the perusal of the " Wonderful Magazine,"
and having in my ear at the same time the bubbling of a
great pot, or rather cauldron, of water, containing what was
by courtesy called a bread pudding; being neither more nor
less than a loaf or two of our bread, which, with a little
sugar mashed up with it, was to serve for my supper. And
there were eyes, not yet asleep, which would look at it out
of their beds, and regard is as a lordly dish. From this
dream of bliss I was roused up on the sudden by a great
cry, and a horrible agony in my legs. A " boy," as a fag
was called, wishing to get something from the other side of
the fire-place, and not choosing either to go round behind
the table, or to disturb the illustrious legs of the monitor,

had endeavored to get under them or between them, and he pulled the great handle of the pot after him. It was a frightful sensation. The whole of my being seemed collected in one fiery torment into my legs. Wood, the Grecian (afterward Fellow of Pembroke, at Cambridge), who was in our ward, and who was always very kind to me (led, I believe, by my inclination for verses, in which he had a great name), came out of his study, and after helping me off with my stockings, which was a horrid operation, the stockings, being very coarse, took me in his arms to the sick ward. I shall never forget the enchanting relief occasioned by the cold air, as it blew across the square of the sick ward. I lay there for several weeks, not allowed to move for some time; and caustics became necessary before I got well. The getting well was delicious. I had no tasks—no master; plenty of books to read: and the nurse's daughter (*absit calumnia*) brought me tea and buttered toast, and encouraged me to play the flute. My playing consisted of a few tunes by rote; my fellow-invalids (none of them in very desperate case) would have it rather than no playing at all; so we used to play and tell stories, and go to sleep, thinking of the blessed sick holiday we should have to-morrow, and of the bowl of milk and bread for breakfast, which was alone worth being sick for. The sight of Mr. Long's probe was not so pleasant. We preferred seeing it in the hands of Mr. Vincent, whose manners, quiet and mild, had double effect on a set of boys more or less jealous of the mixed humbleness and importance of their school. This was most likely the same gentleman of the name of Vincent, who afterward became distinguished in his profession. He was dark, like a West Indian, and I used to think him handsome. Perhaps the nurse's daughter taught me to think so, for she was a considerable observer.

CHAPTER IV.

SCHOOL-DAYS (*continued.*)

Healthy literary training of Christ-Hospital.—Early friendship.—Early
love.—St. James's Park, music, and war.—President West and his
house.—The Thornton family and theirs.—The Dayrells and first love.
Early thoughts of religion.—Jews and their synagogues.—Coleridge
and Lamb.—A mysterious school-fellow.—The greater mystery of
the Fazzer.—Mitchell and Barnes.—Boatings, bathings, and Lady
Craven.—Departure from school.

I AM grateful to Christ-Hospital for its having bred me
up in old cloisters, for its making me acquainted with the
languages of Homer and Ovid, and for its having secured
to me, on the whole, a well-trained and cheerful boyhood.
It pressed no superstition upon me. It did not hinder my
growing mind from making what excursions it pleased into
the wide and healthy regions of general literature. I might
buy as much Collins and Gray as I pleased, and get novels
to my heart's content from the circulating libraries. There
was nothing prohibited but what would have been prohibited
by all good fathers ; and every thing was encouraged which
would have been encouraged by the Steeles, and Addisons,
and Popes ; by the Warburtons, and Atterburys, and Hoad-
leys. Boyer was a severe, nay, a cruel master ; but age and
reflection have made me sensible that I ought always to add
my testimony to his being a laborious, and a conscientious
one. When his severity went beyond the mark, I believe
he was always sorry for it : sometimes I am sure he was.
He once (though the anecdote at first sight may look like a
burlesque on the remark) knocked out one of my teeth with
the back of a Homer, in a fit of impatience at my stammer-
ing. The tooth was a loose one, and I told him as much ;
but the blood rushed out as I spoke : he turned pale, and, on
my proposing to go out and wash the mouth, he said, " Go,
child," in a tone of voice amounting to the paternal. Now

" go, child," from Boyer, was worth a dozen tender speeches from any one else ; and it was felt that I had got an advantage over him, acknowledged by himself.

If I had reaped no other benefit from Christ-Hospital, the school would be ever dear to me from the recollection of the friendships I formed in it, and of the first heavenly taste it gave me of that most spiritual of the affections. I use the word " heavenly " advisedly ; and I call friendship the most spiritual of the affections, because even one's kindred, in partaking of our flesh and blood, become, in a manner, mixed up with our entire being. Not that I would disparage any other form of affection, worshiping, as I do, all forms of it, love in particular, which, in its highest state, is friendship and something more. But if ever I tasted a disembodied transport on earth, it was in those friendships which I entertained at school, before I dreamt of any maturer feeling. I shall never forget the impression it first made on me. I loved my friend for his gentleness, his candor, his truth, his good repute, his freedom even from my own livelier manner, his calm and reasonable kindness. It was not any particular talent that attracted me to him, or any thing striking whatsoever. I should say, in one word, it was his goodness. I doubt whether he ever had a conception of a tithe of the regard ·and respect I entertained for him ; and I smile to think of the perplexity (though he never showed it) which he probably felt sometimes at my enthusiastic expressions ; for I thought him a kind of angel. It was no exaggeration to say, that, take away the unspiritual part of it——the genius and the knowledge——and there is no height of conceit indulged in by the most romantic character in Shakspeare, which surpassed what I felt toward the merits I ascribed to him, and the delight which I took in his society. With the other boys I played antics, and rioted in fantastic jests ; but in his society, or whenever I thought of him, I fell into a kind of Sabbath state of bliss ; and I am sure I could have died for him.

I experienced this delightful affection toward three successive schoolfellows, till two of them had for some time gone out into the world and forgotten me ; but it grew less with

each, and in more than one instance, became rivaled by a new
set of emotions, especially in regard to the last, for I fell in love
with his sister—at least, I thought so. But on the occur-
rence of her death, not long after, I was startled at finding
myself assume an air of greater sorrow than I felt, and at
being willing to be relieved by the sight of the first pretty
face that turned toward me. I was in the situation of the
page in Figaro :

> Ogni donna cangiar di colore ;
> Ogni donna mi fa palpitar.

My friend, who died himself not long after his quitting the
University, was of a German family in the service of the
court, very refined and musical. I likened them to the people in the novels of Augustus La Fontaine ; and with the
younger of the two sisters I had a great desire to play the
part of the hero in the *Family of Halden*.

The elder, who was my senior, and of manners too advanced for me to aspire to, became distinguished in private
circles as an accomplished musician. How I used to rejoice
when they struck their " harps in praise of Bragela !" and
how ill-bred I must have appeared when I stopped beyond
all reasonable time of visiting, unable to tear myself away !
They lived in Spring Gardens, in a house which I have
often gone out of my way to look at ; and, as I first heard
of Mozart in their company, and first heard his marches in
the Park, I used to associate with their idea whatsoever was
charming and graceful.

Maternal notions of war came to nothing before love and
music, and the steps of the officers on parade. The young
ensign with his flag, and the ladies with their admiration of
him, carried every thing before them.

I had already borne to school the air of " *Non piu
andrai ;*" and, with the help of instruments made of paper,
into which we breathed what imitations we could of haut-
boys and clarionets, had inducted the boys into the " pride,
pomp, and circumstance" of that glorious bit of war.

Thus is war clothed and recommended to all of us, and
not without reason, as long as it is a necessity, or as long as

it is something, at least, which we have not acquired knowledge or means enough to do away with.   A bullet is of all pills the one that most requires gilding.

But I will not bring these night-thoughts into the morning of life.   Besides, I am anticipating ; for this was not my first love.   I shall mention that presently.

I have not done with my school-reminiscences ; but in order to keep a straightforward course, and notice simultaneous events in their proper places, I shall here speak of the persons and things in which I took the greatest interest when I was not within schoolbounds.

The two principal houses at which I visited till the arrival of our relations from the West Indies, were Mr. West's (late President of the Royal Academy), in Newman-street, and Mr. Godfrey Thornton's (of the distinguished city family), in Austin-Friars.   How I loved the Graces in one and every thing in the other !   Mr. West (who, as I have already mentioned, had married one of my relations) had bought his house, I believe, not long after he came to England ; and he had added a gallery at the back of it, terminating in a couple of lofty rooms.   The gallery was a continuation of the house-passage, and, together with one of those rooms and the parlor, formed three sides of a garden, very small but elegant, with a grass-plot in the middle, and busts upon stands under an arcade.   The gallery, as you went up it, formed an angle at a little distance to the left, then another to the right, and then took a longer stretch into the two rooms ; and it was hung with the artist's sketches all the way.   In a corner between the two angles was a study-door with casts of Venus and Apollo, on each side of it.   The two rooms contained the largest of his pictures ; and in the farther one, after stepping softly down the gallery, as if reverencing the dumb life on the walls, you generally found the mild and quiet artist at his work ; happy, for he thought himself immortal.

I need not enter into the merits of an artist who is so well known, and has been so often criticised.   He was a man with regular, mild features ; and, though of Quaker origin, had the look of what he was, a painter to a court.

His appearance was so gentlemanly, that, the moment he changed his gown for a coat, he seemed to be full-dressed. The simplicity and self-possession of the young Quaker, not having time enough to grow stiff (for he went early to study at Rome), took up, I suppose, with more ease than most would have done, the urbanities of his new position. And what simplicity helped him to, favor would retain. Yet this man, so well bred, and so indisputably clever in his art (whatever might be the amount of his genius), had received so careless, or so homely an education when a boy, that he could hardly read. He pronounced also some of his words, in reading, with a puritanical barbarism, such as *haive* for *have*, as some people pronounce when they sing psalms. But this was perhaps an American custom. My mother, who both read and spoke remarkably well, would say *haive*, and *shaul* (for *shall*), when she sung her hymns. But it was not so well in reading lectures at the Academy. Mr. West would talk of his art all day long, painting all the while. On other subjects he was not so fluent; and on political and religious matters he tried hard to maintain the reserve common with those about a court. He succeeded ill in both. There were always strong suspicions of his leaning to his native side in politics ; and during Bonaparte's triumph, he could not contain his enthusiasm for the Republican chief, going even to Paris to pay him his homage, when First Consul. The admiration of high colors and powerful effects, natural to a painter, was too strong for him. How he managed this matter with the higher powers in England I can not say. Probably he was the less heedful, inasmuch as he was not very carefully paid. I believe he did a great deal for George the Third with little profit. Mr. West certainly kept his love for Bonaparte no secret ; and it was no wonder, for the latter expressed admiration of his pictures. The artist thought the conqueror's smile enchanting, and that he had the handsomest leg he had ever seen. He was present when the " Venus de Medicis" was talked of, the French having just taken possession of her. Bonaparte, Mr. West said, turned round to those about him, and said, with his eyes lit up, " She's coming !" as if he had

been talking of a living person.   I believe he retained for
the emperor the love that he had had for the First Consul,
a wedded love, " for better for worse."   However, I believe ·
also that he retained it after the Emperor's downfall ; which
is not what every painter did.

But I am getting out of my chronology.   The quiet of
Mr. West's gallery, the tranquil, intent beauty of the statues,
and the subjects of some of the pictures, particularly Death
on the Pale Horse, the Deluge, the Scotch King hunting the
Stag, Moses on Mount Sinai, Christ healing the Sick (a
sketch), Sir Philip Sidney giving up the water to the Dying
Soldier, the Installation of the Knights of the Garter, and
Ophelia before the King and Queen (one of the best things
he ever did), made a great impression upon me.   My mother
and I used to go down the gallery, as if we were treading
on wool.   She was in the habit of stopping to look at some
of the pictures, particularly the Deluge and the Ophelia,
with a countenance quite awe-stricken.   She used also to
point out to me the subjects relating to liberty and patriotism, and the domestic affections.   Agrippina bringing home
the ashes of Germanicus was a great favorite with her.   I
remember, too, the awful delight afforded us by the Angel
slaying the army of Sennacherib ; a bright figure lording it
in the air, with a chaos of human beings below.

As Mr. West was almost sure to be found at work, in
the farthest room, habited in his white woolen gown, so you
might have predicated, with equal certainty, that Mrs. West
was sitting in the parlor, reading.   I used to think, that if
I had such a parlor to sit in, I should do just as she did.   It
was a good-sized room, with two windows looking out on the
little garden I spoke of, and opening to it from one of them
by a flight of steps.   The garden with its busts in it, and
the pictures which you know were on the other side of its
wall, had an Italian look.   The room was hung with engravings and colored prints.   Among them was the Lion
Hunt, from Rubens ; the Hierarchy with the Godhead, from
Raphael, which I hardly thought it right to look at ; and
two screens by the fireside, containing prints (from Angelica
Kauffman, I think, but I am not sure that Mr. West him-

self was not the designer) of the Loves of Angelica and Medoro, which I could have looked at from morning to night. Angelica's intent eyes, I thought, had the best of it; but I thought so without knowing why. This gave me a love for Ariosto before I knew him. I got Hoole's translation, but could make nothing of it. Angelica Kauffman seemed to me to have done much more for her namesake. She could see farther into a pair of eyes than Mr. Hoole with his spectacles. This reminds me that I could make as little of Pope's Homer, which a schoolfellow of mine was always reading, and which I was ashamed of not being able to like. It was not that I did not admire Pope; but the words in his translation always took precedence in my mind of the things, and the unvarying sweetness of his versification tired me before I knew the reason. This did not hinder me afterward from trying to imitate it; nor from succeeding; that is to say as far as everybody else succeeds, and writing smooth verses. It is Pope's wit and closeness that are the difficult things, and that make him what he is; a truism, which the mistakes of critics on divers sides have made it but too warrantable to repeat.

Mrs. West and my mother used to talk of old times, and Philadelphia, and my father's prospects at court. I sat apart with a book, from which I stole glances at Angelica. I had a habit at that time of holding my breath, which forced me every now and then to take long sighs. My aunt would offer me a bribe not to sigh. I would earn it once or twice; but the sighs were sure to return. These wagers I did not care for; but I remember being greatly mortified when Mr. West offered me half-a-crown if I would solve the old question of " Who was the father of Zebedee's children ?" and I could not tell him. He never made his appearance till dinner, and returned to his painting room directly after it. And so at tea-time. The talk was very quiet; the neighborhood quiet; the servants quiet; I thought the very squirrel in the cage would have made a greater noise any where else. James the porter, a fine tall fellow, who figured in his master's pictures as an apostle, was as quiet as he was strong. Standing for his picture had become a sort of religion with him.

Even the butler, with his little twinkling eyes, full of pleasant conceit, vented his notions of himself in half tones and whispers. This was a strange fantastic person. He got my brother Robert to take a likeness of him, small enough to be contained in a shirt pin. It was thought that his twinkling eyes, albeit not young, had some fair cynosure in the neighborhood. What was my brother's amazement, when, the next time he saw him, the butler said, with a face of enchanted satisfaction, " Well, sir, you see !" making a movement at the same time with the frill at his waistcoat. The miniature that was to be given to the object of his affections, had been given accordingly. It was in his own bosom.

But, notwithstanding my delight with the house at the west end of the town, it was not to compare with my beloved one in the city. There was quiet in the one ; there were beautiful statues and pictures ; and there was my Angelica for me with her intent eyes, at the fireside. But besides quiet in the other, there was cordiality, and there was music, and a family brimful of hospitality and good-nature, and dear Almeria T. (now Mrs. P——e), who in vain pretends that she has become aged, which is what she never did, shall, would, might, should, or could do. Those were indeed holidays, on which I used to go to Austin-Friars. The house (such, at least, are my boyish recollections) was of the description I have been ever fondest of, large, rambling, old-fashioned, solidly built, resembling the mansions about Highgate and other old villages.

It was furnished as became the house of a rich merchant and a sensible man, the comfort predominating over the costliness. At the back was a garden with a lawn ; and a private door opened into another garden, belonging to the Company of Drapers ; so that, what with the secluded nature of the street itself, and these verdant places behind it, it was truly *rus in urbe*, and a retreat. When I turned down the archway, I held my mother's hand tighter with pleasure, and was full of expectation, and joy, and respect. My first delight was in mounting the staircase to the rooms of the young ladies, setting my eyes on the comely and bright countenance of my fair friend, with her romantic name, and

turning over for the hundredth time, the books in her library.
What she did with the volumes of the *Turkish Spy*, what
they meant, or what amusement she could extract from them,
was an eternal mystification to me. Not long ago, meeting
with a copy of the book accidentally, I pounced upon my old
acquaintance, and found him to contain better and more
amusing stuff than people would suspect from his dry look
and his obsolete politics.*

The face of tenderness and respect with which Almeria
used to welcome my mother, springing forward with her fine
buxom figure to supply the strength which the other wanted,
and showing what an equality of love there may be between
youth and middle-age, and rich and poor, I should never
cease to love her for, had she not been, as she was, one of
the best-natured persons in the world in every thing. I have
not seen her now for a great many years; but, with that
same face, whatever change she may pretend to find in it,
she will go to heaven; for it is the face of her spirit. A
good heart never grows old.

Of George T——, her brother, who will pardon this
omission of his worldly titles, whatever they may be, I have
a similar kind of recollection, in its proportion; for, though
we knew him thoroughly, we saw him less. The sight of
his face was an additional sunshine to my holiday. He
was very generous and handsome-minded; a genuine human
being.

Mrs. T——, the mother, a very lady-like woman, in a
delicate state of health, we usually found reclining on a sofa,
always ailing, but always with a smile for us. The father,
a man of a large habit of body, panting with asthma, whom
we seldom saw but at dinner, treated us with all the family
delicacy, and would have me come and sit next him, which
I did with a mixture of joy and dread; for it was painful
to hear him breathe. I dwell the more upon these atten-

---

* The *Turkish Spy* is a sort of philosophical newspaper, in volumes; and, under a mask of bigotry, speculates very freely on all
subjects. It is said to have been written by an Italian Jesuit of the
name of Marana. The first volume has been attributed, however, to
Sir Roger Manley, father of the author of the *Atalantis;* and the rest
to Dr. Midgeley, a friend of his.

tions, because the school that I was in held a sort of equivocal rank in point of what is called respectability; and it
was no less an honor to another, than to ourselves, to know
when to place us upon a liberal footing.   Young as I was,
I felt this point strongly; and was touched with as grateful
a tenderness toward those who treated me handsomely, as
I retreated inwardly upon a proud consciousness of my
Greek and Latin, when the supercilious would have hum-
bled me.   Blessed house!   May a blessing be upon your
rooms, and your lawn, and your neighboring garden, and
the quiet old monastic name of your street! and may it
never be a thoroughfare! and may all your inmates be
happy!   Would to God one could renew, at a moment's
notice, the happy hours we have enjoyed in past times, with
the same circles, and in the same houses!   A planet with
such a privilege would be a great lift nearer heaven.   What
prodigious evenings, reader, we would have of it!   What
fine pieces of childhood, of youth, of manhood—ay, and of
age, as long as our friends lasted.

The old gentleman in Gil Blas, who complained that the
peaches were not so fine as they used to be when he was
young, had more reason than appears on the face of it.   He
missed not only his former palate, but the places he ate them
in, and those who ate them with him.   I have been told,
that the cranberries I have met with since must have been
as fine as those I got with the T.'s; as large and as juicy;
and that they came from the same place.   For all that, I
never ate a cranberry-tart since I dined in Austin-Friars.

I should have fallen in love with A. T——, had I been
old enough.   As it was, my first flame, or my first notion
of a flame, which is the same thing in those days, was for
my giddy cousin Fanny Dayrell, a charming West Indian.
Her mother, the aunt I spoke of, had just come from Barbadoes with her two daughters and a sister.   She was a
woman of a princely spirit; and having a good property, and
every wish to make her relations more comfortable, she did
so.   It became holiday with us all.   My mother raised her
head; my father grew young again; my cousin Kate
(Christina rather, for her name was not Catherine; Chris-

tina Arabella was her name) conceived a regard for one of
my brothers, and married him ; and for my part, besides
my pictures and Italian garden at Mr. West's, and my beloved old English house in Austin-Friars, I had now another
paradise in Great Ormond-street.

My aunt had something of the West Indian pride, but all
in a good spirit, and was a mighty cultivator of the gentili-
ties, inward as well as outward.   I did not dare to appear
before her with dirty hands, she would have rebuked me so
handsomely.   For some reason or other, the marriage of my
brother and his cousin was kept secret a little while.   I
became acquainted with it by chance, coming in upon a
holiday, the day the ceremony took place.   Instead of keeping me out of the secret by a trick, they very wisely resolved
upon trusting me with it, and relying upon my honor.   My
honor happened to be put to the test, and I came off with
flying colors.   It is to this circumstance I trace the religious idea I have ever since entertained of keeping a secret.
I went with the bride and bridegroom to church, and
remember kneeling apart and weeping bitterly.   My tears
were unaccountable to them.   Doubtless they were owing
to an instinctive sense of the great change that was taking
place in the lives of two human beings, and of the unalter-
ableness of the engagement.   Death and Life seem to come
together on these occasions, like awful guests at a feast, and
look one another in the face.

It was not with such good effect that my aunt raised my
notions of a schoolboy's pocket-money to half-crowns, and
crowns, and half-guineas.   My father and mother were both
as generous as daylight ; but they could not give what they
had not.   I had been unused to spending, and accordingly
I spent with a vengeance.   I remember a ludicrous instance.
The first half-guinea that I received brought about me a
consultation of companions to know how to get rid of it.
One shilling was devoted to pears, another to apples, another
to cakes, and so on, all to be bought immediately, as they
were ; till coming to the sixpence, and being struck with a
recollection that I ought to do something useful with that,
I bought sixpenn'orth of shoe-strings : these, no doubt, van-

ished like the rest.   The next half-guinea came to the
knowledge of the master : he interfered, which was one of
his proper actions ; and my aunt practiced more self-denial
in future.

Our new family from abroad were true West Indians, or,
as they would have phrased it, " true Barbadians born."
They were generous, warm tempered, had great good-nature ;
were proud, but not unpleasantly so ; lively, yet indolent ;
temperately epicurean in their diet ; fond of company, and
dancing, and music ; and lovers of show, but far from with-
holding the substance.   I speak chiefly of the mother and
daughters.   My other aunt, an elderly maiden, who piqued
herself on the delicacy of her hands and ankles, and made
you understand how many suitors she had refused (for which
she expressed any thing but repentance, being extremely
vexed), was not deficient in complectional good-nature ; but
she was narrow-minded, and seemed to care for nothing in
the world but two things : first, for her elder niece Kate,
whom she had helped to nurse ; and second, for a becoming
set-out of coffee and buttered toast, particularly of a morning, when it was taken up to her in bed, with a suitable
equipage of silver and other necessaries of life.   Yes ; there
was one more indispensable thing—slavery.   It was frightful to hear her small mouth and little mincing tones assert
the necessity not only of slaves, but robust, corporal punishment to keep them to their duty.   But she did this, because
her want of ideas could do no otherwise.   Having had slaves,
she wondered how any body could object to so natural and
lady-like an establishment.   Late in life, she took to fancying
that every polite old gentleman was in love with her ; and
thus she lived on, till her dying moment, in a flutter of
expectation.

The black servant must have puzzled this aunt of mine
sometimes.   All the wonder of which she was capable, he
certainly must have roused, not without a " quaver of con-
sternation."   This man had come over with them from the
West Indies.   He was a slave on my aunt's estate, and as
such he demeaned himself, till he learned that there was no
such thing as a slave in England ; that the moment a man

set his foot on English ground, he was free. I can not help smiling to think of the bewildered astonishment into which his first overt act in consequence of this knowledge, must have put my poor aunt Courthope (for that was her Christian name). Most likely it broke out in the shape of some remonstrance about his fellow-servants. He partook of the pride common to all the Barbadians, black as well as white; and the maid-servants tormented him. I remember his coming up in the parlor one day, and making a ludicrous representation of the affronts put upon his office and person, interspersing his chattering and gesticulations with explanatory dumb show. One of them was a pretty girl, who had manœuvred till she got him stuck in a corner; and he insisted upon telling us all that she said and did. His respect for himself had naturally increased since he became free; but he did not know what to do with it. Poor Samuel was not ungenerous, after his fashion. He also wished, with his freedom, to acquire a freeman's knowledge, but stuck fast at pothooks and hangers. To frame a written B he pronounced a thing impossible. Of his powers on the violin he made us more sensible, not without frequent remonstrances, which it must have taken all my aunt's good-nature to make her repeat. He had left two wives in Barbadoes, one of whom was brought to bed of a son a little after he came away. For this son he wanted a name, that was new, sounding, and long. They referred him to the reader of Homer and Virgil. With classical names he was well acquainted, Mars and Venus being among his most intimate friends, besides Jupiters and Adonises, and Dianas with large families. At length we succeeded with Neoptolemus. He said he had never heard it before; and he made me write it for him in a great text hand, that there might be no mistake.

My aunt took a country-house at Merton, in Surrey, where I passed three of the happiest weeks of my life. It was the custom at our school, in those days, to allow us only one set of unbroken holidays during the whole time we were there—I mean, holidays in which we remained away from school by night as well as by day. The period was always in August. Imagine a schoolboy passionately fond

of the green fields, who had never slept out of the heart of
the city for years.   It was a compensation even for the pang
of leaving my friend ; and then what letters I would write
to him.   And what letters I did write !   What full measure
of affection pressed down, and running over !   I read, walked, had a garden and orchard to run in ; and fields that I
could have rolled in, to have my will of them.

My father accompanied me to Wimbledon to see Horne
Tooke, who patted me on the head.   I felt very differently
under his hand, and under that of the bishop of London,
when he confirmed a crowd of us in St. Paul's.   Not that
I thought of politics, though I had a sense of his being a
patriot ; but patriotism, as well as every thing else, was
connected in my mind with something classical, and Horne
Tooke held his political reputation with me by the same
tenure that he held his fame for learning and grammatical
knowledge.   " The learned Horne Tooke" was the designation by which I styled him in some verses I wrote ; in which
verses, by the way, with a poetical license which would have
been thought more classical by Queen Elizabeth than my
master, I called my aunt a " nymph."   In the ceremony of
confirmation by the bishop, there was something too official,
and like a dispatch of business, to excite my veneration.
My head only anticipated the coming of his hand, with a
thrill in the scalp : and when it came, it tickled me.

My cousins had the celebrated Dr. Calcott for a music-
master.   The doctor, who was a scholar and a great reader,
was so pleased with me one day for being able to translate
the beginning of Xenophon's Anabasis (one of our school-
books), that he took me out with him to Nunn's the bookseller's in Great Queen-street, and made me a present of
Schrevelius's Lexicon."   When he came down to Merton,
he let me ride his horse.   What days were those !   Instead
of being roused against my will by a bell, I jumped up with
the lark, and strolled " out of bounds."   Instead of bread
and water for breakfast, I had coffee and tea, and buttered
toast : for dinner, not a hunk of bread and a modicum of
hard meat, or a bowl of pretended broth ; but fish, and fowl,
and noble hot joints, and puddings, and sweets, and Guava

jellies, and other West Indian mysteries of peppers and pre-
serves, and wine ; and then I had tea ; and I sat up to supper like a man, and lived so well, that I might have been
very ill, had I not run about all the rest of the day.

My strolls about the fields with a book were full of happiness ! only my dress used to get me stared at by the villa-
gers. Walking one day by the little river Wandle, I came
upon one of the loveliest girls I ever beheld, standing in the
water with bare legs, washing some linen. She turned as
she was stooping, and showed a blooming oval face with blue
eyes, on either side of which flowed a profusion of flaxen
locks. With the exception of the color of the hair, it was
like Raphael's own head turned into a peasant girl's. The
eyes were full of gentle astonishment at the sight of me ;
and mine must have wondered no less. However, I was
prepared for such wonders. It was only one of my poetical
visions realized, and I expected to find the world full of
them. What she thought of my blue skirts and yellow
stockings, is not so clear. She did not, however, taunt me
with my " petticoats," as the girls in the streets of London
would do, making me blush, as I thought they ought to have
done instead. My beauty in the brook was too gentle and
diffident ; at least I thought so, and my own heart did not
contradict me. I then took every beauty for an Arcadian,
and every brook for a fairy stream ; and the reader would
be surprised, if he knew to what an extent I have a similar
tendency still. I find the same possibilities by another path.

I do not remember whether an Abbé Paris, who taught
my cousins French, used to see them in the country ; but I
never shall forget him in Ormond-street. He was an emi-
grant, very gentlemanly, with a face of remarkable benignity,
and a voice that became it. He spoke English in a slow
manner, that was very graceful. I shall never forget his
saying one day in answer to somebody who pressed him on
the subject, and in the mildest of tones, that without doubt
it was impossible to be saved out of the pale of the Catholic
Church.

One contrast of this sort reminds me of another. My
aunt Courthope had something growing out on one of her

knuckles, which she was afraid to let a surgeon look at. There was a Dr. Chapman, a West Indian physician, who came to see us, a person of great suavity of manners, with all that air of languor and want of energy which the West Indians often exhibit. He was in the habit of inquiring, with the softest voice in the world, how my aunt's hand was; and coming one day upon us in the midst of dinner, and sighing forth his usual question, she gave it him over her shoulder to look at. In a moment she shrieked, and the swelling was gone. The meekest of doctors had done it away with his lancet.

I had no drawback on my felicity at Merton, with the exception of an occasional pang at my friend's absence, and a new vexation that surprised and mortified me. I had been accustomed at school to sleep with sixty boys in the room, and some old night fears that used to haunt me were forgotten. No Mantichoras there!—no old men crawling on the floor! What was my chagrin, when on sleeping alone, after so long a period, I found my terrors come back again!—not, indeed, in all the same shapes. Beasts could frighten me no longer; but I was at the mercy of any other ghastly fiction that presented itself to my mind, crawling or ramping. I struggled hard to say nothing about it; but my days began to be discolored with fears of my nights; and with unutterable humiliation I begged that the footman might be allowed to sleep in the same room. Luckily, my request was attended to in the kindest and most reconciling manner. I was pitied for my fears, but praised for my candor—a balance of qualities which, I have reason to believe, did me a service far beyond that of the moment. Samuel, who, fortunately for my shame, had a great respect for fear of this kind, had his bed removed accordingly into my room. He used to entertain me at night with stories of Barbadoes and the negroes; and in a few days I was reassured and happy.

It was then (oh, shame that I must speak of fair lady after confessing a heart so faint!)—it was then that I fell in love with my cousin Fan. However, I would have fought all her young acquaintances round for her, timid as I was, and little inclined to pugnacity.

Fanny was a lass of fifteen, with little laughing eyes, and a mouth like a plum. I was then (I feel as if I ought to be ashamed to say it) not more than thirteen, if so old; but I had read Tooke's Pantheon, and came of a precocious race. My cousin came of one too, and was about to be married to a handsome young fellow of three-and-twenty. I thought nothing of this, for nothing could be more innocent than my intentions. I was not old enough, or grudging enough, or whatever it was, even to be jealous. I thought every body must love Fanny Dayrell; and if she did not leave me out in permitting it, I was satisfied. It was enough for me to be with her as long as I could; to gaze on her with delight, as she floated hither and thither; and to sit on the stiles in the neighboring fields, thinking of Tooke's Pantheon. My friendship was greater than my love. Had my favorite schoolfellow been ill, or otherwise demanded my return, I should certainly have chosen his society in preference. Three-fourths of my heart were devoted to friendship; the rest was in a vague dream of beauty, and female cousins, and nymphs, and green fields, and a feeling which, though of a warm nature, was full of fear and respect.

Had the jade put me on the least equality of footing as to age, I know not what change might have been wrought in me; but though too young herself for the serious duties she was about to bring on her, and full of sufficient levity and gayety not to be uninterested with the little black-eyed schoolboy that lingered about her, my vanity was well paid off by hers, for she kept me at a distance by calling me *petit garçon*. This was no better than the assumption of an elder sister in her teens over a younger one; but the latter feels it, nevertheless; and I persuaded myself that it was particularly cruel. I wished the Abbé Paris at Jamaica with his French. There would she come in her frock and tucker (for she had not yet left off either), her curls dancing, and her hands clasped together in the enthusiasm of something to tell me, and when I flew to meet her, forgetting the difference of ages, and alive only to my charming cousin, she would repress me with a little fillip on the cheek, and say, " Well, *petit garçon*, what do you think of that?" The worst of it was, that this odious French phrase sat insufferably well upon her plump little mouth. She and I used to gather peaches before the house were up. I held the ladder for her; she mounted like a fairy; and when I stood doating on her, as she looked down and threw the fruit in my lap, she would cry, " *Petit garçon*, you will let 'em all drop !" On my return to school, she gave me a locket for a keepsake, in the shape of a heart; which was the worst thing she ever did to the *petit garçon*, for it touched me on my weak side, and looked like a sentiment. I believe I should have had serious thoughts of becoming melancholy, had I not, in returning to school, returned to my friend, and so found means to occupy my craving for sympathy. However, I wore the heart a long while. I have sometimes thought there was more in her French than I imagined; but I believe not. She naturally took herself for double my age, with a lover of three-and-twenty. Soon after her marriage, fortune separated us for many years. My passion had almost as soon died away; but I have loved the name of Fanny ever since; and when I met her again, which was under circumstances of trouble on her part, I could not see her without such an emotion as I was fain to confess to a person " near and dear," who forgave me for it; which made me love the forgiver the more. Yes ! the " black ox " trod on the fairy foot of my light-hearted cousin Fan; of her, whom I could no more have thought of in conjunction with sorrow, than of a ball-room with a tragedy. To know that she was rich and admired, and abounding in mirth and music, was to me the same thing as to know that she existed. How often did I afterward wish myself rich in turn, that I might have restored to her all the graces of life ! She was generous, and would not have denied me the satisfaction.

This was my first love. That for a friend's sister was my second, and not so strong ; for it was divided with the admiration of which I have spoken for the Park music and " the soldiers." Nor had the old tendency to mix up the clerical with the military service been forgotten. Indeed, I have never been without a clerical tendency ; nor, after what I have written for the genial edification of my fellow-

creatures, and the extension of charitable and happy thoughts
in matters of religion, would I be thought to speak of it without even a certain gravity, not compromised or turned into
levity, in my opinion, by any cheerfulness of tone with which
it may happen to be associated ; for Heaven has made smiles
as well as tears ; has made laughter itself, and mirth ; and
to appreciate its gifts thoroughly is to treat none of them
with disrespect, or to affect to be above them. The wholly
gay, and the wholly grave spirit is equally but half the
spirit of a right human creature.

I mooted points of faith with myself very early, in couse-
quence of what I heard at home. The very inconsistencies
which I observed round about me in matters of belief and
practice, did but the more make me wish to discover in what
the right spirit of religion consisted : while, at the same time,
nobody felt more instinctively than myself, that forms were
necessary to preserve essence. I had the greatest respect
for them, wherever I thought them sincere. I got up
imitations of religious processions in the school-room, and
persuaded my coadjutors to learn even a psalm in the original Hebrew, in order to sing it as part of the ceremony.
To make the lesson as easy as possible, it was the shortest
of all the psalms, the hundred and seventeenth, which consists but of two verses. A Jew, I am afraid, would have
been puzzled to recognize it ; though, perhaps, I got the
tone from his own synagogue ; for I was well acquainted
with that place of worship. I was led to dislike Catholic
chapels, in spite of their music and their paintings, by what
I had read of Inquisitions, and by the impiety which I found
in the doctrine of eternal punishment—a monstrosity which
I never associated with the Church of England, at least not
habitually. But identifying no such dogmas with the Jews,
who are indeed free from them (though I was not aware of
that circumstance at the time), and reverencing them for
their ancient connection with the Bible, I used to go with
some of my companions to the synagogue in Duke's Place ;
where I took pleasure in witnessing the semi-catholic pomp
of their service, and in hearing their fine singing ; not without something of a constant astonishment at their wearing

their hats. This custom, however, kindly mixed itself up
with the recollection of my cocked hat and band. I
was not aware that it originated in the immovable eastern
turban.

These visits to the synagogue did me, I conceive, a great
deal of good. They served to universalize my notions of
religion, and to keep them unbigoted. It never became
necessary to remind me that Jesus was himself a Jew. I
have also retained through life a respectful notion of the
Jews as a body.

There were some school rhymes about " pork upon a fork,"
and the Jews going to prison. At Easter, a strip of bordered paper was stuck on the breast of every boy, containing the words " He is risen. It did not give us the slightest thought of what it recorded. It only reminded us of an
old rhyme, which some of the boys used to go about the
school repeating :

> He is risen, he is risen,
> All the Jews must go to prison.

A beautiful Christian deduction ! Thus has charity itself
been converted into a spirit of antagonism ; and thus it is
that the antagonism, in the progress of knowledge, becomes
first a pastime and then a jest.

I never forgot the Jews' synagogue, their music, their
tabernacle, and the courtesy with which strangers were
allowed to see it. I had the pleasure, before I left school,
of becoming acquainted with some members of their community, who were extremely liberal toward other opinions,
and who, nevertheless, entertained a sense of the Supreme
Being far more reverential than I had observed in any
Christian, my mother excepted. My feelings toward them
received additional encouragement from the respect shown to
their history in the paintings of Mr. West, who was any thing
but a bigot himself, and who often had Jews to sit to him.
I contemplated Moses and Aaron, and the young Levites, by
the sweet light of his picture-rooms, where every body trod
about in stillness, as though it was a kind of holy ground ;
and if I met a Rabbi in the street, he seemed to me a man

coming, not from Bishopsgate or Saffron Hill, but out of the remoteness of time.

I have spoken of the distinguished individuals bred at Christ-Hospital, including Coleridge and Lamb, who left the school not long before I entered it. Coleridge I never saw till he was old. Lamb I recollect coming to see the boys, with a pensive, brown, handsome, and kingly face, and a gait advancing with a motion from side to side, between involuntary consciousness and attempted ease. His brown complexion may have been owing to a visit in the country; his air of uneasiness to a great burden of sorrow. He dressed with a quaker-like plainness. I did not know him as Lamb; I took him for a Mr. "Guy," having heard somebody address him by that appellative, I suppose in jest.

The boy whom I have designated in these notices as C———n, and whose intellect in riper years became clouded, had a more than usual look of being the son of old parents. He had a reputation among us, which, in more superstitious times, might have rendered him an object of dread. We thought he knew a good deal out of the pale of ordinary inquiries. He studied the weather and the stars, things which boys rarely trouble their heads with; and as I had an awe of thunder, which always brought a reverential shade on my mother's face, as if God had been speaking, I used to send to him on close summer days, to know if thunder was to be expected.

In connection with this mysterious schoolfellow, though he was the last person, in some respects, to be associated with him, I must mention a strange epidemic fear which occasionally prevailed among the boys, respecting a personage whom they called the Fazzer.

The Fazzer was known to be nothing more than one of the boys themselves. In fact, he consisted of one of the most impudent of the bigger ones; but as it was his custom to disguise his face, and as this aggravated the terror which made the little boys hide their own faces, his participation of our common human nature only increased the supernatural fearfulness of his pretensions. His office as Fazzer consisted in being audacious, unknown, and frighten-

ing the boys at night; sometimes by pulling them out of
their beds; sometimes by simply *fazzing* their hair ("faz
zing" meant pulling or vexing, like a goblin); sometimes
(which was horriblest of all) by quietly giving us to understand, in some way or other, that the "Fazzer was out,"
that is to say, out of his own bed, and then being seen (by
those who dared to look) sitting, or otherwise making his
appearance, in his white shirt, motionless and dumb.   It
was a very good horror, of its kind.   The Fazzer was our
Dr. Faustus, our elf, our spectre, our Flibbertigibbet, who
"put knives in our pillows and halters in our pews."   He
was Jones, it is true, or Smith; but he was also somebody
else—an anomaly, a duality, Smith and sorcery united.   My
friend Charles Ollier should have written a book about him.
He was our Old Man of the Mountain, and yet a common
boy.   .

One night I thought I saw this phenomenon under circumstances more than usually unearthly.   It was a fine
moonlight night; I was then in a ward the easements of
which looked (as they still look) on the church-yard.   My
bed was under the second window from the east, not far
from the statue of Edward the Sixth.   Happening to wake
in the middle of the night, and cast up my eyes, I saw, on
a bed's head near me, and in one of these casements, a figure
in its shirt, which I took for the Fazzer.   The room was
silent; the figure motionless; I fancied that half the boys
in the ward were glancing at it, without daring to speak.
It was poor C———n, gazing at that lunar orb, which
might afterwerd be supposed to have malignantly fascinated
him.

Contemporary with C———n was Wood, before mentioned, whom I admired for his verses, and who was afterward
Fellow of Pembroke College, Cambridge, where I visited
him, and found him, to my astonishment, a head shorter than
myself.   Every upper boy at school appears a giant to a
little one.   "Big boy" and senior are synonymous.   Now
and then, however, extreme smallness in a senior scholar
gives a new kind of dignity, by reason of the testimony it
bears to the ascendency of the intellect.   It was the custom

for the monitors at Christ-Hospital, during prayers before meat, to stand fronting the tenants of their respective wards, while the objects of their attention were kneeling.   Looking up, on one of these occasions, toward a new monitor who was thus standing, and whose face was unknown to me (for there were six hundred of us, and his ward was not mine), I thought him the smallest boy that could ever have attained to so distinguished an eminence.   He was little in person, little in face, and he had a singularly juvenile east of features even for one so *petite*.

It was Mitchell, the translator of Aristophanes.   He had really attained his position prematurely.   I rose afterward to be next to him in the school ; and from a grudge that existed between us, owing probably to reserve, which I thought pride on his part, and to an ardency which he may have considered frivolous on mine, we became friends.   Circumstances parted us in after life ; I became a Reformist, and he a Quarterly Reviewer ; but he sent me kindly remembrances not long before he died.   I did not know he was declining ; and it will ever be a pain to me to reflect, that delay conspired with accident to hinder my sense of it from being known to him; especially as I learned that he had not been so prosperous as I supposed.   He had his weaknesses as well as myself, but they were mixed with conscientious and noble qualities.   Zealous as he was for aristocratical government, he was no indiscriminate admirer of persons in high places ; and, though it would have bettered his views in life, he had declined taking orders, from nicety of religious scruple.   Of his admirable scholarship I need say nothing.

Equally good scholar, but of a less zealous temperament, was Barnes, who stood next me on the Deputy-Grecian form, and who was afterward identified with the sudden and striking increase of the *Times* newspaper in fame and influence.   He was very handsome when young, with a profile of Grecian regularity ; and was famous among us for a certain dispassionate humor, for his admiration of the works of Fielding, and for his delight, nevertheless, in pushing a narrative to its utmost, and drawing upon his stores of fancy

for intensifying it ; an amusement for which he possessed an
understood privilege.   It was painful in after-life to see his
good looks swallowed up in corpulency, and his once handsome mouth thrusting its under lip out, and panting with
asthma.   I believe he was originally so well constituted, in
point of health and bodily feeling, that he fancied he could
go on all his life without taking any of the usual methods to
preserve his comfort.   The editorship of the *Times*, which
turned his night into day, and would have been a trying
burden to any man, completed the bad consequences of his
negligence ; and he died painfully before he was old.   Barnes
wrote elegant Latin verse, a classical English style, and
might assuredly have made himself a name, in wit and
literature, had he cared much for any thing beyond his glass
of wine and his Fielding.

What pleasant days have I not passed with him, and
other schoolfellows, bathing in the New River, and boating
on the Thames.   He and I began to learn Italian together ;
and any body not within the pale of the enthusiastic, might
have thought us mad, as we went shouting the beginning
of Metastasio's ode to Venus, as loud as we could bawl, over
the Hornsey-fields.   I can repeat it to this day, from those
first lessons.

> Scendi propizia
>   Col tuo splendore,
> O bella Venere,
>   Madre d'Amore ;
> Madre d'Amore,
>   Che sola sei
> Piacer degli uomini,
>   E degli dei.*

On the same principle of making invocations as loud as
possible, and at the same time of fulfilling the prophecy of a
poet, and also for the purpose of indulging ourselves with an
echo, we used to lie upon our oars at Richmond, and call,
in the most vociferous manner, upon the spirit of Thomson
to " rest."

* " Descend propitious with thy brightness, O beautiful Venus,
Mother of Love ; Mother of Love, who alone art the pleasure of men
and of gods."

Remembrance oft shall haunt the shore,
  When Thames in summer wreaths is drest,
And oft suspend the dashing oar
  To bid his gentle spirit rest.
    Collins's Ode on the Death of Thomson.

It was more like " perturbing" his spirit than laying it.

One day Barnes fell overboard, and, on getting into the boat again, he drew a little edition of Seneca out of his pocket, which seemed to have become fat with the water. It was like an extempore dropsy.

Another time, several of us being tempted to bathe on a very hot day, near Hammersmith, and not exercising suf-ficient patience in selecting our spot, we were astonished at receiving a sudden lecture from a lady. She was in a hat and feathers, and riding-habit; and as the grounds turned out to belong to the Margravine of Anspach (Lady Craven), we persuaded ourselves that our admonitrix, who spoke in no measured terms, was her Serene Highness herself. The obvious reply to her was, that if it was indiscreet in us not to have chosen a more sequestered spot, it was not exces-sively the reverse in a lady to come and rebuke us. I re-lated this story to my acquaintance, Sir Robert Ker Porter, who knew her. His observation was, that nothing wonder-ful was to be wondered at in the Margravine.

I was fifteen when I put off my band and blue skirts for a coat and neckcloth. I was then first Deputy-Grecian, and I had the honor of going out of the school in the same rank, at the same age, and for the same reason, as my friend Charles Lamb. The reason was that I hesitated in my speech. I did not stammer half so badly as I used; and it is very seldom that I halt at a syllable now; but it was understood that a Grecian was bound to deliver a public speech before he left school, and to go into the church after-ward; and as I could do neither of these things, a Grecian I could not be. So I put on my coat and waistcoat, and, what was stranger, my hat; a very uncomfortable addi-tion to my sensations. For eight years I had gone bare-headed; save now and then, a few inches of pericranium, when the little cap, no larger than a crumpet, was stuck

on one side, to the mystification of the old ladies in the
streets.

I then cared as little for the rains as I did for any thing
else. I had now a vague sense of worldly trouble, and of a
great and serious change in my condition; besides which, I
had to quit my old cloisters, and my playmates, and long
habits of all sorts; so that, what was a very happy moment
to schoolboys in general, was to me one of the most painful
of my life. I surprised my schoolfellows and the master
with the melancholy of my tears. I took, leave of my books,
of my friends, of my seat in the grammar-school, of my good-
hearted nurse and her daughter, of my bed, of the cloisters,
and of the very pump out of which I had taken so many delicious draughts, as if I should never see them again, though
I meant to come every day. The fatal hat was put on ; my
father was come to fetch me.

> We, hand in hand, with strange new steps and slow,
> Through Holborn took our meditative way.

CHAPTER V.

FOR some time after I left school, I did nothing but visit my schoolfellows, haunt the book-stalls, and write verses. My father collected the verses; and published them with a large list of subscribers, numbers of whom belonged to his old congregations. I was as proud perhaps of the book at that time, as I am ashamed of it now. The French Revolution, though the worst portion of it was over, had not yet shaken up and re-invigorated the sources of thought all over Europe. At least I was not old enough, perhaps was not able, to get out of the trammels of the regular imitative poetry, or versification rather, which was taught in the schools. My book was a heap of imitations, all but absolutely worthless. But absurd as it was, it did me a serious mischief; for it made me suppose that I had attained an end, instead of not having reached even a commencement; and thus caused me to waste in imitation a good many years which I ought to have devoted to the study of the poetical art, and of nature. Coleridge has praised Boyer for teaching us to laugh at " muses," and " Castalian streams ;" but he ought rather to have lamented that he did not teach us how to love them wisely, as he might have done had he really known any thing about poetry, or loved Spenser and the old poets, as he thought he admired the new. Even Coleridge's juvenile poems were none the better for Boyer's training. As to

mine, they were for the most part as mere trash as anti-Cas-
talian heart could have desired.   I wrote "odes" because
Collins and Gray had written them, "pastorals" because
Pope had written them, "blank verse" because Akenside
and Thomson had written blank verse, and a "Palace of
Pleasure" because Spenser had written a "Bower of Bliss."
But in all these authors I saw little but their words, and
imitated even those badly.   I had nobody to bid me to go
to the nature which had originated the books.   Coleridge's
lauded teacher put into my hands, at one time, the life of
Pope by Ruffhead (the worst he could have chosen), and at
another (for the express purpose of cultivating my love of
poetry) the *Irene* and other poems of Dr. Johnson ! Pope's
smooth but unartistical versification spell-bound me for a long
time.   Of Johnson's poem I retained nothing but the epigram
beginning "Hermit hoar—"

> " Hermit hoar, in solemn cell,
>   Wearing out life's evening gray,
> Strike thy bosom, sage, and tell
>   What is bliss, and which the way.

> " Thus I spoke, and speaking, sighed,
>   Scarce repressed the starting tear,
> When the hoary sage replied,
>   Come, my lad, and drink some beer."

This was the first epigram of the kind which I had seen;
and it had a cautionary effect upon me to an extent which
its author might hardly have desired.   The grave Dr. Johnson and the rogue Ambrose de Lamela, in *Gil Blas*, stood
side by side in my imagination as unmaskers of venerable
appearances.

Not long after the publication of my book, I visited two
of my school-fellows, who had gone to Cambridge and Oxford.   The repute of it, unfortunately, accompanied me, and
gave a foolish increase to my self-complacency.   At Oxford,
I was introduced to Kett, the poetry professor, a good-natured man, with a face like a Houhynnm (Swift should have
thought it a pattern for humanity).   It was in the garden
of his college (Trinity); and he expressed a hope that I
should feel inspired then " by the muse of Warton."   I was

not acquainted with the writings of Warton at that time ; and perhaps my ignorance was fortunate ; for it was not till long after my acquaintance with them, that I saw further into their merits, than the very first anti-commonplaces would have discerned, and as I had not acquired even those at that period, and my critical presumption was on a par with my poetical, I should probably have given the professor to understand, that I had no esteem for that kind of second-hand inspiration. I was not aware that my own was precisely of the same kind, and as different from Warton's as poverty from acquirement.

At Oxford, my love of boating had nearly cost me my life. I had already had a bit of a taste of drowning in the river Thames, in consequence of running a boat too hastily on shore ; but it was nothing to what I experienced on this occasion. The schoolfellow whom I was visiting was the friend whose family lived in Spring Gardens. We had gone out in a little decked skiff and not expecting disasters in the gentle Isis, I had fastened the sail-line, of which I had the direction, in order that I might read a volume which I had with me, of Mr. Cumberland's novel called "Henry." My friend was at the helm. The wind grew a little strong ; and we had just got into Iffley Reach, when I heard him exclaim, "Hunt, we are over." The next moment I was under the water, gulping it, and giving myself up for lost The boat had a small opening in the middle of the deck, under which I had thurst my feet ; this circumstance had carried me over with the boat, and the worst of it was, I found I had got the sail-line round my neck. My friend, who sat on the deck itself, had been swept off, and got comfortably to shore, which was at a little distance.

My bodily sensations were not so painful as I should have fancied they would have been. My mental reflections were very different, though one of them, by a singular meeting of extremes, was of a comic nature. I thought that I should never see the sky again, that I had parted with all my friends, and that I was about to contradict the proverb which said that a man who was born to be hung, would never be drowned ; for the sail-line, in which I felt entangled, seemed destined to perform for me both the offices. On a sudden, I found an oar in my hand, and the next minute I was climbing, with assistance, into a wherry, in which there sat two Oxonians, one of them helping me, and loudly and laughingly differing with the other, who did not at all like the rocking of the boat, and who assured me, to the manifest contradiction of such senses as I had left, that there was no room. This gentleman is now no more; and I shall not mention his name, because I might do injustice to the memory of a brave man struck with a panic. The name of his companion, if I mistake not, was Russel. I hope he was related to an illustrious person of the same name, to whom I have lately been indebted for what may have been another prolongation of my life.

On returning to town, which I did on the top of an Oxford coach, I was relating this story to the singular person who then drove it (Bobart, who had been a collegian), when a man who was sitting behind surprised us with the excess of his laughter. On asking him the reason, he touched his hat, and said, "Sir, I'm his footman." Such are the delicacies of the livery, and the glorifications of their masters with which they entertain the kitchen.

This Bobart was a very curious person. I have noticed him in the *Indicator*, in the article on "Coaches." He was a descendant of a horticultural family, who had been keepers of the Physic-Garden at Oxford, and one of whom palmed a rat upon the learned world for a dragon, by stretching out its skin into wings. Tillimant Bobart (for such was the name of our charioteer) had been at college himself, probably as a sizer; but having become proprietor of a stage-coach, he thought fit to be his own coachman; and he received your money and touched his hat like the rest of the fraternity. He had a round red face, with eyes that stared, and showed the white; and having become, by long practice, an excellent capper of verses, he was accustomed to have bouts at that pastime with the collegians whom he drove. It was curious to hear him whistle and grunt, and urge on his horses with the other customary euphonics of his tribe, and then see him flash his eye round upon the capping gentleman who sat behind him, and quote his never-failing line out of Virgil and Horace. In the evening (for he only drove his coach half way to London) he divided his solace after his labors, between his book and his brandy-and-water; but I am afraid with a little too much of the brandy, for his end was not happy.* There was eccentricity in the family, without any thing much to show for it. The Bobart who invented the dragon, chuckled over the secret for a long time with a satisfaction that must have cost him many falsehoods; and the first Bobart that is known, used to tag his beard with silver on holidays.

If female society had not been wanting, I should have longed to reside at an university; for I have never seen trees, books, and a garden to walk in, but I saw my natural home, provided there was no "monkery" in it. I have always thought it a brave and great saying of Mohammed, "There is no monkery in Islam."

> "From women's eyes this doctrine I derive:
> They are the books, the arts, the academes,
> Which show, contain, and nourish all the world."

Were I to visit the universities now, I should explore every corner, and reverently fancy myself in the presence of every great and good man that has adorned them; but the most important people to young men are one another; and I was content with glancing at the haunts of Addison, and Warton in Oxford, and at those of Gray, Spenser, and Milton, in Cambridge. Oxford, I found, had greatly the advantage of Cambridge in point of country. You could understand well enough how poets could wander about Iffley and Woodstock; but when I visited Cambridge, the nakedness of the land was too plainly visible under a sheet of snow, through which gutters of ditches ran, like ink, by the side of leafless sallows, which resembled huge pincushions stuck on posts. The town, however, made amends; and Cambridge has the

---

* On the information of Mr. George Hooper, of Oxford, who kindly volunteered the communication as a reader of the *Indicator*, and sent me a very curious letter on the subject; with details, however, that were rather of private than public interest.

advantage of Oxford in a remarkable degree, as far as regards eminent names.   England's two greatest philosophers,
Bacon and Newton, and (according to Tyrwhitt), three out
of its four great poets, were bred there, besides double the
number of minor celebrities.   Oxford even did not always
know " the goods the gods provided."   It repudiated Locke ;
alienated Gibbon ; and had nothing but angry sullenness and
hard expulsion to answer to the inquiries which its very or-
dinances encouraged in the sincere and loving spirit of
Shelley.

Yet they are divine places, both ; full of grace and beauty,
and scholarship ; of reverent antiquity, and ever young nature
and hope.   Their faults, if of worldliness in some, are those
of time and of conscience in more, and if the more pertinacious
on those accounts, will merge into a like conservative firmness, when still nobler developments are in their keeping.
So at least I hope ; and so may the fates have ordained ;
keeping their gowns among them as a symbol that learning
is indeed something which ever learns ; and instructing them
to teach love and charity, and inquiry, with the same accomplished authority, as that with which they have taught
assent.

My book was unfortunately successful every where, particularly in the metropolis.   The critics were extremely
kind ; and, as it was unusual at that time to publish at so
early a period of life, my age made me a kind of " Young
Roscius" in authorship.   I was introduced to literati, and
shown about among parties.   My father taking me to
see Dr. Raine, Master of the Charter-house, the doctor, who
was very kind and pleasant, but who probably drew none
of our deductions in favor of the young writer's abilities,
warned me against the perils of authorship ; adding as a final
dehortative, that " the shelves were full."   It was not till
we came away, that I thought of an answer, which I conceived would have " annihilated" him.   " Then, sir" (I
should have said), " we will make another."   Not having
been in time with this repartee, I felt all that anguish of
undeserved and unnecessary defeat, which has been so pleasantly described in the *Miseries of Human Life*.   This,

thought I, would have been an answer befitting a poet, and calculated to make a figure in biography.

A mortification that I encountered at a house in Cavendish-square affected me no less, though it surprised me a good deal more. I had been held up, as usual, to the example of the young gentlemen, and the astonishment of the young ladies, when, in the course of the dessert, one of mine host's daughter's, a girl of exuberant spirits, and not of the austerest breeding, came up to me, and, as if she had discovered that I was not so young as I pretended to be, exclaimed, "What a beard you have got!" at the same time convincing herself of the truth of her discovery by taking hold of it! Had I been a year or two older, I should have taken my revenge. As it was, I know not how I behaved, but the next morning I hastened to have a beard no longer.

I was now a man, and resolved not to be out of countenance next time. Not long afterward, my grandfather sensible of the new fame of his family, but probably alarmed at the fruitless consequences to which it might lead, sent me word, that if I would come to Philadelphia, "he would make a man of me." I sent word, in return, that "men grew in England as well as America;" an answer which repaid me for the loss of my repartee at Dr. Raine's. I was very angry with him for his niggardly conduct to my mother. I could not help, for some time, identifying the whole American character with his; and I still have a tendency to do so, in spite of relationship. I would fain think it unjust; and of course it is so, as far as regards individuals. For the rest, I must refer for my vindication to Pennsylvanian bond-holders, southern slave-holders, and to my friends the United States booksellers, who do us so much honor in taking our books, and giving us nothing in exchange. I love Emerson, and Bryant, and Lowell, and some others, and all Philadelphia women in particular, for the sake of my mother; but as a nation, I can not get it out of my head, that the Americans are Englishmen with the poetry and romance taken out of them; and that there is one great counter built along their coast from north to south, behind which they are all standing like so many linendrapers.

F*

They will be far otherwise, I have no doubt, in time, and this unchristian opinion of them have come to nothing.

Partly on the same account, I acquired a dislike for my grandfather's friend Dr. Franklin, author of *Poor Richard's Almanack:* a heap, as it appeared to me, of " Scoundrel maxims." *   I think I now appreciate Dr. Franklin as I ought; but although I can see the utility of such publications as his Almanack for a rising commercial state, and hold it useful as a memorandum to uncalculating persons like myself, who happen to live in an old one, I think it has no business either in commercial nations long established, or in others who do not found their happiness in that sort of power.   Franklin, with all his abilities, is but at the head of those who think that man lives " by bread alone."   He will commit none of the follies, none of the intolerances, the absence of which is necessary to the perfection of his system ; and in setting his face against these, he discountenances a great number of things very inimical to higher speculations. But he was no more a fit representative of what human nature largely requires, and may reasonably hope to attain to, than negative represents positive, or the clearing away a ground in the back-settlements, and setting to work upon it, represents the work in its completion.   Something of the pettiness and materiality of his first occupation always stuck

---

* Thomson's phrase, in the *Castle of Indolence*, speaking of a miserly money-getter :

> " ' A penny saved is a penny got ;'
> Firm to this scoundrel maxim keepeth he,
> Ne of its rigor will he bate a jot,
> Till it hath quench'd his fire and and banishèd his pot."

The reader will not imagine that I suppose all money-makers to be of this description.   Very gallant spirits are to be found, among them, who only take to this mode of activity for want of a better, and are as generous in disbursing as they are vigorous in acquiring.   You may always know the common run, as in other instances, by the soreness with which they feel attacks on the body corporate.

For the assertion that Dr. Franklin cut off his son with a shilling, my only authority is family tradition.   It is observable, however, that the friendliest of his biographers are not only forced to admit that he seemed a little too fond of money, but notice the mysterious secrecy in which his family history is involved.

to him.   He took nothing for a truth or a matter-of-faet that he could not handle, as it were, like his types : and yet, like all men of this kind, he was liable, when put out of the ordinary pale of his calculations, to fall into the greatest errors, and substitute the integrity of his reputation for that of whatsoever he chose to do.   From never doing wrong in little things, he conceived that he could do no wrong in great ; and, in the most deliberate act of his life, he showed he had grievously mistaken himself.   He was, I allow, one of the *cardinal* great men of his time.   He was Prudence. But he was not what he took himself for——all the other Virtues besides ; and, inasmuch as he was deficient in those, he was deficient even in his favorite one.   He was not Temperance ; for, in the teeth of his capital recommendations of that virtue, he did not scruple to get burly and big with the enjoyments that he cared for.   He was not Justice ; for he knew not how to see fair play between his own wisdom and that of a thousand wants and aspirations, of which he knew nothing : and he cut off his son with a shilling, for differing with him in politics.   Lastly, he was not Fortitude ; for having few passions and no imagination, he knew not what it was to be severely tried ; and if he had been there is every reason to conclude, from the way in which he treated his son, that his self-love would have been the part in which he felt the torture ; that as his Justice was only arithmetic, so his Fortitude would have been nothing but stubbornness.

If Franklin had been the only great man of his time, he would merely have contributed to make the best of a bad system, and so hurt the world by prolonging it ; but, luckily, there were the French and English philosophers besides, who saw farther than he did, and provided for higher wants. I feel grateful to him, for one, inasmuch as he extended the sphere of liberty, and helped to clear the earth of the weeds of sloth and ignorance, and the wild beasts of superstition ; but when he comes to build final homes for us, I rejoice that wiser hands interfere.   His line and rule are not every thing ; they are not even a tenth part of it.   Cocker's numbers are good ; but those of Plato and Pythagoras have their merits too, or we should have been made of dry bones and tangents, and not had the fancies in our heads, and the hearts beating in our bosoms, that make us what we are. We should not even have known that Cocker's numbers were worth any thing; nor would Dr. Franklin himself have played on the harmonica, albeit he must have done it in a style very different from that of Milton or Cimarosa. Finally, the writer of this passage on the Doctor would not have ventured to give his opinion of so great a man in so explicit a manner. I should not have ventured to give it, had I not been backed by so many powerful interests of humanity, and had I not suffered in common, and more than in common, with the rest of the world, from a system which, under the guise of economy and social advantage, tends to double the love of wealth and the hostility of competition, to force the best things down to a level with the worst, and to reduce mankind to the simplest and most mechanical law of their nature, divested of its heart and soul—the law of being in motion. Most of the advantages of the present system of money-making, which may be called the great *lay* superstition of modern times, might be obtained by a fifth part of the labor, if more equally distributed. Yet all the advantages could not be so obtained; and the system is necessary as a portion of the movement of time and progress, and as the ultimate means of dispensing with its very self.

Among those with whom my book made me acquainted, was the late Rev. Mr. Maurice, of the British Museum, author of " Indian Antiquities." I mention him more partie- ularly, as I do others, because he had a character of his own, and makes a portrait. I had seen an engraving of him, representing a slender, prim-eyed, enamel faced person, very tightly dressed and particular, with no expression but that of propriety. What was my surprise, when I beheld a short, chubby, good-humored companion, with boyish features, and a lax dress and manner, heartily glad to see you, and tender over his wine! He was a sort of clerical Horace. He might, by some freak of patronage, have been made a bishop; and he thought he deserved it for having proved the identity of the Hindoo with the Christian Trinity, which was the object of his book! But he began to despond on

that point, when I knew him ; and he drank as much wine
for sorrow, as he would, had he been made a bishop, for joy.
He was a man of a social and overflowing nature ; more
fit, in truth, to set an example of charity than faith ; and
would have made an excellent Bramin of the Rama-Deeva
worship.

Maurice's Hymns to the Gods of India were as good as
Sir William Jones's, and his attention to the amatory theology of the country (allowing for his deficiency in the language) as close.   He was not so fortunate as Sir William
in retaining a wife whom he loved.   I have heard him
lament, in very genuine terms, his widowed condition, and
the task of finishing the great manuscript catalogue of the
Museum books, to which his office had bound him.   This
must have been a torture, physical as well as moral ; for he
had weak eyes, and wrote with a magnifying-glass as big
round as the palm of his hand.   With this, in a tall thick
handwriting, as if painting a set of rails, he was to finish
the folio catalogues, and had produced the seven volumes of
Indian Antiquities !   Nevertheless, he seemed to lament his
destiny, rather in order to accommodate the weakness of his
lachrymal organs, than out of any mental uneasiness ; for
with the aspect he had the spirits of a boy ; and his laughter would follow his tears with a happy incontinence.   He
was always catching cold, and getting well of it after dinner.

Many a roast fowl and bottle of wine have I enjoyed with
Thomas Maurice in his rooms at the British Museum ; and
if I thought the reader, as well as myself, had not a regard
for him, I would not have opened their doors.   They were
in a turret in the court-yard walls, and exist, alas ! no
longer.   I never passed them, without remembering how he
used to lay down his magnifying-glass, take both my hands,
and condescend to anticipate the pleasant chat we should
have about authors and books over his wine ; I say, condescend, because, though he did not affect any thing of that
sort, it was a remarkable instance of his good-nature, and
his freedom from pride, to place himself on a level in this
manner with a youth in his teens, and pretend that I
brought him as much amusement as he gave.   Owing to

the exclusive notions I entertained of friendship, I mystified
him by answering the "Dear sirs" of his letters in a more
formal manner. I fear it induced him to make unfavorable
comparisons of my real disposition with my behavior at
table ; and it must be allowed, that having no explanation
on the subject, he had a right to be mystified. Somehow
or other (I believe it was because a new Dulcinea called me
elsewhere), the acquaintance dropped, and I did not see him
for many years.

He died, notwithstanding his wine and his catarrhs, at a
good old age, writing verses to the last, and showing what a
young heart he retained by his admiration of nature : and
undoubtedly this it was that enabled him to live so long ;
for though the unfeeling are apt to outlast the sensitive dur
ing a sophisticate and perplexing state of society, it is as
tonishing how long a cordial pulse will keep playing, if allowed
reasonably to have its way. Were the lives of mankind as
natural as they should be, and their duties rendered as cheerful, the Maurices and Horaces would outlast all the formalists
buttoned up in denial, as surely as the earth spins round, and
the pillars fall.

I wish I could relate half the stories Mr. Maurice told
me. He told them well, and I should have been glad to
repeat them in his own words. I recollect but one, which
I shall tell for his sake, though it is not without a jest. I
hope it is not old. He said there was a gentleman, not very
robust, but an enthusiast for nature and good health, who
entertained a prodigious notion of the effects of smelling to
fresh earth.* Accordingly, not to go too nicely about the
matter, but to do it like a man, he used to walk every morning

---

* Bacon had a notion of this sort, and would have a piece of earth
brought him fresh out of the ground to smell to ; but then he put wine
to it. I fancy I hear Mr. Maurice exclaiming, "Ah, he was a great
man !" There was a pomp and altitude in the ways of Bacon, and
all in the highest taste, that serves almost to reconcile us to Cowley's
conceit, in styling him "Nature's Lord Chancellor." His house and
gardens were poetically magnificent. He had the flowers in season
always put upon his table ; sometimes had music in the next room
while he was writing ; and would ride out in an open chariot during
the rain, with his head bare, saying, "he felt the spirit of the universe
upon him !"

to Primrose-hill; and, digging a hole of a good depth in the
ground, prostrate himself, and put his head in it. The longer
he kept his head immersed, the more benefit he thought he
derived ; so that he would lie for several minutes, and look
like a Persian adoring the sun. One day some thieves set
upon him, and, retaining his head under that salutary re
striction, picked his pockets.

Mr. Maurice got me permission to read in the Museum ;
which I did regularly for some time. It was there I began
to learn Italian. I obtained the same privilege for a person
who became one of its most enthusiastic visitors, and who is
worthy describing. His name is Llwyd (for he would account it treason to his country to write it Lloyd), and he is
author, among other pieces, of a poem entitled " Beaumaris
Bay," which obtained a great deal of praise from the critics.
I say " is," because I hope he is alive to read this account
of himself, and to attribute it (as he assuredly will do) to its
proper motives. My Llwyd was probably between thirty
and forty when I knew him. His face and manner of
speaking were as Ancient British as he could desire ; but
these merits he possessed in common with others. What
rendered him an extraordinary person was, that he raised
himself, by dint of his talents and integrity, from the situation of a gentleman's servant to a footing with his superiors,
and they were generous and wise enough to acknowledge it.
From what I was told, nothing could be better done on all
sides. They encouraged, and, I believe, enabled him to
make good his position; and he gave the best proof of his
right to it, by the delicacy of his acquiescence. His dress
was plain and decent, equally remote from sordidness and
pretension ; and his manners possessed that natural good-
breeding which results from the wish to please and the consciousness of being respected. Mr. Llwyd came to London
at certain periods, took an humble lodging, and passed his
time in visiting his friends, and reading at the Museum.
His passion was for the antiquities of his native country. If
you looked over his book, it was most probably full of the
coat-armor of Wynnes and Prices.

I was indebted to Mr. Llwyd for an introduction to his

friend Mr. Owen, translator of the *Paradise Lost* into Welsh,
Both of them were of the order of Bards ; and Mr. Owen
carried the same seal of his British origin in his face and
manners, and appeared to possess the same simplicity and
goodness.   Furthermore, he had a Welsh harp in his room,
and I had the satisfaction of hearing him play upon it.   He
was not very like Gray's bard : and instead of Conway's flood,
and a precipice, and an army coming to cut our throats, we
had tea and bread and butter, and a snug parlor with books
in it.   Notwithstanding my love of Gray, and a considerable wish to see a proper ill-used bard, I thought this a better thing, though I hardly know whether my friends did.
I am not sure, with all their good-nature, whether they
would not have preferred a good antiquarian death, with the
opportunity of calling King Edward a rascal, and playing
their harps at him, to all the Saxon conveniences of modern
times.

But I must speak a little of events as well as persons.

The respect which, in matters of religion, I felt for the
" spirit which giveth life," in preference to the "letter which
killeth," received a curious corroboration from a circumstance
which I witnessed on board a Margate hoy.   Having nothing
to do, after the publication of my poor volume, but to read
and to look about me, a friend proposed an excursion to
Brighton.   We were to go first to Margate, and then walk
the rest of the way by the sea-side, for the benefit of
the air.

We took places accordingly in the first hoy that was
about to sail, and speedily found ourselves seated and moving.
We thought the passengers a singularly staid set of people
for holiday-makers, and could not account for it.   The impression by degrees grew so strong, that we resolved to
inquire into the reason ; and it was with no very agreeable
feelings, that we found ourselves fixed for the day on board
what was called the " Methodist hoy."   The vessel, it
seems, was under the particular patronage of the sect of
that denomination ; and it professed to sail " by Divine
Providence."

Dinner brought a little more hilarity into the faces of these children of heaven. One innocently proposed a game at riddles; another entertained a circle of hearers by a question in arithmetic; a third (or the same person, if I remember— a very dreary gentleman) raised his voice into some remarks on "atheists and deists," glancing, while he did it, at the small knot of the uninitiated who had got together in self-defense; on which a fourth gave out a hymn of Dr. Watts's, which says that

> "Religion never was designed
> To make our pleasures less."

It was sung, I must say in a tone of the most impartial misery, as if on purpose to contradict the opinion.

Thus passed the hours, between formality. and eating and drinking, and psalm-singing, and melancholy attempts at a little mirth, till night came on; when our godly friends vanished below into their berths. The wind was against us: we beat out to sea, and had a taste of some cold autumnal weather. Such of us as were not prepared for this, adjusted ourselves as well as we could to the occasion, or paced about the deck to warm ourselves, not a little amused with a small crew of sailors belonging to the vessel, who sat together singing songs in a low tone of voice, in order that the psalm-singers below might not hear them.

During one of these pacings about the deck, my foot came in contact with a large bundle which lay as much out of the way as possible, but which I had approached unawares. On stooping to see what it was, I found it was a woman. She was sleeping, and her clothes were cold and damp.

As the captain could do nothing for her, except refer me to the "gentlefolks" below, in case any room could be made for her in their dormitory, I repaired below accordingly; and with something of a malicious benevolence, persisted in waking every sleeper in succession, and stating the woman's case.

Not a soul would stir. They had paid for their places: the woman should have done the same; and so they left her to the care of the "Providence," under which they sailed.

I do not wish to insinuate by this story that many excellent people have not been Methodists.   All I mean to say is, that here was a whole Margate hoy full of them ; that they had feathered their nests well below ; that the night was trying ; that to a female it might be dangerous ; and that not one of them, nevertheless, would stir to make room for her.

As Methodism is a fact of the past, and of the present, I trust it may have had its uses.   The degrees of it are various, from the blackest hue of what is called Calvinistic Methodism to colors little distinguishable from the mildest and pleasantest of conventional orthodoxy.   Accidents of birth, breeding, brain, heart, and temperament make worlds of difference in this respect, as in all others.   But where the paramount doctrine of a sect, whatever it may profess to include, is Self-preservation, and where this paramount doctrine, as it needs must when actually paramount, blunts in very self-defense the greatest final sympathies with one's fellow-creatures, the transition of ideas is easy from unfeelingness in a future state to unfeelingness in the present ; and it becomes a very little thing indeed to let a woman lie out in the cold all night, while saints are snoozing away in comfort.

My companion and I, much amused, and not a little indignant, took our way from Ramsgate along the coast, turning cottages into inns as our hunger compelled us, sleeping at night the moment we laid our heads on our pillows, and making such prodigious breakfasts, that in one instance we had a consultation whether we should muster up face enough to ask for more toast.   The rapid answer of the waiter, and his total unconsciousness of our feelings, highly delighted us.   We did not consider, that the vaster the orders, the more reasonable he would think us.

We passed Pegwell Bay, famous for shrimps ; Sandwich, once famous for oysters ; Deal, where I thought of the porpoises ; Dover, where we looked over the cliff, visited the castle, and were saluted by something that came tinkling down in the air (a prisoner's money-box on a string) ; Folkestone, Hythe, Dymchurch ; New Romney, an old place ;

Pevensey, where we poked about the ruins of a castle; Lewes and the river Ouse, a name that seems common to muddy places; Beachey-Head, where Charlotte Smith picked flowers and wrote pretty sonnets; and so came to Brighton, where we put up at the "Ship," and got acquainted with a regular inn-living gentleman.

This personage had a red face, a good appetite, and some prevailing ailment which he soothed with sea-air, and exasperated with good living. He had his meals set forth in the nicest manner; was thin and irritable, though good-natured; seemed to pass half of his morning in thinking of what he should eat, and seeing to it himself; and was very glad after dinner if you would talk to him, and amuse him, and listen to what he thought wholesome, and judicious, and *comme il faut.*

I recollect nothing else of Brighton, except that the Prince of Wales used to be there. Perhaps this was the reason why our red-faced friend chose it for his watering-place. He was just the man to hover on the borders of high life, and love to repose himself by the side of a polite, a princely, and an epicurean satisfaction. I should take him to have been a retired confectioner; or a clerk in Doctors Commons, or the Herald's Office; or the son of some agent of all work, who had claims on the nobility, which he took out in a sense of the connection.

At Dover, while being shown through the corridors in the rock, we were struck by a deep voice which suddenly opened above our heads. Looking up, we saw a head and shoulders leaning out of a corridor above, and reading a book by the light of an orifice still higher. It was somebody reading the Bible to some soldiers. Such at least is my recollection.

At Pevensey, a landlord on a Sunday morning was so charmed with our exploits in the breakfast line, that he did all he could to make us stop dinner by enlarging on the merits of the village preacher. He lamented the loss we should have of so admirable a sermon; said every body came to hear him; that we were in luck to be on the spot, &c. At length, finding his rhetoric of no avail on the spiritual side, he concluded by describing the charming piece of beef in his larder.

Not so hospitable was a farm-house in Pevensey Marsh. We reached it benighted, and being much fatigued, and desirous of going no farther, knocked and re-knocked for a chance of admission, but in vain. We saw, through a hole in the door, a party of men and women seated by a hearth ; but they would not attend to us. At length, on our knocking louder, and bawling through the hole, they bade us, with insolent speeches, to be gone. We departed in disgust, shaking the dust (or mud) off our feet, and wondering at the state of existing virtue, when such honest people as ourselves could be refused a night's lodging. But to say nothing of want of room, honest, or at any rate legal people, were perhaps those they most objected to. They may have taken us for emissaries of the custom-house. The whole region thereabouts was a great anticipator of free-trade.

These little incidents and characters that we met with in our journey, reminded us of passages in Fielding and his brother novelists. They lay in the same path of reality. Fielding and Smollett did but meet with similar things, and describe them better. One little passage, insignificant in itself, or only amusing from its apparent caricature, was identical with one that we had met with in books ; and I here relate it, to show how a seeming caricature may be simple matter of fact. Inquiring our way of a countryman, he began his answer by inquiring in turn which way we came. On obtaining that favorite and superfluous piece of information, he directed us to go by "Miss Shore's house." We asked whereabouts we should have the pleasure of seeing Miss Shore's house, and what sort of house it was. "Lord !" cried he, in amazement, " What ! don't you know Miss Shore's house ?"

These absurd answers were precisely the same they had been a hundred years before ; probably a thousand or ten thousand. Chaucer met with them on the road to Canterbury. Kow Moo gave them in China to Confucius. They are the last local oracles that will retreat before the diffusion of knowledge !

The length of this journey, which did us good, we reckoned to be a hundred and twelve miles ; and we did it in
four days; which was not bad walking. But the brother
whom I have mentioned as still living, has gone a hundred
miles in two. He also, when a lad, kept up at a kind of
trotting pace with a friend's horse all the way from Finchley
to Pimlico. His limbs were admirably well set.

The friend who was my companion in this journey had
not been long known to me ; but he was full of good qualities. He died a few years afterward in France, where he
unhappily found himself among his countrymen whom
Bonaparte so iniquitously detained at the commencement
of the second war. He was brother of my old friend Henry
Robertson, treasurer of Covent Garden Theatre, in whose
company and that of Vincent Novello, Charles Cowden
Clarke, and other gifted and estimable men, I have enjoyed some of the most harmonious evenings of my life, in
every sense of the word. Toward the latter part of his
detention he wrote me a letter which I delayed answering,
till answer was of no use ; and I mention the circumstance,
and shall notice another instance or two of procrastination on
my part, in case they may serve, even on one single occasion,
to give a casting vote in favor of promptness to some reader,
who may be doubting whether he shall procrastinate or not.
For out of a single moment so delayed may spring hundreds
full of regret. I have already noticed one, in speaking of a
schoolfellow. A third delay in writing a letter caused me
still greater pain on a similar account ; and for nearly fifty
years I have had a pang now and then come over me for
not having posted a letter which was given me for that
purpose by my mother. It was to my eldest brother, who
had been " wild." He was then in America, and has never
been heard of since. I never posted that letter at all ; and
finding it months afterward in my possession I did, what I
hope nobody will believe me capable of doing on any dis-
similar occasion, opened it, in order to see what amount of
evil I may have caused, and to make the confession of having done so to the writer, in case of necessity. Fortunately
it was only a letter of affection and general advice, and I

said nothing about it.   But as my mother, for aught I know
to the contrary, never again heard of her son, how was I to
be certain that the want of the letter might not have done
him some injury, and caused anguish to herself from his
silence ?   I do not wish to make mountains of molehills, or
to pretend that I may never have caused pain to others, of
a worse nature than this.   Perhaps I have, though with as
little intention ; for deliberately, or apart from unforeseen
consequences of thoughtlessness and vanity, I never distressed
human being ; and as I have undergone my distresses in
turn, and hope I have not lived altogether for nothing, I
comfort myself and am comforted, as I would have all the
world comfort one another.   I have found myself in my time
on jarring ground with acquaintances ; I have been preposterously misrepresented by enemies ; but I never ended with
losing the good-will of friends.   I must add, as some diminution of my offense in not answering the above letters, that I
had always intended to do so, and that the delay was partly
caused by my wishing to do it in the fullest manner ; but
what signify intentions, half occasioned, perhaps, by a sense
of our importance, if a friend is to die under the impression
of his being neglected ?

Let me revert to a pleasanter recollection.   The companion of my journey to Brighton, and another brother of
his, who was afterward in the commissariat (they are all
dead, except my friend of Covent Garden), set up a little
club, to which I belonged, called the "Elders," from our re
gard for the wine of that name, with hot goblets of which
we finished the evening.   Not the wine so called, which you
buy in the shops, and which is a mixture of brandy and ver-
juice ; but the vintage of the genuine berry, which is
admired wherever it is known, and which the ancients unquestionably symbolized under the mystery of the Bearded
Bacchus, the senior god of that name,

Brother of Bacchus, *elder* born.

The great Boerhaave held the tree in such pleasant reverence for the multitude of its virtues, that he is said to have
taken off his hat whenever he passed it.

Be this as it may, so happily it sent us to our beds, with such an extraordinary twofold inspiration of Bacchus and Somnus, that falling to sleep we would dream half an hour after of the last jest, and wake up again in laughter.

CHAPTER VI

PLAYGOING AND VOLUNTEERS.

Threatened invasion by the French.—The St. James's Volunteers.—
Singular debut of their colonel.—Satire of Foote.—A taste of campaigning.—Recollections of the stage at the beginning of the present
century.—Farley, De Camp, Miss De Camp, Emery, Kelly and
Mrs. Crouch, Catalini, Mrs. Billington, Madame Grassini, Braham.
Pasta and Lablache, female singers in general; Ambrogetti, Vestris
the dancer, Parisot; singing and dancing in former times and present; Jack Banister, Fawcett, Munden, Elliston, Mathews, Dowton,
Cooke, the Kembles and Mrs. Siddons, and Mrs. Jordan.—Playgoing in youth.—Critical playgoing.—Playgoing in general not what
it was.—Social position of actors in those times.—John Kemble and
a noble lord at a book-sale.—Earl Spencer.

A KNOCK at the doors of all England woke us up from
our dreams.   It was Bonaparte, threatening to come among
us, and bidding us put down " that glass."

The " Elders," in common with the rest of the world,
were moved to say him nay, and to drink, and drill themselves, to his confusion.

I must own that I never had the slightest belief in this
coming of Bonaparte.   It did, I allow, sometimes appear to
me not absolutely impossible ; and very strange it was to
think that some fine morning I might actually find myself
face to face with a parcel of Frenchmen in Kent or Sussex,
instead of playing at soldiers in Piccadilly.   But I did not
believe in his coming ; first, because I thought he had far
wiser things to attend to ; secondly, because he made such
an ostentatious show of it ; and thirdly, because I felt, that
whatever might be our party politics, it was not in the nature
of things English to allow it.   Nobody, I thought, could believe it possible, who did but see and hear the fine, unaffected, manly young fellows, that composed our own regiment of
volunteers, the St. James's, and whose counterparts had arisen
in swarms all over the country.   It was too great a jest.

And with all due respect for French valor, I think so to this day.

The case was not the same as in the time of the Normans. The Normans were a more advanced people than the Saxons; they possessed a familiar and family interest among us; and they had even a right to the throne. But in the year 1802, the French and English had, for centuries, been utterly distinct as well as rival nations; the latter had twice beaten the French on French ground, and under the greatest disadvantages; how much less likely were they to be beaten on their own, under every circumstance of exasperation? They were an abler-bodied nation than the French; they had been bred up, however erroneously, in a contempt for them, which (in a military point of view) was salutary, when it was not careless; and, in fine, here were all these volunteers, as well as troops of the line, taking the threat with an ease too great even to laugh at it, but at the same time sedulously attending to their drills, and manifestly resolved, if the struggle came, to make a personal business of it, and see which of the two nations had the greatest pluck.

The volunteers would not even take the trouble of patronizing a journal that was set up to record their movements and to flatter their self-respect. A word of praise from the king, from the commander-in-chief, or the colonel of the regiment, was well enough; it was all in the way of business, but why be told what they knew, or be encouraged when they did not require it? Wags used to say of the journal in question, which was called the *Volunteer,* that it printed only one number, sold only one copy, and that this copy had been purchased by a volunteer drummer-boy. The boy, seeing the paper set out for sale, exclaimed, " The *Volunteer!* why, I'm a volunteer;" and so he bought that solitary image of himself. The boy was willing to be told that he was doing something more than playing at soldiers; but what was this to the men?

This indifferent kind of self-respect and contentment did not hinder the volunteers, however, from having a good deal of pleasant banter of one another among themselves, or from feeling that there was something now and then among them

ridiculous in respect to appearances. A gallant officer in
our regiment, who was much respected, went among us by
the name of Lieutenant Molly, on account of the delicacy of
his complexion. Another, who was a strict disciplinarian,
and had otherwise a spirit of love for the profession, as
though he had been a born soldier, was not spared allusions
to his balls of perfumery. Our major (now no more), was
an undertaker in Piccadilly, of the name of Downs, very fat
and jovial, yet active withal, and a good soldier. He had
one of those lively, juvenile faces that are sometimes observed
in people of a certain sleek kind of corpulency. This ample
field officer was " cut and come again" for jokes of all sorts.
Nor was the colonel himself spared, though he was a highly
respectable nobleman, and nephew to an actual troop-of-the-
line conqueror, the victor of Montreal. But this requires a
paragraph or two to itself.

We had been a regiment for some time, without a colonel.
The colonel was always about to be declared, but declared
he was not ; and meantime we mustered about a thousand
strong, and were much amazed, .and, perhaps, a little
indignant. At length the moment arrived—the colonel
was named ; he was to be introduced to us ; and that
nothing might be wanting to our dignity, he was a lord, and
a friend of the minister, and nephew to the victor aforesaid.

Our parade was the court-yard of Burlington House.
The whole regiment attended. We occupied three sides of
the ground. In front of us were the great gates, longing to
be opened. Suddenly the word is given, " My lord is at
hand !" Open burst the gates—up strikes the music. " Present arms !" vociferates the major.

In dashes his lordship, and is pitched right over his horse's
head to the ground.

It was the most unfortunate anticlimax that could have
happened. Skill, grace, vigor, address, example, ascendency,
mastery, victory, all were, in a manner, to have been presented to us in the heroical person of the noble colonel ; and
here they were, prostrated at our feet—ejected—cast out—
humiliated—ground to the earth ; subjected (for his merciful

construction) to the least fellow-soldier that stood among us, upright on his feet.

The construction, however, was accorded. Every body felt indeed, that the greatest of men might have been subjected to the accident. It was the horse, not he, that was in fault—it was the music—the ringing of the arms, &c. His spirit had led him to bring with him too fiery a charger. Bucephalus might have thrown Alexander at such a moment. A mole-hill threw William the Third. A man might conquer Bonaparte, and yet be thrown from his horse. And the conclusion was singularly borne out in another quarter; for no conqueror, I believe, whose equitation is ascertained, ever combined more numerous victories with a greater number of falls from his saddle, than his lordship's illustrious friend, the Duke of Wellington.

During our field-days, which sometimes took place in the neighborhood celebrated by Foote in his *Mayor of Garrat*, it was impossible for those who were acquainted with his writings, not to think of his city trained-bands and their dreadful "marchings and counter-marchings from Acton to Ealing, and from Ealing back again to Acton." We were not "all robbed and murdered," however, as we returned home, "by a single footpad." We returned, not by the Ealing stage, but in right warlike style, marching and dusty. We had even, one day, a small taste of the will and appetite of campaigning. Some of us, after a sham-fight, were hastening toward Acton, in a very rage of hunger and thirst, when we discerned coming toward us a baker with a basket full of loaves. To observe the man; to see his loaves scattored on the ground; to find ourselves, each with one of them under his arm, tearing the crumb out, and pushing on for the village, heedless of the cries of the pursuing baker, was (in the language of the novelists) the work of a moment. Next moment we found ourselves standing in the cellar of an Acton alehouse, with the spigots torn out of the barrels, and every body helping himself as he could. The baker and the beer-man were paid, but not till we chose to attend to them; and I fully comprehended, even from this small specimen of the will and pleasure of soldiers, what savages they could become on graver occasions.

In this St. James's regiment of volunteers were three persons whom I looked on with great interest, for they were actors. They were Farley, Emery, and De Camp, all well-known performers at the time. The first, I believe, is still living. He was a celebrated melo-dramatic-actor, remarkable for combining a short, sturdy person with energetic activity; for which reason, if I am not mistaken, in spite of his shortness and his sturdiness, he had got into the light infantry company, where I think I have had the pleasure of standing both with him and Mr. De Camp. With De Camp certainly. The latter was brother of Miss De Camp, afterward Mrs. Charles Kemble, an admirable actress in the same line as Farley, and in such characters as *Beatrice* and *Lucy Lockitt*. She had a beautiful figure, fine, large, dark eyes, and elevated features, fuller of spirit than softness, but still capable of expressing great tenderness. Her brother was nobody in comparison with her, though he was clever in his way, and more handsome. But it was a sort of effeminate beauty, which made him look as if he ought to have been the sister, and she the brother. It was said of him, in a comprehensive bit of alliteration, that he "failed in fops, but there was fire in his footmen."

The third of these histrionic patriots, Mr. Emery, was one of the best actors of his kind the stage ever saw. He excelled, not only in Yorkshiremen, and other rustical comic characters, but in parts of homely tragedy, such as criminals of the lower order, whose conscious guilt he exhibited with such a lively, truthful mixture of clownishness in the mode and intensity in the feeling, as made a startling and terrible picture of the secret passions to which all classes of men are liable.

Emery was also an amateur painter—of landscape, I believe, and of no mean repute. He was a man of a middle height, rather tall, perhaps, than otherwise, and with quiet, respectable manners; but with something of what is called a pudding face, and an appearance on the whole not unlike a gentleman farmer. You would not have supposed there was so much emotion in him ; though he had purpose, too, in his look ; and he died early.

I have been tempted to dilate somewhat on these gentle-men ; for though I made no acquaintance with them pri-vately, I was now beginning to look with peculiar interest on the stage, to which I had already wished to be a con-tributor, and of which I was then becoming a critic. I had written a tragedy, a comedy, and a farce ; and my Spring Garden friends had given me an introduction to their ac-quaintance, Mr. Kelly, of the Opera House, with a view to having the farce brought out by some manager with whom he was intimate. I remember lighting upon him at the door of his music-shop, or saloon, at the corner of the lane in Pall Mall, where the Arcade now begins, and giving him my letter of introduction and my farce at once. He had a quick, snappish, but not ill-natured voice, and a flushed, handsome, and good-humored face, with the hair about his ears. The look was a little rakish or so, but very agreeable.

Mr. Kelly was extremely courteous to me ; but what he said of the farce, or did with it, I utterly forget. Himself I shall never forget ; for as he was the first actor I ever beheld any where, so he was one of the first whom I saw on the stage. Actor, indeed, he was none, except inasmuch as he was an acting singer, and not destitute of a certain spirit in every thing he did. Neither had he any particular power as a singer, nor even a voice. He said it broke down while he was studying in Italy ; where, indeed, he had sung with applause. The little snappish tones I spoke of, were very manifest on the stage : he had short arms, as if to match them, and a hasty step : and yet, notwithstanding these drawbacks, he was heard with pleasure, for he had taste and feeling. He was a delicate composer, as the music in *Blue Beard* evinces ; and he selected so happily from other composers, as to give rise to his friend Sheridan's banter, that he was an " importer of music and composer of wines" (for he once took to being a wine-merchant). While in Ireland, during the early part of his career, he adapted a charming air of Martini's to English words, which, under under the title of *Oh, thou wert born to please me*, he sang with Mrs. Crouch to so much effect, that not only was it always called for three times, but no play was suffered to be performed without it. It should be added, that Mrs. Crouch was a lovely woman, as well as a beautiful singer, and that the two performers were in love. I have heard them sing it myself, and do not wonder at the impression it made on the susceptible hearts of the Irish. Twenty years afterward, when Mrs. Crouch was no more, and while Kelly was singing a duet in the same country with Madame Catalani, a man in the gallery cried out, " Mr. Kelly, will you be good enough to favor us with *Oh, thou wert born to please me ?*" The audience laughed ; but the call went to the heart of the singer, and probably came from that of the honest fellow who made it. The man may have gone to the play in his youth, with somebody whom he loved by his side, and heard two lovers, as happy as himself, sing what he now wished to hear again.

Madame Catalani was also one of the singers I first remember. I first heard her at an oratorio, where happening to sit in a box right opposite to where she stood, the leaping forth of her amazingly powerful voice absolutely startled me. Women's voices on the stage are apt to rise above all others, but Catalani's seemed to delight in trying its strength with choruses and orchestras ; and the louder they became, the higher and more victorious she ascended. In fact, I believe she is known to have provoked and enjoyed this sort of contest. I suspect, however, that I did not hear her when she was at her best or sweetest. My recollection is, that with a great deal of taste and brilliancy, there was more force than feeling. She was a Roman, with the regular Italian antelope face (if I may so call it) ; large eyes, with a sensitive, elegant nose, and lively expression.

Mrs. Billington also appeared to me to have more brilliancy of execution than depth of feeling. She was a fat beauty, with regular features, and may be seen drawn to the life, in a portrait in Mr. Hogarth's *Memoirs of the Musical Drama*, where she is frightfully dressed in a cropped head of hair, and a waist tucked under her arms—the fashion of the day.

Not so Grassini. a large but perfectly well-made as well

as lovely woman, with black hair and eyes, and a countenance as full of feeling as her divine contralto voice. Largeness, or what is called fineness of person, was natural to her,
and did not hinder her from having a truly feminine appearance. She was an actress as well as singer. She acted
Proserpina in Winter's beautiful opera, and might have remained in the recollection of any one who heard and beheld
her, as an image of the goddess she represented. My friend,
Vincent Novello, saw the composer when the first performance of the piece was over, stoop down (he was a very tall
man) and kiss Mrs. Billington's hand for her singing in the
character of *Ceres*. I wonder he did not take Grassini in his
arms. She must have had a fine soul, and would have
known how to pardon him. But perhaps he did.

With Billington used to perform Braham, who is still in
some measure before the public, and from whose wonderful
remains of power in his old age they may judge what he
must have been in his prime. I mean, with regard to
voice ; for as to general manner and spirit, it is a curious
fact, that, except when he was in the act of singing, he
used to be a remarkably insipid performer; and that it was
not till he was growing elderly, that he became the animated person we now see him. This, too, he did all on a
sudden, to the amusement as well as astonishment of the
beholders. When he sang, he was always animated. The
probability is, that he had been bred up under masters who
were wholly untheatrical, and that something had occurred to
set his natural spirit reflecting on the injustice they had
done him ; though, for a reason which I shall give presently, the theatre, after all, was not the best field for his abilities. He had wonderful execution as well as force, and his
voice could also be very sweet, though it was too apt to betray something of that nasal tone which has been observed
in Jews, and which is, perhaps, quite as much, or more, a
habit in which they have been brought up, than a consequence of organization. The same thing has been noticed
in Americans ; and it might not be difficult to trace it to
moral, and even to moneyed causes ; those, to-wit, that induce people to retreat inwardly upon themselves ; into a

sense of their shrewdness and resources; and to clap their finger in self-congratulation upon the organ through which it pleases them occasionally to intimate as much to a bystander, not choosing to trust it wholly to the mouth.

Perhaps it was in some measure the same kind of breeding (I do not say it in disrespect, but in reference to matters of caste, far more discreditable to Christians than Jews) which induced Mr. Braham to quit the Italian stage, and devote himself to his popular and not very refined style of bravura-singing on the English. It was what may be called the loud-and-soft style. There was admirable execution; but the expression consisted in being very soft on the words *love, peace*, &c., and then bursting into roars of triumph on the words *hate, war*, and *glory*. To this pattern Mr. Braham composed many of the songs written for him; and the public were enchanted with a style which enabled them to fancy that they enjoyed the highest style of the art, while it required only the vulgarest of their perceptions. This renowned vocalist never did himself justice except in the compositions of Handel. When he stood in the concert-room or the oratorio, and opened his mouth with plain, heroic utterance in the mighty strains of *Deeper and deeper still*, or, *Sound an alarm*, or, *Comfort ye my people*, you felt indeed that you had a great singer before you. His voice which too often sounded like a horn vulgar, in the catch-penny lyrics of Tom Dibdin, now became a veritable trumpet of grandeur and exaltation; the tabernacle of his creed seemed to open before him in its most victorious days; and you might have fancied yourself in the presence of one of the sons of Aaron, calling out to the host of people from some platform occupied by their prophets.

About the same time Pasta made her first appearance in England, and produced no sensation. She did not even seem to attempt any. Her nature was so truthful, that, having as yet no acquirements to display, it would appear that she did not pretend she had. She must either have been prematurely put forward by others, or, with an instinct of her future greatness, supposed that the instinct itself would be recognized. When she came the second time, after com-

pleting her studies, she took rank at once as the greatest
genius in her line which the Italian theatre in England had
witnessed. She was a great tragic actress; and her singing, in point of force, tenderness, and expression, was equal
to her acting. All noble passions belonged to her; and her
very scorn seemed equally noble, for it trampled only on
what was mean. When she measured her enemy from head
to foot, in *Tancredi*, you really felt for the man, at seeing
him so reduced into nothingness. When she made her entrance on the stage, in the same character—which she did
right in front of the audience, midway between the side
scenes, she waved forth her arms, and drew them quietly together again over her bosom, as if she sweetly, yet modestly, embraced the whole house. And when, in the part of Medea,
she looked on the children she was about to kill, and tenderly
parted their hair, and seemed to mingle her very eyes in
lovingness with theirs, uttering, at the same time, notes of
the most wandering and despairing sweetness, every gentle
eye melted into tears. She wanted height, and had some
what too much flesh; but it seemed the substance of the very
health of her body, which was otherwise shapely. Her
head and bust were of the finest classical mould. An occasional roughness in her lower tones did but enrich them with
passion, as people grow hoarse with excess of feeling; and
while her voice was in its prime, even a little incorrectness
now and then in the notes would seem the consequence of
a like boundless emotion; but, latterly, it argued a failure
of ear, and consoled the mechanical artists who had been
mystified by her success. In every other respect, perfect
truth, graced by idealism, was the secret of Pasta's greatness. She put truth first always; and, in so noble and
sweet a mind, grace followed it as a natural consequence.

With the exception of Lablache, that wonderful bass singer, full of might as well as mirth, in whom the same truth,
accompanied in some respects by the same grace of feeling,
has suffered itself to be overlaid with comic fat (except when
he turns it into an heroic amplitude with drapery), I remember no men on our Italian stage equal to the women. Women

have carried the palm out and out, in acting, singing, and
dancing.   The pleasurable seems more the forte of the sex ;
and the opera house is essentially a palace of pleasure, even in
its tragedy.   Bitterness there can not but speak sweetly ; there
is no darkness, and no poverty ; and every death is the death
of the swan.   When the men are sweet, they either seem
feeble, or, as in the case of Rubini, have execution without
passion.   Naldi was amusing , Tramezzani was elegant ;
Ambrogetti (whose great big calves seemed as if they ought
to have saved him from going into La Trappe) was a fine
dashing representative of Don Juan, without a voice.   But
what were these in point of impression on the public, compared with the woman I have mentioned, or even with vo-
luptuous Fodor, with amiable Sontag, with charming Mali-
bran (whom I never saw), or with adorable Jenny Lind
(whom, as an Irishman would say, I have seen still less ;
for not to see her appears to be a deprivation beyond all
ordinary conceptions of musical loss and misfortune) ?

As to dancers, male dancers are almost always *gawkies*,
compared with female.   One forgets the names of the best
of them ; but who, that ever saw, has forgotten Heberle, or
Cerito, or Taglioni ?   There was a great noise in France
about the Vestrises ; particularly old Vestris ; but (with all
due respect to our gallant neighbors) I have a suspicion that
he took the French in with the gravity and *imposingness* of
his twirls.   There was an imperial demand about Vestris,
likely to create for him a corresponding supply of admiration.
The most popular dancers of whom I have a recollection,
when I was young, were Deshayes, who was rather an elegant posture-master than dancer, and Madame Parisot, who
was very thin, and always smiling.   I could have seen little
dancing in those times, or I should have something to say of
the Presles, Didelots, and others, who turned the heads of the
Yarmouths and Barrymores of the day.   Art, in all its
branches, has since grown more esteemed ; and I suspect,
that neither dancing nor singing ever attained so much grace
and beauty as they have done within the last twenty years.
The Farinellis and Pacchierottis were a kind of monsters of
execution.   There were tones, also, in their voices which, in

all probability, were very touching. But, to judge from their printed songs, their chief excellence lay in difficult and ever-lasting roulades. And we may guess, even now, from the prevailing character of French dancing, that difficulty was the great point of conquest with Vestris. There was no such graceful understanding between the playgoers and the performers, no such implied recognition of the highest principles of emotion, as appears to be the case in the present day with the Taglionis and Jenny Linds.

To return to the English boards ; the first actor whom I remember seeing upon them was excellent Jack Bannister. He was a handsome specimen of the best kind of Englishman—jovial, manly, good-humored, unaffected, with a great deal of whim and drollery, but never passing the bounds of the decorous ; and when he had made you laugh heartily as some yeoman or seaman in a comedy, he could bring the tears into your eyes for some honest sufferer in an afterpiece. He gave you the idea of a good fellow, a worthy household humorist, whom it would be both pleasant and profitable to live with ; and this was his real character. He had a taste for pictures, and settled down into a good English gout and the love of his family. I saw him one day hobbling with a stick in Gower-street, where he lived, and the same evening performing the part either of the young squire, Tony Lumpkin, in *She Stoops to Conquer*, or of Acres, in the Comedy of the *Rivals*, I forget which ; but in either character he would be young to the last. Next day he would perform the old father, the Brazier, in Colman's sentimental comedy, *John Bull ;* and every body would see that it was a father indeed who was suffering.

This could not be said of Fawcett in the same character, who roared like a Bull, but did not feel like John. He was affecting, too, in his way ; but it was after the fashion of a great noisy boy, whom you can not help pitying for his tears, though you despise him for his vulgarity. Fawcett had a harsh, brazen face, and a voice like a knife-grinder's wheel. He was all pertness, coarseness, and effrontory, but with a great deal of comic force ; and whenever he came trotting on to the stage (for such was his walk) and pouring forth his harsh, 1apid words, with his nose in the air, and a facetious grind in his throat, the audience were prepared for a merry evening.

Munden was a comedian famous for the variety and significance of his grimaces, and for making something out of nothing by a certain intensity of contemplation. Lamb, with exquisite wit, described him in one sentence, by saying, that he " beheld a leg of mutton in its quiddity." If he laid an emphasis on the word " Holborn," or " button," he did it in such a manner that you thought there was more in " Holborn," or " button," than it ever before entered into your head to conceive. I have seen him, while playing the part of a vagabond loiterer about inn-doors, look at, and gradually approach, a pot of ale on a table from a distance, for ten minutes together, while he kept the house in roars of laughter by the intense idea which he dumbly conveyed of its contents, and the no less intense manifestation of his cautious but inflexible resolution to drink it. So, in acting the part of a credulous old antiquary, on whom an old beaver is palmed for the " hat of William Tell," he reverently put the hat on his head, and then solemnly walked to and fro with such an excessive sense of the glory with which he was crowned, such a weight of reflected heroism, and accumulation of Tell's whole history on that single representative culminating point, elegantly halting every now and then to put himself in the attitude of one drawing a bow, that the spectator could hardly have been astonished had they seen his hair stand on end, and carry the hat aloft with it. But I must not suffer myself to be led into these details.

Lewis was a comedian of the rarest order, for he combined whimsicality with elegance, and levity with heart. He was the fop, the lounger, the flatterer, the rattlebrain, the sower of wild oats ; and in all he was the gentleman. He looked on the stage what he was off it, the companion of wits and men of quality. It is pleasant to know that he was a descendant of Erasmus Lewis, the secretary of Lord Oxford, and friend of Pope and Swift. He was airiness personified. He had a light person, light features, a light voice, a smile that showed the teeth, with good-humored eyes ; and a genial levity pervaded his action, to the very tips of his delicately-gloved fingers. He drew on his glove like a gentleman, and then darted his fingers at the ribs of the character he was talking with, in a way that carried with it whatever was suggestive, and sparkling, and amusing. When he died, they put up a classical Latin inscription to his memory, about *elegantiæ* and *lepores* (whims and graces); and you felt that no man better deserved it. He had a right to be recorded as the type of airy genteel comedy.

Elliston was weightier both in manner and person; and he was a tragedian as well as comedian. Not a great tragedian, though able to make a serious and affecting impression; and when I say weightier in comedy than Lewis, I do not mean heavy; but that he had greater bodily substance and force. In Sir Harry Wildair, for instance, he looked more like the man who could bear rakery and debauch. The engraved portrait of him in a coat bordered with fur is very like. He had dry as well as genial humor, was an admirable representative of the triple hero in *Three and the Deuce*, of Charles Surface, Don Felix, the Duke in the *Honeymoon*, and of all gallant and gay lovers of a robust order, not omitting the most cordial. Indeed, he was the most genuine lover that I ever saw on the stage. No man approached a woman as he did—with so flattereng a mixture of reverence and passion—such closeness without insolence, and such a trembling energy in his words. His utterance of the single word "charming" was a volume of rapturous fervor. I speak, of course, only of his better days. Latterly, he grew flustered with imprudence and misfortune; and from the accounts I have heard of his acting, nobody who had not seen him before could have guessed what sort of man he had been. Elliston, like Lewis, went upon the stage with advantages of training and connections. He was nephew of Dr. Elliston, master of one of the colleges at Cambridge; and he was educated at Saint Paul's school.

These are the actors of those days whom I recollect with the greatest pleasure. I include Fawcett, because he was identified with some of the most laughable characters in farce.

To touch on some others. Liston was renowned for an exquisitely ridiculous face and manner, rich with half-conscious, half-unconscious absurdity. The whole piece became *Listonized* the moment he appeared. People longed for his coming back, in order that they might doat on his oily, mantling face, and laugh with him and at him.

Mathews was a genius in mimicry, a facs-imile in mind as well as manner ; and he was a capital Sir Fretful Plagiary. It was a sight to see him looking wretchedly happy at his victimizers, and digging deeper and deeper into his mortification at every fresh button of his coat that he buttoned up.

Dowton was perfect in such characters as Colonel Oldboy and Sir Anthony Absolute. His anger was no petty irritability, but the boiling of a rich blood, and of a will otherwise genial. He was also by far the best Falstaff.

Cooke, a square-faced, hook-nosed, .wide-mouthed, malignantly smiling man, was intelligent and peremptory, and a hard hitter : he seized and strongly kept your attention ; but he was never pleasant. He was too entirely the satirist, the hyprocite, and the villain. He loved too fondly his own caustic and rascally words, so that his voice, which was otherwise harsh, was in the *habit* of melting and dying away inwardly in the secret satisfaction of its smiling malignity. As to his vaunted tragedy, it was a mere reduction of Shakspeare's poetry into indignant prose. He limited every character to its worst qualities ; and had no idealism, no affections, no verse.

Kemble was a god compared with Cooke, as far as the ideal was concerned ; though, on the other hand, I never could admire Kemble, as it was the fashion to do. He was too artificial, too formal, too critically and deliberately conscious. Nor do I think that he had any genius whatsoever. His power was all studied acquirement. It was this indeed, by the help of a stern Roman aspect, that made the critics like him. It presented, in a noble shape, the likeness of their own capabilities.

Want of genius could not be imputed to his sister, Mrs. Siddons. I did not see her, I believe, in her best days ;

but she must always have been a somewhat masculine beauty ; and she had no love in her, apart from other passions. She was a mistress, however, of lofty, of queenly, and of appalling tragic effect. Nevertheless, I could not but think that something of too much art was apparent even in Mrs. Siddons ; and she failed, I think, in the highest points of refinement. When she smelt the blood on her hand, for instance, in *Macbeth*, in the scene where she walked in her sleep, she made a face of ordinary disgust, as though the odor was offensive to the senses, not appalling to the mind.

Charles Kemble, who had an ideal face and figure, was the nearest approach I ever saw to Shakespeare's gentlemen, and to heroes of romance. He also made an excellent Cassio. But with the exception of Mrs. Siddons, who was declining, all the reigning school of tragedy had retrograded rather than otherwise, toward the times that preceded Garrick ; and the consequence was, that when Kean brought back nature and impulse, he put an end to it at once, as Garrick had put an end to Quin.

In comedy nature had never been wanting ; and there was one comic actress, who was nature herself in one of her most genial forms. This was Mrs. Jordan ; who, though she was neither beautiful, nor handsome, nor even pretty, nor accomplished, nor " a lady," nor any thing conventional or *comme il faut* whatsoever, yet was so pleasant, so cordial, so natural, so full of spirits, so healthily constituted in mind and body, had such a shapely leg withal, so charming a voice, and such a happy and happy-making expression of countenance, that she appeared something superior to all those requirements of acceptability, and to hold a patent from nature herself for our delight and good opinion. It is creditable to the feelings of society in general, that allowances are made for the temptations to which the stage exposes the sex ; and in Mrs. Jordan's case these were not diminished by a sense of the like consideration due to princely restrictions, and to the manifest domestic dispositions of more parties than one. But she made even Methodists love her. A touching story is told of her apologizing to a poor man of that persuasion for having relieved him. He had

asked her name ; and she expressed a hope that he would
not feel offended when the name was told him.   On hearing
it, the honest Methodist (he could not have been one on
board the hoy) shed tears of pity and admiration, and trusted
that he could not do wrong in begging a blessing on her
head.

[*Serious Reviewer, interrupting.*   But, my good sir,
suppose some of your female readers should take it into their
heads to be Mrs. Jordan ?

Author.   Oh, my good sir, don't be alarmed.   My female
readers are not persons to be so much afraid for, as you seem
to think yours are.   The stage itself has taught them large
measures both of charity and discernment.   They have not
been so locked up in restraint, as to burst out of bounds the
moment they see a door open for consideration.]

Mrs. Jordan was inimitable in exemplifying the consequences of too much restraint in ill-educated Country-Girls,
in romps, in hoydens, and in wards on whom the mercenary have designs.   She wore a bib and tucker, and pinafore,
with a bouncing propriety, fit to make the boldest spectator
alarmed at the idea of bringing such a household responsibility on his shoulders.   To see her when thus attired shed
blubbering tears for some disappointment, and eat all the
while a great thick slice of bread and butter, weeping, and
moaning, and munching, and eying at every bite the part
she meant to bite next, was a lesson against will and appetite
worth a hundred sermons of our friends on board the hoy ;
and, on the other hand, they could assuredly have done and
said nothing at all calculated to make such an impression in
favor of amiableness as she did, when she acted in gentle,
generous, and confiding characters.   The way in which she
would take a friend by the cheek and kiss her, or make up
a quarrel with a lover, or coax a guardian into good-humor,
or sing (without accompaniment) the song of *Since then I'm
doom'd*, or *In the Dead of the Night*, trusting, as she had
a right to do, and as the house wished her to do, to the sole
effect of her sweet, mellow, and loving voice—the reader will
pardon me, but tears of pleasure and regret come into my
eyes at the recollection, as if she personified whatsoever was

happy at that period of life, and which has gone like herself.
The very sound of the little familiar word *bud* from her lips
(the abbreviation of husband), as she packed it closer, as it
were, in the utterance, and pouted it up with fondness in
the man's face, taking him at the same time by the chin,
was a whole concentrated world of the power of loving.

That is a pleasant time of life, the play-going time in
youth, when the coach is packed full to go to the theatre,
and brothers and sisters, parents and lovers (none of whom,
perhaps, go very often) are all wafted together in a flurry
of expectation ; when the only wish as they go (except with
the lovers) is to go as fast as possible, and no sound is so
delightful as the cry of " Bill of the Play ;" when the smell
of links in the darkest and muddiest winter's night is charming ; and the steps of the coach are let down ; and a roar
of hoarse voices round the door, and *mud-shine* on the pavement, are accompanied with the sight of the warm-looking
lobby which is about to be entered ; and they enter, and
pay, and ascend the pleasant stairs, and begin to hear the
silence of the house, perhaps the first jingle of the music ;
and the box is entered amidst some little awkwardness in
descending to their places, and being looked at ; and at
length they sit, and are become used to by their neighbors,
and shawls and smiles are adjusted, and the play-bill is
handed round or pinned to the cushion, and the gods are
a little noisy, and the music veritably commences, and at
length the curtain is drawn up, and the first delightful syllables are heard :

" Ah ! my dear Charles, when did you see the lovely
Olivia ?"

" Oh ! my dear Sir George, talk not to me of Olivia. The
cruel guardian," &c.

Anon the favorite of the party makes his appearance, and
then they are quite happy ; and next day, besides his own
merits, the points of the dialogue are attributed to him as if
he was their inventor.   It is not Sir Harry, or old Dornton,
or Dubster, who said this or that; but "Lewis," "Munden,"
or "Keeley."   They seem to think the wit really originated
with the man who uttered it so delightfully.

Critical play-going is very inferior in its enjoyments to this. It must of necessity blame as well as praise ; it becomes difficult to please ; it is tempted to prove its own merits, instead of those of its entertainers ; and the enjoyments of self-love, besides, perhaps, being ill-founded, and subjecting it to the blame which it bestows, are sorry substitutes, at the best, for hearty delight in others. Never, after I had taken critical pen in hand, did I pass the thoroughly-delightful evenings at the playhouse which I had done when I went only to laugh or be moved. I had the pleasure, it is true, of praising those whom I admired ; but the retributive uneasiness of the very pleasure of blaming attended it ; the consciousness of self, which on all occasions except loving ones, contains a bitter in its sweet, put its sorry obstacle in the way of an unembarrassed delight ; and I found the days flown when I retained none but the good passages of plays and performers, and when I used to carry to my old school-fellows rapturous accounts of the farces of Colman, and the good-natured comedies of O'Keefe.

I speak of my own feelings, and at a particular time of life ; but forty or fifty years ago, people of all times of life were much greater play-goers than they are now. They dined earlier ; they had not so many newspapers, clubs, and piano-fortes; the French Revolution only tended at first to endear the nation to its own habits ; it had not yet opened a thousand new channels of thought and interest ; nor had railroads conspired to carry people, bodily as well as mentally, into as many analogous directions. Every thing was more concentrated, and the various classes of society felt a greater concern in the same amusements. Nobility, gentry, citizens, princes, all were frequenters of theaters, and even more or less acquainted personally with the performers. Nobility intermarried with them ; gentry, and citizens too, wrote for them ; princes conversed and lived with them. Sheridan, and other members of parliament, were managers as well as dramatists. It was Lords Derby, Craven, and Thurlow that sought wives on the stage. Two of the most popular minor dramatists were Cobb, a clerk in the India House, and Birch, the pastry-cook. If Mrs. Jordan lived

with the Duke of Clarence (William IV.) as his mistress,
nobody doubts that she was as faithful to him as a wife.
His brother, the Prince of Wales (George the Fourth), besides his intimacy with Sheridan and the younger Colman,
and to say nothing of Mrs. Robinson, took a pleasure in conversing with Kemble, and was the personal patron of O'Keefe
and of Kelly.   The Kembles, indeed, as Garrick had been,
were received every where, among the truly best circles; that
is to say, where intelligence was combined with high breeding : and they deserved it ; for whatever difference of opinion may be entertained as to the amount of genius in the
family, nobody who recollects them will dispute that they
were a remarkable race, dignified and elegant in manners,
with intellectual tendencies, and in point of aspect very like
what has been called " God Almighty's nobility."

I remember once standing behind John Kemble and a
noble lord at a sale.   It was the celebrated book-sale of the
Duke of Roxburgh ; and by the same token I recollect another person that was present, of whom more by-and-by.
The player and the nobleman were conversing, the former
in his high, dignified tones, the latter in a voice which I
heard but indistinctly.   Presently, the actor turned his noble
profile to his interlocutor, and on his moving it back again,
the man of quality turned his.   What a difference ! and
what a voice !   Kemble's voice was none of the best ; but,
like his profile, it was nobleness itself compared with that of
the noble lord.   I had taken his lordship for a young man,
by the trim cut of his body and of his clothes, the " fall in"
of his back and the smart way in which he had stuck his
hat on the top of his head ; but when I saw his profile and
heard his voice, I seemed to have before me a premature old
one.   His mouth seemed toothless ; his voice was a hasty
mumble.   Without being aquiline, the face had the appearance of being what may be called an old " nose-and-mouth
face."   The suddenness with which it spoke added to the
surprise.   It was like a flash of decrepitude on the top of a
young body.

This was the sale at which the unique copy of Boccacio
fetched a thousand and four hundred pounds.   It was bought

by the Marquis of Blandford (the late Duke of Marlborough) in competition with Earl Spencer, who conferred with his son, Lord Althorp, and gave it up. So at least I understand, for I was not aware of the conference, or of the presence of Lord Althorp (afterward minister, and late Earl Spencer). I remember his father well at the sale, and how he sat at the further end of the auctioneer's table with an air of intelligent indifference, leaning his head on his hand so as to push up the hat a little from off it. I beheld with pleasure in his person the pupil of Sir William Jones and brother of Coleridge's Duchess of Devonshire. It was curious and scarcely pleasant, to see two Spencers thus bidding against one another, even though the bone of contention was a book, and the ghost of their illustrious kinsman, the author of the *Faerie Queene*, might have been gratified to see what book it was, and how high the prices of old folios had risen. What satisfaction the marquis got out of his victory, I can not say. The earl, who, I believe, was a genuine lover of books, could go home, and reconcile himself to his defeat by reading the work in a cheaper edition.

I shall have occasion to speak of Mr. Kemble again presently, and of subseouent actors by-and-by.

CHAPTER VII.

ESSAYS IN CRITICISM.

Acquaintance with the British classics, and contribution of a series of articles to an evening paper.—Colman and Bonnell Thornton.—Goldsmith again.—Reading of novels.—Objections to history.—Voltaire.—Youthful theology.—The News.—Critical essays on the performers of the London theatres.—John Kemble and his whims of pronunciation.

I HAD not been as misdirected in the study of prose as in that of poetry. It was many years before I discovered what was requisite in the latter. In the former, the very commonplaces of the schoolmaster tended to put me in the right path, for (as I have already intimated) he found the *Spectator* in vogue, and this became our standard of prose writing.

It is true (as I have also mentioned) that in consequence of the way in which we were taught to use them by the schoolmaster, I had become far more disgusted than delighted with the charming papers of Addison, and with the exaction of moral observations on a given subject. But the seed was sown, to ripen under pleasanter circumstances; and my father, with his usual good-natured impulse, making me a present one day of a set of the British classics, which attracted my eyes on the shelves of Harley, the bookseller in Cavendish-street, the tenderness with which I had come to regard all my school-recollections, and the acquaintance which I now made for the first time with the lively papers of the *Connoisseur*, gave me an entirely fresh and delightful sense of the merits of essay writing. I began to think that when Boyer crumpled up and chucked away my "themes" in a passion, he had not done justice to the honest weariness of my anti-formalities, and to their occasional evidences of something better.

The consequence was a delighted perusal of the whole set of classics (for I have ever been a "glutton of books"); and this was followed by my first prose endeavors in a series of papers called the *Traveler*, which appeared in the evening paper of that name (now the *Globe*), under the signature of " Mr. Town, *junior*, Critic and Censor-general"—the senior Mr. Town, with the same titles, being no less a person than my friend of the *Connoisseur*, with whom I thus had the boldness to fraternize.   I offered them with fear and trembling to the editor of the *Traveler*, Mr. Quin, and was astonished at the gayety with which he accepted them.   What astonished me more was a perquisite of five or six copies of the paper, which I enjoyed every Saturday when my essays appeared, and with which I used to re-issue from Bolt Court in a state of transport.   I had been told, but could not easily conceive, that the editor of a new evening paper would be happy to fill up his pages with any decent writing ; but Mr. Quin praised me besides ; and I could not behold the long columns of type, written by myself, in a public paper, without thinking there must be some merit in them, besides that of being a stop-gap.

Luckily, the essays were little read ; they were not at all noticed in public ; and I thus escaped the perils of another permature laudation for my juvenility.   I was not led to repose on the final merits either of my prototype or his imitator.   The *Connoisseur*, nevertheless, gave me all the transports of a first love.   His citizen at Vauxhall, who says at every mouthful of beef, " There goes twopence ;" and the creed of his unbeliever, who " believes in all unbelief," competed for a long time in my mind with the humor of Goldsmith.   I was also greatly delighted with the singular account of himself, in the dual number, with which he concludes his work, shadowing forth the two authors of it in one person :

" Mr. Town (says he) is a fair, black, middle-sized, very short person.   He wears his own hair, and a periwig.   He is about thirty years of age, and not more than four-and-twenty.   He is a student of the law and a bachelor of physic.   He was bred at the University of Oxford; where, having taken no less than three degrees, he looks down on many learned professors as his inferiors; yet, having been there but little longer than to take the first degree of bachelor of arts, it has more than once happened that the censor-general of all England has been reprimanded by the censor of his college for neglecting to furnish the usual essay, or (in the collegiate phrase) the theme of the week."

Probably these associations with school-terms, and with a juvenile time of life, gave me an additional liking for the *Connoisseur*. The two-fold author, which he thus describes himself, consisted of Bonnell Thornton, afterward the translator of Plautus, and Colman, the dramatist, author of the *Jealous Wife*, and translator of Terence. Colman was the "very short person" of four-and-twenty, and Thornton was the bachelor of physic, though he never practiced. The humor of these writers, compared with Goldsmith's, was caricature, and not deep ; they had no pretensions to the genius of the *Vicar of Wakefield :* but they possessed great animal spirits, which are a sort of merit in this climate ; and this was another claim on my regard. The name of Bonnell Thornton (whom I had taken to be the sole author of the *Connoisseur*) was for a long time, with me, another term for animal spirits, humor, and wit. I then discovered that there was more smartness in him than depth ; and had I known that he and Colman had ridiculed the odes of Gray, I should, perhaps, have made the discovery sooner ; though I was by no means inclined to confound parody with disrespect. But the poetry of Gray had been one of my first loves ; and I could as soon have thought of friendship or of the grave with levity, as of the friend of West, and the author of the *Elegy* and the *Bard*.

An amusing story is told of Thornton, which may show the quick and ingenious, but, perhaps, not very feeling turn of his mind. It is said that he was once discovered by his father sitting in a box at the theatre, when he ought to have been in his rooms at college. The old gentleman addressing him accordingly, that youngster turned in pretended amazement to the people about him, and said, "Smoke old wigsby, who takes me for his son." Thornton, senior, upon this, indignantly hastens out of the box, with the manifest intention of setting off for Oxford, and finding the rooms vacant. Thornton, junior, takes double post-horses, and is there before him, quietly sitting in his chair.

He rises from it on his father's appearance, and cries, " Ah, dear sir, is it you? To what am I indebted for this unexpected pleasure?"

Goldsmith enchanted me. I knew no end of repeating passages out of the *Essays* and the *Citizen of the World*, such as the account of the Club, with its babel of talk; of Beau Tibbs, with his dinner of ox-cheek which " his grace was so fond of;" and of the wooden-legged sailor, who regarded those that were luckly enough to have their "legs shot off" on board king's ships (which entitled them to a penny a day), as being "born with golden spoons in their mouths." Then there was his correct, sweet style ; the village-painting in his poems ; the *Retaliation*, which though on an artificial subject, seemed to me (as it yet seems) a still more genuine effusion ; and, above all, the *Vicar of Wakefield*, with Burchell, whom I adored ; and Moses, whom I would rather have been cheated with, than prosper; and the Vicar himself in his cassock, now presenting his "Treatise against Polygamy" (in the family picture) to his wife, habited as Venus ; and now distracted for the loss of his daughter Sophia, who is seduced by the villainous baronet. I knew not whether to laugh at him, or cry with him, most.

These, with Fielding and Smollett, Voltaire, Charlotte Smith, Bage, Mrs. Radcliffe, and Augustus La Fontaine, were my favorite prose authors. I had subscribed, while at school, to the famous circulating library in Leadenhall-street, and I have continued to be such a glutton of novels ever since, that, except where they repel me in the outset with excessive wordiness, I can read their three-volume enormities to this day without skipping a syllable; though I guess pretty nearly all that is going to happen, from the mysterious gentleman who opens the work in the dress of a particular century, down to the distribution of punishments and the drying up of tears in the last chapter. I think the authors wonderfully clever people, particularly those who write most; and I should like the most contemptuous of their critics to try their hand at doing something half as engaging.

Should any chance observer of these pages (for I look upon my customary perusers as people of deeper insight), pronounce such a course of reading frivolous, he will be exasperated to hear, that, had it not been for reverence to opinion, I should have been much inclined at that age (as, indeed, I am still) to pronounce the reading of far graver works frivolous ; history, for one. I read every history that came in my way, and could not help liking good old Herodotus, ditto Villani, picturesque, festive Froissart, and accurate and most entertaining, though artificial Gibbon. But the contradictions of historians in general, their assumption of a dignity for which I saw no particular grounds, their unphilosophic and ridiculous avoidance (on that score) of personal anecdote, and, above all, the narrow-minded and time-serving confinement of their subject to wars and party-government (for there are time-servings, as there are fashions, that last for centuries), instinctively repelled me. I felt, though I did not know, till Fielding told me, that there was more truth in the verisimilitudes of fiction than in the assumptions of history ; and I rejoiced over the story told of Sir Walter Raleigh, who, on receiving I forget how many different acounts of an incident that occurred under his own windows, laughed at the idea of his writing a *History of the World.*

But the writer who made the greatest impression on me was Voltaire. I did not read French at that time, but I fell in with the best translation of some of his miscellaneous works ; and I found in him not only the original of much which I had admired in the style and pleasantry of my favorite native authors, Goldsmith in particular (who adored him), but the most formidable antagonist of absurdities which the world had seen ; a discloser of lights the most overwhelming, in flashes of wit ; a destroyer of the strongholds of superstition, that were never to be built up again, let the hour of renovation seem to look forth again as it might. I was transported with the gay courage and unquestionable humanity of this extraordinary person, and I soon caught the tone of his cunning implications and provoking turns. He did not frighten me. I never felt for a moment, young as I was, and Christianly brought up, that true religion would suffer at his hands. On the contrary, I had been bred up (in my home circle) to look for reforms in religion ; I had been led to desire the best

and gentlest form of it, unattended with threats and horrors :
and if the school orthodoxy did not countenance such expect-
ations, it took no pains to discountenance them.   I had pri-
vately accustomed myself, of my own further motion, to doubt
and to reject every doctrine, and every statement of facts,
that went counter to the plainest precepts of love, and to the
final happiness of all the creatures of God.   I could never
see, otherwise, what Christianity could mean, that was not
meant by a hundred inferior religions ; nor could I think it
right and holy to accept of the greatest hopes, apart from
that universality—*Fiat justitia, ruat cœlum.*   I was prepared to give up heaven itself (as far as it is possible for
human hope to do so) rather than that any thing so unhea-
venly as a single exclusion from it should exist.   Therefore,
to me, Voltaire was a putter down of a great deal that was
wrong, but of nothing that was right.   I did not take him
for a builder ; neither did I feel that he knew much of the
sanctuary which was inclosed in what he pulled down.   He
found a heap of rubbish pretending to be the shrine itself
and he set about denying its pretensions, and abating it as a
nuisance, without knowing, or considering (at least I thought
so) what there remained of beauty and durability, to be disclosed on its demolition.   I fought for him, then and afterward, with those who challenged me to the combat ; and I
was for some time driven to take myself for a Deist in the
most ordinary sense of the word, till I had learned to know
what a Christian truly was, and so arrived at opinions on
religious matters in general, which I shall notice at the conclusion of these volumes.

It is a curious circumstance respecting the books of Voltaire—the greatest writer upon the whole that France has
produced, and undoubtedly the greatest name in the eighteenth century ; that to this moment they are far less known
in England than talked of; so much so, that, with the exception of a few educated circles, chiefly of the upper class,
and exclusively among the men even in those, he has not
only been hardly read at all, even by such as have talked of
him with admiration, or loaded him with reproach, but the
portions of his writings that have had the greatest effect on

the world are the least known among readers the most popularly acquainted with him. The reasons of this remarkable
ignorance respecting so great a neighbor——one of the movers
of the world, and an especial admirer of England, are to be
found, first, in the exclusive and timid spirit, under the guise
of strength, which came up with the accession of George the
Third : second, as a consequence of this spirit, a studious
ignoring of the Frenchman in almost all places of education,
the colleges and foundations in particular ; third, the Anti-
Gallican spirit which followed and exasperated the prejudice
against the French Revolution ; and fourth, the very translation and popularity of two of his novels, the *Candide* and
Zadig, which, though no by means among his finest productions, had yet enough wit and peculiarity to be accepted
as sufficing specimens of him, even by his admirers. Unfortunately, one of these, the *Candide*, contained some of his
most licentious and even revolting writing. This enabled
his enemies to adduce it as a sufficing specimen on their own
side of the question ; and the idea of him which they succeeded in imposing upon the English community in general,
was that of a mere irreligious scoffer, who was opposed to
every thing good and serious, and who did but mingle a little
frivolous wit with an abundance of vexatious, hard-hearted,
and disgusting effrontery.

There is, it is true, a verison, purporting to be that of his
whole works, by Smollett, Thomas Franklin, and others,
which is understood to have been what is called a bookseller's job ; but I never met with it except in an old catalogue ; and I believe it was so dull and bad, that readers
instinctively recoiled from it as an incredible representation
of any thing lively. The probability is, that Smollett only
lent his name ; and Franklin himself may have done as
little, though the "translator of Sophocles," (as he styled
himself) was well enough qualified to misrepresent any kind
of genius.

Be this as it may, I have hardly ever met, even in literary circles, with persons who knew any thing of Voltaire, except through the medium of these two novels, and of later
school editions of his two histories of Charles the Twelfth

and Peter the Great; books, which teachers of all sorts, in
his own country, have been gradually compelled to admit
into their courses of reading, by national pride and the im-
perative growth of opinion.   Voltaire is one of the three
great tragic writers of France, and excels in pathos; yet
not one Englishman in a thousand knows a syllable of his
tragedies, or would do any thing but stare to hear of his
pathos.   Voltaire inducted his countrymen into a knowledge
of English science and metaphysics, nay, even of English
poetry; yet Englishmen have been told little about him
in connection with them, except of his disagreements with
Shakspeare.   Voltaire created a fashion for English thinking, manner, and policy, and fell in love with the simplicity
and truthfulness of their very Quakers; and yet, I will venture
to say, the English knew far less of all this, than they do of a
licentious poem with which he degraded his better nature in
burlesquing the history of Joan of Arc.

There are, it is admitted, two sides to the character of
Voltaire; one licentious, merely scoffing, saddening, defective
in sentiment, and therefore wanting the inner clew of the
beautiful to guide him out of the labyrinth of scorn and perplexity; all owing, be it observed, to the errors which he
found prevailing in his youth, and to the impossible demands
which they made on his acquiescence; but the other side of
his character is moral, cheerful, beneficent, prepared to en-
counter peril, nay, actually encountering it in the only true
Christian causes, those of toleration and charity, and raising
that voice of demand for the advancement of reason and justice which is now growing into the whole voice of Europe.
He was the only man, perhaps, that ever existed, who represented in his single person the entire character, with one
honorable exception (for he was never sanguinary), of the
nation in which he was born; nay, of its whole history,
past, present, and to come.   He had the licentiousness of the
old monarchy under which he was bred; the cosmopolite ardor
of the revolution, the science of the consulate and the "sav-
ans," the unphilosophic love of glory of the empire, the
worldly wisdom (without pushing it into folly) of Louis
Philippe, and the changeful humors, the firmness, the weak-

ness, the flourishing declamation, the sympathy with the poor, the *bonhomie*, the unbounded hopes, of the best actors in the extraordinary scenes now acting before the eyes of Europe in this present year 1850. As he himself could not construct as well as he could pull down ; so neither do his countrymen, with all the goodness and greatness among them, appear to be less truly represented by him in that particular than in others ; but in pulling down he had the same vague desire of the best that could set up ; and when he was most thought to oppose Christianity itself, he only did it out of an impatient desire to see the law of love triumphant, and was only thought to be the adversary of its spirit, because his revilers knew nothing of it themselves.

Voltaire, in an essay written by himself in the English language, has said of Milton, in a passage which would do honor to our best writers, that when the poet saw the Adamo of Andreini at Florence, he " pierced through the absurdity of the plot to the hidden majesty of the subject." It may be said of himself, that he pierced through the conventional majesty of a great many subjects, to the hidden absurdity of the plot. He laid the ax to a heap of savage abuses ; pulled the corner-stones out of dungeons and inquisitions : bowed and mocked the most tyrannical absurdities out of countenance ; and raised one prodigious peal of laughter at superstition, from Naples to the Baltic. He was the first man who got the power of opinion and common sense openly recognized as a reigning authority ; and who made the acknowledgment of it a point of wit and cunning, even with those who had hitherto thought they had the world to themselves.

An abridgement that I picked up of the *Philosophical Dictionary* (a translation), was for a long while my textbook, both for opinion and style. I was also a great admirer of *L'Ingenu, or the Sincere Huron*, and of the *Essay on the Philosophy of History*. In the character of the *Sincere Huron* I thought I found a resemblance to my own, as most readers do in those of their favorites : and this piece of self-love helped me to discover as much good-heartedness in Voltaire as I discerned wit. *Candide*, I confess, I could not like. I enjoyed passages ; but the laughter was not as good-humored as usual ; there was a view of things in it which I never entertained then or afterward, and into which the author had been led, rather in order to provoke Leibnitz, than because it was natural to him ; and, to crown my unwilling dislike, the book had a coarseness, apart from graceful and pleasurable ideas, which I have never been able to endure. There were passages in the abridgment of the *Philosophical Dictionary* which I always passed over ; but the rest delighted me beyond measure. I can repeat things out of it now, and will lay two or three of the points before the reader, as specimens of what made such an impression upon me. They are in Voltaire's best manner ; which consists in an artful intermixture of the conventional dignity and real absurdity of what he is exposing, the tone being as grave as the dignity seems to require, and the absurdity coming out as if unintentionally.

Speaking of the *Song of Solomon* (of which by-the-way, his criticism is very far from being in the right, though he puts it so pleasantly), he thinks he has the royal lover at a disadvantage with his comparisons of noses to towers, and eyes to fishpools ; and then concludes with observing, " All this, it must be confessed, is not in the taste of the Latin poets ; *but then a Jew is not obliged to write like Virgil.*" Now, it would not be difficult to show that Eastern and Western poetry had better be two things than one ; or, at least, that they have a right to be so, and can lay claim to their own beauties ; but, at the same time, it is impossible to help laughing at this pretended admission *in Solomon's favor*, and the cunning introduction of the phrase " *a Jew*," contrasted with the dignity of the name of Virgil.

In another part of the same article on Solomon, where he speaks of the many thousands of chariots which the Jewish monarch possessed (a quantity that certainly have a miraculous appearance, though, perhaps, explainable by a good scholar), he says he can not conceive, for the life of him, what Solomon did with such a multitude of carriages, " unless," adds he, " it was to take *the ladies of his seraglio* an airing on the borders of the lake Genesareth, or along the brook Cedron ; a charming spot, *except* that it is dry nine months in the year, *and the ground a little stony.*" At these passages I used to roll with laughter ; and I can not help laughing now, writing as I am, alone by my fireside. They tell nothing, except against those who confound every thing the most indifferent, relating to the great men of the Bible, with something sacred ; and who have thus done more harm to their own distinctions of sacred and profane, than all which has been charged on the ridicule they occasion.

The last quotation shall be from the admirable article on *War* which made a profound impression on me. You can not help laughing at it : the humor is high and triumphant ; but the laugh ends in very serious reflections on the nature of war, and on the very doubtful morality of those who make no scruple, when it suits them, of advocating the infliction of calamity in some things, while they protest against the least hazard of it in others. Voltaire notices the false and frivolous pretensions upon which princes subject their respective countries to the miseries of war, purely to oblige their own cupidity and ambition. One of them, he says, finds in some old document a claim or pretense of some relation of his to some piece of land in the possession of another. He gives the other notice of his claim ; the other will not hear of it : so the prince in question "picks up a great many men who have nothing to do and nothing to lose ; *binds their hats with coarse white worsted, five sous to the ell ;* turns them to the right and left ; *and marches away with them to glory.*" Now, the glory and the white worsted, the potentate who is to have an addition to his coffers, and the poor soul who is to be garnished for it with a halo of bobbin, "five sous to the ell," here come into admirable contrast. War may be necessary on some occasions, till a wiser remedy be found ; and ignoble causes may bring into play very noble passions ; but it is desirable that the world should take the necessity of no existing system for granted, which is accompanied with horrible evils. This is a lesson which Voltaire has taught us ; and it is invaluable. Our author terminates his ridicule on War with a sudden and startling apostrophe to an eminent preacher on a very different subject. The familiar tone of the reproof is very pleasant. " Bourdaloue, a very bad sermon have you made against love ; against that passion which consoles and restores the human race ; but not a word, bad or good, have you said against this passion that tears us to pieces." (I quote from memory, and am not sure of my words in this extract ; but the spirit of them is the same). He adds, that all the miseries ever produced in the world by love, do not come up to the calamities occasioned by a single campaign. If he means love in the abstract, unconnected with the systems by which it has been regulated in different parts of the world, he is probably in the right; but the miscalculation is enormous, if he includes those. The ninety-six thousand prostitutes alone in the streets of London, which we are told are the inevitable accompaniment, and even safeguard, of the virtuous part of our system (to say nothing of the tempers, the jealousies, the chagrins, the falsehoods, the quarrels, and the repeated murders which afflict and astonish us even in that), most probably experience more bitterness of heart, every day of their lives, than is caused by any one campaign, however wild and flagitious.

Besides Voltaire and the *Connoisseur*, I was very fond at that time of *Johnson's Lives of the Poets*, and a great reader of Pope. My admiration of the *Rape of the Lock* led me to write a long mock-heroic poem, entitled the *Battle of the Bridal Ring*, the subject of which was a contest between two rival orders of spirits, on whom to bestow a lady in marriage. I venture to say, that it would have been well spoken of by the critics, and was not worth a penny. I recollect one couplet, which will serve to show how I mimicked the tone of my author. It was an apostrophe to Mantua,

> " Mantua, of great and small the long renown,
> That now a Virgil giv'st, and now a gown."

Dryden I read, too, but not with that relish for his nobler versification which I afterward acquired. To dramatic reading, with all my love of the theatre, I have already mentioned my disinclination ; yet, in the interval of my departure from school, and my getting out of my teens, I

wrote two farces, a comedy, and a tragedy ; and the plots
of all (such as they were) were inventions. The hero of
my tragedy was the *Earl of Surrey* (Howard, the poet),
who was put to death by Henry the Eighth. I forget what
the comedy was upon. The title of one of the farces was
the *Beau Miser*, which may explain the nature of it. The
other was called *A Hundred a Year*, and turned upon a
hater of the country, who, upon having an annuity to that
amount given him, on condition of his never going out of
London, becomes a hater of the town. In the last scene,
his annuity died a jovial death in a country tavern ; the
bestower entering the room just as my hero had got on a
table, with a glass in his hand, to drink confusion to the
metropolis. All these pieces were, I doubt not, as bad as
need be. About thirty years ago, being sleepless one night
with a fit of enthusiasm, in consequence of reading about the
Spanish play of the *Cid*, in Lord Holland's *Life of Guillen
de Castro*, I determined to write a tragedy on the same
subject, which was accepted at Drury-lane. Perhaps the
conduct of this piece was not without merit, the conclusion
of each act throwing the interest into the succeeding one ;
but I had great doubts of all the rest of it ; and on receiving
it from Mr. Elliston to make an alteration in the third act,
very judiciously proposed by him, I looked the whole of the
play over again, and convinced myself it was unfit for the
stage. I therefore withheld it. I had painted my hero too
after the beau-ideal of a modern reformer, instead of the
half-godlike, half-bigoted soldier that he was. I began afterward to re-cast the play, but grew tired and gave it up.
The *Cid* would make a delicious character for the stage, or
in any work ; not, indeed, as Corneille declaimed him, nor
as inferior writers might adapt him to the reigning taste ;
but taken, I mean, as he was, with the noble impulses he
received from nature, the drawbacks with which a bigoted
age qualified them, and the social and open-hearted pleasantry (not the least evidence of his nobleness) which brings
forth his heart, as it were, in flashes through the stern armor.
But this would require a strong hand, and readers capable
of grappling with it. In the mean time, they should read

of him in Mr. Southey's *Chronicle of the Cid* (an admirable summary from the old Spanish writers), and in the delightful verses at the end of it, translated from an old Spanish poem by Mr. Hookham Frere, with a triumphant force and fidelity, that you know to be true to the original at once.

About the period of my writing the above essays, circumstances introduced me to the acquaintance of Mr. Bell, the proprietor of the *Weekly Messenger*. In his house in the Strand I used to hear of politics and dramatic criticism, and of the persons who wrote them. Mr. Bell had been well known as a bookseller, and a speculator in elegant typography. It is to him the public are indebted for the small edition of the Poets that preceded Cooke's, and which, with all my predilections for that work, was unquestionably superior to it. Besides, it included Chaucer and Spenser. The omission of these in Cooke's edition was as unpoetical a sign of the times, as the present familiarity with their names is the reverse. It was thought a mark of good sense : as if good sense, in matters of literature, did not consist as much in knowing what was poetical in poetry, as brilliant in wit. Bell was upon the whole a remarkable person. He was a plain man, with a red face, and a nose exaggerated by intemperance ; and yet there was something not unpleasing in his countenance, especially when he spoke. He had sparkling black eyes, a good-natured smile, gentlemanly manners, and one of the most agreeable voices I ever heard. He had no acquirements, perhaps not even grammar ; but his taste in putting forth a publication, and getting the best artists to adorn it, was new in those times, and may be admired in any ; and the same taste was observable in his house. He knew nothing of poetry. He thought the *Della Cruscans* fine people, because they were known in the circles ; and for Milton's *Paradise Lost* he had the same epithet as for Mrs. Crouch's face, or the phaeton of Major Topham : he thought it "pretty." Yet a certain liberal instinct, and turn for large dealing, made him include Chaucer and Spenser in his edition ; he got Stothard to adorn the one, and Mortimer the other ; and in the midst, I suspect, of very

equivocal returns, published a *British Theatre*, with em-
bellishments, and a similar edition of the plays of Shakspeare—the incorrectest work, according to Mr. Chalmers,
that ever issued from the press.

Unfortunately for Mr. Bell, he had as great a taste for
neat wines and ankles as for pretty books ; and, to crown
his misfortunes, the Prince of Wales, to whom he was bookseller, once did him the honor to partake of an entertainment
at his house. He afterward became a bankrupt. He was
one of those men whose temperament and turn for enjoyment throw a sort of grace over whatsoever they do, standing them in stead of every thing but prudence, and sometimes even supplying them with the consolations which imprudence itself has forfeited. After his bankruptcy he set
up a newspaper, which became profitable to every body but
himself. He had become so used to lawyers and bailiffs
that the more his concerns flourished, the more his debts
flourished with them. It seemed as if he would have been
too happy without them ; too exempt from the cares that
beset the prudent. The first time I saw him he was standing in a chemist's shop, waiting till the road was clear for
him to issue forth. He had a toothache, for which he held
a handkerchief over his mouth ; and, while he kept a sharp
look-out with his bright eye, was alternatley groaning in a
most gentlemanly manner over his gums, and addressing
some polite words to the shopman. I had not then been
introduced to him, and did not know his person ; so that the
effect of his voice upon me was unequivocal. I liked him
for it, and wished the bailiff at the devil.*

* An intelligent compositor (Mr. J. P. S. Bicknell), who had been
a noter of curious passages in his time, informs me, that Bell was the
first printer who confined the small letter *s* to its present shape, and
rejected altogether the older form, *ſ*. He tells me, that this innovation,
besides the handsomer form of the new letter, was "a boon to both
master-printers and the compositor, inasmuch as it lessened the amount
of capital necessary to be laid out under the old system, and saved to
the workman no small portion of his valuable time and labor."

My informant adds, as a curious instance of conservative tendency
on small points, that Messrs. Rivington having got as far as three
sheets, on a work of a late Bishop of Durham, in which the new plan
was adopted, the Bishop sent back the sheets, in order to have the old

In the office of the *Weekly Messenger*, I saw one day a
person who looked the epitome of squalid authorship.   He
was wretchedly dressed and dirty ; and the rain, as he took
his hat off, came away from it as from a spout.   This was
a man of the name of Badini, who had been poet at the
Opera, and was then editor of the *Messenger*.   He was
afterward sent out of the country under the Alien Act, and
became reader of the English papers to Bonaparte.   His
intimacy with some of the first families in the country,
among whom he had been a teacher, is supposed to have
been of use to the French government.   He wrote a good
idiomatic English style, and was a man of abilities.   I had
never before seen a *poor author*, such as are described in
books ; and the spectacle of the reality startled me.   Like
most authors, however, who are at once very poor and very
clever, his poverty was his own fault.   When he received
any money he disappeared, and was understood to spend it
in alehouses.   We heard that in Paris he kept his carriage.
I have since met with authors of the same squalid description ; but they were destitute of ability, and had no more
right to profess literature as a trade than alchemy.   It is
from these that the common notions about the poverty of
the tribe are taken.   One of them, poor fellow ! might have
cut a figure in Smollett.   He was a proper ideal author,
in rusty black, out at elbows, thin and pale.   He brought
me an ode about an eagle ; for which the publisher of a
magazine, he said, had had "the inhumanity" to offer him
half a crown.   His necessity for money he did not deny ;
but his great anxiety was to know whether, as a poetical
composition, his ode was not worth more.   "Is that *poetry*,
sir ?" cried he : "that's what I want to know—is that
poetry?" rising from his chair, and staring and trembling
in all the agony of contested excellence.

letter·restored, which compelled the booksellers to get a new supply
from the type-foundry, the font containing the venerable f having been
thrown away.

Mr. Bicknell also informs me, that when Bell set up his newspaper,
the *Weekly Messenger* (which had a wood-cut at the top of it, of a newsman blowing his horn), he is said to have gone to a masquerade in the
newsman's character, and distributed prospectuses to the company.

My brother John, at the beginning of the year 1805, set up a paper, called the *News*, and I went to live with him in Brydges-street, and write the theatricals in it.

It was the custom at that time for editors of papers to be intimate with actors and dramatists. They were often proprietors, as well as editors; and, in that case, it was not expected that they should escape the usual intercourse, or wish to do so. It was thought a feather in the cap of all parties; and with their feathers they tickled one another. The newspaper man had consequence in the green-room, and plenty of tickets for his friends; and he dined at amusing tables. The dramatist secured a good-natured critique in his journal, sometimes got it written himself, or, according to Mr. Reynolds, was even himself the author of it. The actor, if he was of any eminence, stood upon the same ground of reciprocity; and not to know a pretty actress would have been a want of the knowing in general. Upon new performers, and upon writers not yet introduced, a journalist was more impartial; and sometimes, where the proprietor was in one interest more than another, or for some personal reason grew offended with an actor, or set of actors, a criticism would occasionally be hostile, and even severe. An editor, too, would now and then suggest to his employer the policy of exercising a freer authority, and obtain influence enough with him to show symptoms of it. I believe Bell's editor, who was more clever, was also more impartial than most critics; though the publisher of the *British Theatre*, and patron of the *Della Cruscans*, must have been hampered with literary intimacies. The best chance for an editor, who wished to have any thing like an opinion of his own, was the appearance of a rival newspaper with a strong theatrical connection. Influence was here threatened with diminution. It was to be held up on other grounds; and the critic was permitted to find out that a bad play was not good, or an actress's petticoat of the lawful dimensions.

Puffing and plenty of tickets, were, however, the system of the day. It was an interchange of amenities over the dinner-table; a flattery of power on the one side, and puns on the other; and what the public took for a criticism on a

play, was a draft upon the box-office, or reminiscences of last
Thursday's salmon and lobster-sauce. The custom was, to
write as short and as favorable a paragraph on the new
piece as could be; to say that Bannister was "excellent,"
and Mrs. Jordan "charming"; to notice the "crowded
house," or invent it if necessary; and to conclude by observing that "the whole went off with *éclat.*" For the rest, it
was a critical religion in those times to admire Mr. Kemble;
and at the period in question Master Betty had appeared,
and been hugged to the hearts of the town as the young
Roscius.

We saw that independence in theatrical criticism would
be a great novelty. We announced it, and nobody believed
us: we stuck to it, and the town believed every thing we
said. The proprietors of the *News*, of whom I knew so little
that I can not recollect with certainty any one of them, very
handsomely left me to myself. My retired and scholastic
habits kept me so; and the pride of success confirmed my
independence with regard to others. I was then in my twentieth year, an early age at that time for a writer. The
usual exaggeration of report made me younger than I was:
and after being a "young Roscius" political, I was now
looked upon as one critical. To know an actor personally
appeared to me a vice not to be thought of; and I would
as lief have taken poison as accepted a ticket from the
theaters.

Good God! To think of the grand opinion I had of myself
in those days, and what little reason I had for it! Not to
accept the tickets was very proper, considering that I bestowed more blame than praise. There was also more good-nature than I supposed in not allowing myself to know any
actors; but the vanity of my position had greater weight
with me than any thing else, and I must have proved it to
discerning eyes by the small quantity of information I brought
to my task, and the ostentation with which I produced it.
I knew almost as little of the drama as the young Roscius
himself. Luckily, I had the advantage of him in knowing
how unfit *he* was for his office; and, probably, he thought
me as much so, though he could not have argued upon it;

for I was in the minority respecting his merits, and the balance was then trembling on the beam : the *News*, I believe, hastened the settlement of the question. I wish with all my heart we had let him alone, and he had got a little more money. However, he obtained enough to create him a provision for life. His position, which appeared so brilliant at first, had a remarkable cruelty in it. Most men begin life with struggles, and have their vanity sufficiently knocked about the head and shoulders to make their kinder fortunes the more welcome. Mr. Betty had his sugar first, and his physic afterward. He began life with a double childhood, with a new and extraordinary felicity added to the natural enjoyments of his age ; and he lived to see it speedily come to nothing, and to be taken for an ordinary person. I am told that he acquiesces in his fate, and agrees that the town were mistaken. If so, he is no ordinary person still, and has as much right to our respect for his good sense, as he is declared on all hands to deserve it for his amiableness. I have an anecdote of him to both purposes, which exhibits him in a very agreeable light. Hazlitt happened to be at a party where Mr. Betty was present; and in coming away, when they were all putting on their great-coats, the critic thought fit to complement the dethroned favorite of the town, by telling him that he recollected him in old times, and had been " much pleased with him." Betty looked at his memorialist, as much as to say, " You don't tell me so !" and then starting into a tragical attitude, exclaimed, " Oh, memory ! memory !"

I was right about Master Betty, and I am sorry for it ; though the town was in fault, not he. I think I was right also about Kemble ; but I have no regret upon that score. He flourished long enough after my attacks on his majestic dryness and deliberate nothings ; and Kean would have taken the public by storm, whether they had been prepared for him or not :

" One touch of nature makes the whole world kin."

Kemble faded before him, like a tragedy ghost. I never denied the merits which that actor possessed. He had the

look of a Roman ; made a very good ideal, though not
a very real Coriolanus, for his pride was not sufficiently
blunt and unaffected : and in parts that suited his natural
deficiency, such as Penruddock and the Abbé de l'Epée,
would have been altogether admirable and interesting, if you
could have forgotten, that their sensibility, in his hands, was
not so much repressed, as wanting.   He was no more to be
compared to his sister, than stone is to flesh and blood.
There was much of the pedagogue in him.   He made a fuss
about trifles ; was inflexible on a pedantic reading : in short,
was rather a teacher of elocution than an actor ; and not a
good teacher on that account.   There was merit in his
idealism as far as it went.   He had at least faith in something classical and scholastic, and he made the town partake
of it ; but it was all on the surface—a hollow trophy : and
I am persuaded, that he had no idea in his head but of a
stage Roman, and the dignity he added to his profession.

But if I was right about Kemble, whose admirers I plagued
enough, I was not equally so about the living dramatists,
whom I plagued more.   I laid all the deficiences of the
modern drama to their account, and treated them like a parcel of mischievous boys, of whom I was the schoolmaster and
whipper-in.   I forgot that it was I who was the boy, and
that they knew twenty times more of the world than I did.
Not that I mean to say their comedies were excellent, or
or that my commonplaces about the superior merits of Con-
greve and Sheridan were not well-founded ; but there was
more talent in their " five-act farces" than I supposed ; and
I mistook, in great measure, the defect of the age—its dearth
of dramatic character—for that of the writers who were to
draw upon it.   It is true, a great wit, by a laborious process, and the help of his acquirements, might extract a play
or two from it, as was Sherdian's own case ; but there was
a great deal of imitation even in Sheridan, and he was fain
to help himself to a little originality out of the characters of
his less formalized countrymen, his own included.

It is remarkable, that the three most amusing dramatists
of the last age, Sheridan, Goldsmith, and O'Keeffe, were all
Irishmen, and all had characters of their own.   Sheridan,

after all, was Swift's Sheridan come to life again in the person of his grandson, with the oratory of Thomas Sheridan, the father, superadded and brought to bear. Goldsmith, at disadvantage in his breeding, but full of address with his pen, drew upon his own absurdities and mistakes, and filled his dramas with ludicrous perplexity. O'Keeffe was all for whim and impulse, but not without a good deal of conscience; and, accordingly, in his plays we have a sort of young and pastoral taste of life in the very midst of its sophistications. Animal spirits, quips and cranks, credulity, and good intention, are triumphant throughout, and make a delicious mixture. It is a great credit to O'Keeffe, that he ran sometimes close upon the borders of the sentimental drama, and did it not only with impunity but advantage; but sprightliness and sincerity enable a man to do every thing with advantage.

It was a pity that as much could not be said of Mr. Colman, who, after taking more license in his writings than any body, became a licenser *ex officio*, and seemed inclined to license nothing but cant. When this writer got into the sentimental, he made a sad business of it, for he had no faith in sentiment. He mouthed and overdid it, as a man does when he is telling a lie. At a farce he was admirable; and he remained so to the last, whether writing or licensing.

Morton seemed to take a color from the writers all round him, especially from O'Keeffe and the sentimentalists. His sentiment was more in earnest than Colman's, yet, somehow, not happy either. There was a gloom in it, and a smack of the Old Bailey. It was best when he put it in a shape of humor, as in the paternal and inextinguishable *tailorism* of Old Rapid, in a *Cure for the Heart-Ache*. Young Rapid, who complains that his father "sleeps so slow," is also a pleasant fellow, and worthy of O'Keeffe. He is one of the numerous crop that sprang up from *Wild Oats*, but not in so natural a soil.

The character of the modern drama at that time was singularly commercial; nothing but gentlemen in distress, and hard landlords, and generous interferers, and fathers who got a great deal of money, and sons who spent it. I remember one play in particular, in which the whole wit ran upon

prices, bonds, and post-obits.   You might know what the
pit thought of their pound notes by the ostentatious indifference with which the heroes of the pieces gave them away,
and the admiration and pretended approval with which the
spectators observed it.   To make a present of a hundred
pounds was as if a man had uprooted and given away an
Egyptian pyramid.

Mr. Reynolds was not behindhand with his brother dramatists in drawing upon the taste of the day for gains and distresses.   It appears by his Memoirs, that he had too much
reason for so doing.   He was, perhaps, the least ambitious,
and the least vain (whatever charges to the contrary his
animal spirits might have brought on him), of all the writers
of that period.   In complexional vivacity he certainly did
not yield to any of them ; his comedies, if they were fugitive,
were genuine representations of fugitive manners, and went
merrily to their death ; and there is one of them, the *Dramatist*, founded upon something more lasting, which promises
to remain in the collections, and deserves it : which is not a
little to say of any writer.   I never wish for a heartier laugh
than I have enjoyed, since I grew wiser, not only in seeing,
but in reading the vagaries of his dramatic hero, and his
mystifications of " Old Scratch."   When I read the good-
humored Memoirs of this writer the other day, I felt quite
ashamed of the ignorant and boyish way in which I used to
sit in judgment upon his faults, without being aware of what
was good in him ; and my repentance was increased by the
very proper manner in which he speaks of his critics, neither
denying the truth of their charges in letter, nor admitting
them altogether in spirit ; in fact, showing that he knew
very well what he was about, and that they, whatsoever
they fancied to the contrary, did not.

Mr. Reynolds, agreeably to his sense and good-humor,
never said a word to his critics at the time.   Mr. Thomas
Dibdin, not quite so wise, wrote me a letter, which Incledon,
I am told, remonstrated with him for sending, saying, it
would do him no good with the " d——d boy."   And he was
right.   I published it, with an answer, and only thought
that I made dramatists " come bow to me."   Mr. Colman

attacked me in a prologue, which, by a curious chance, **Faw-cett** spoke right in my teeth, the box I sat in happening to be directly opposite him. I laughed at the prologue; and only looked upon **Mr. Colman** as a great monkey pelting me with nuts, which I ate. Attacks of this kind were little calculated to obtain their end with a youth who persuaded himself that he wrote for nothing but the public good; who mistook the impression which any body of moderate talents can make with a newspaper, for the result of something peculiarly his own; and who had just enough scholarship to despise the want of it in others. I do not pretend to think that the criticisms in the *News* had no merit at all. They showed an acquaintance with the style of Voltaire, Johnson, and others; were not unagreeably sprinkled with quotation; and, above all, were written with more care and attention than was customary with newspapers at that time. The pains I took to round a period with nothing in it, or to invent a simile that should appear off-hand, would have done honor to better stuff.

A portion of these criticisms subsequently formed the appendix of an original volume on the same subject, entitled *Critical Essays on the Performers of the London Theatres.* I have the book now before me; and if I thought it had a chance of survival, I should regret and qualify a good deal of uninformed judgment in it respecting the art of acting, which, with much inconsistent recommendation to the contrary, it too often confounded with a literal, instead of a liberal imitation of nature. I particularly erred with respect to comedians like Munden, whose superabundance of humor and expression I confounded with farce and buffoonery. Charles Lamb taught me better.

There was a good deal of truth, however, mixed up with these mistakes. One of the things on which I was always harping, was Kemble's vicious pronunciation. Kemble had a smattering of learning, and a great deal of obstinacy. He was a reader of old books; and having discovered that pronunciation had not always been what it was, and that in one or two instances the older was metrically better than the new (as in the case of the word *aches*, which was orig-

inally a dissyllable—*aitches*), he took upon him to reform
it in a variety of cases, where propriety was as much against
him as custom.   Thus the vowel *e* in the word " merchant,"
in defiance of its Latin etymology, he insisted upon pronouncing according to its French derivative, *marchant*.   " Innocent" he called *innocint ;* " conscience" (in defiance even
of his friend Chaucer), *conshince ;* " virtue," in proper
slip-slop, *varchue ;* " fierce," *furse ;* " beard," *bird ;* " thy,"
thĕ (because we generally call " my," *mĕ*) ; and " odious,"
" hideous," and " perfidious," became *ojus, hijjus,* and
perfijjus.

Nor were these all.   The following banter, in the shape
of an imaginary bit of conversation between an officer and
his friend was, literally, no caricature :

A. Ha! captain how dost?   (1) *The* appearance would be much
improved by a little more attention to *the* (2) *bird*.
B. Why, so I think : there's no (3) *sentimint* in a *bird*.   But then
it serves to distinguish a soldier, and there is no doubt much military
(4) *varchue* in looking (5) *furful.*
A. But, the girls, Jack, the girls!   Why, *the* mouth is enough to
banish kissing from the (6) *airth* (7) *etairnally.*
B. In (8) *maircy*, no more of that!   Zounds, but the shopkeepers
and the (9) *marchants* will get the better of us with the dear souls !
However, as it is now against military law to have a tender countenance, and as some *birds*, I thank heaven, are of a tolerable (10) *quăl-
ity*, I must make a *varchue* of necessity ; and as I can't look soft for
the love of my girl, I must e'en look (11) *hijjus* for the love of my
country."

———

(1) thy; (2) beard; (3) sentiment; (4) virtue; (5) fearful; (6)
earth; (7) eternally; (8) mercy; (9) merchants; (10) quality (with
the *a* as in *universality*) ; (11) hideous.

CHAPTER VIII.

SUFFERING AND REFLECTION.

Nervous illness and conclusions therefrom.—Mystery of the universe.
—Hypochondriacal recreations.—A hundred and fifty rhymes on a
trissyllable.—Pastoral innocence.—A didactic yeoman.—"Hideous
sight" of Dr. Young.—Action the cure for sedentary ailments.—
Boating ; a fray on the Thames.—Magical effect of the word " Law."
—Return of health and enjoyment.

But the gay and confident spirit in which I began this
critical career received a check, of which none of my
friends suspected the anguish, and very few were told.
I fell into a melancholy state of mind, produced by ill
health.

I thought it was owing to living too well ; and as I had
great faith in temperance, I went to the reverse extreme ;
not considering, that temperance implies moderation in self-
denial, as well as in self indulgence. The consequence was
a nervous condition, amounting to hypochondria, which lasted me several' months. I experienced it twice afterward,
each time more painfully than before, and for a much longer
period ; but I have never had it since ; and I am of opinion
that I need not have had it at all, had I gone at once to
a physician, and not repeated the mistake of being over
abstinent.

I mention the whole circumstance for the benefit of others.
The first attack came on me with palpitations of the heart.
These I got rid of by horseback. I forget what symptoms
attended the approach of the second. The third was produced by sitting out of doors too early in the spring. I attempted to outstarve them all, but egregiously failed. In
one instance, I took wholly to a vegetable diet, which made
me so weak and giddy, that I was forced to catch hold of
rails in the streets to hinder myself from falling. In another, I confined myself for some weeks to a milk diet, which

did nothing but jaundice my complexion. In the third, I took a modicum of meat, one glass of wine, no milk except in tea, and no vegetables at all ; but though I did not suffer quite so much mental distress from this regimen as from the milk, I suffered more than from the vegetables, and for a much longer period than with either. To be sure, I continued it longer ; and, perhaps, it gave me greater powers of endurance ; but for upward of four years, without intermission, and above six years in all, I underwent a burden of wretchedness, which I afterward felt convinced I need not have endured for as many weeks, perhaps not as many days, had I not absurdly taken to the extreme I spoke of in the first instance, and then as absurdly persisted in seeking no advice, partly from fear of hearing worse things foretold me, and partly from a hope of wearing out of the calamity by patience. At no time did my friends guess to what amount I suffered. They saw that my health was bad enough, and they condoled with me accordingly ; but cheerful habits enabled me to retain an air of cheerfulness, except when I was alone ; and I never spoke of it but once, which was to my friend Mitchell, whom I guessed to have undergone something of the kind.

And what was it that I suffered ? and on what account? On no account. On none whatsoever, except my ridiculous super-abstinence, and my equally ridiculous avoidance of speaking about it. The very fact of having no cause whatsoever, was the thing that most frightened me. I thought that if I had but a cause, the cause might have been removed or palliated ; but to be haunted by a ghost which was not even ghostly, which was something I never saw, or could even imagine, this, I thought, was the most terrible thing that could befall me. I could see no end to the perscontions of an enemy, who was neither visible nor even existing !

Causes for suffering, however, came. Not, indeed, the worst, for I was neither culpable nor superstitious. I had wronged nobody ; and I now felt the inestimable benefit of having had cheerful opinions given me in religion. But I plagued myself with things which are the pastimes of better states of health, and the pursuits of philosophers. I mooted with myself every point of metaphysics which could get into a head into which they had never been put. I made a cause of causes for anxiety, by inquiring into causation, and outdid the Vicar of Wakefield's Moses, in being my own Sanchoniathan and Berosus on the subject of the cosmogony! I jest about it now; but, oh! what pain was it to me then! and what pangs of biliary will and impossibility I underwent in the endeavor to solve these riddles of the universe! I felt, long before I knew Mr. Wordsworth's poetry,

> "the burthen and the mystery
> Of all this unintelligible world."

I reverence the mystery still, but I no longer feel the burden, because for these five-and-thirty years I have known how to adjust my shoulders to it by taking care of my health. I should rather say because healthy shoulders have no such burden to carry. The elements of existence, like the air which we breathe, and which would otherwise crush us, are so nicely proportioned to one another within and around them, that we are unconsciously sustained by them, not thoughtfully oppressed.

One great benefit, however, resulted to me from this suffering. It gave me an amount of reflection, such as in all probability I never should have had without it; and if readers have derived any good from the graver portion of my writings, I attribute it to this experience of evil. It taught me patience; it taught me charity (however imperfectly I may have exercised either); it taught me charity even toward myself; it taught me the worth of little pleasures, as well as the dignity and utility of great pains; it taught me that evil itself contained good; nay, it taught me to doubt whether any such thing as evil, considered in itself, existed; whether things altogether, as far as our planet knows them, could have been so good without it; whether the desire, nevertheless, which nature has implanted in us for its destruction, be not the signal and the means to that end; and whether its destruction, finally, will not prove its existence, in the mean time, to have been necessary to the very bliss that supersedes it.

I have been thus circumstantial respecting this illness, or series of illnesses, in the hope that such readers as have not had experience or reflection enough of their own to dispense with the lesson, may draw the following conclusions from sufferings of all kinds, if they happen to need it :

First. That however any suffering may seem to be purely mental, body alone may occasion it ; which was undoubtedly the case in my instance.

Second. That as human beings do not originate their own bodies or minds, and as yet very imperfectly know how to manage them, they have a right to all the aid or comfort they can procure, under any sufferings whatsoever.

Third. That whether it be the mind or body that is ailing, or both, they may save themselves a world of perplexity and of illness by going at once to a physician.

Fourth. That till they do so, or in case they are unable to do it, a recourse to the first principles of health is their only wise proceeding ; by which principles I understand air and exercise, bathing, amusements, and whatsoever else tends to enliven and purify the blood.

Fifth. That the blackest day may have a bright morrow ; for my last and worst illness suddenly left me, probably in consequence of the removal, though unconsciously, of some internal obstruction ; and it is now for the long period above mentioned that I have not had the slightest return of it, though I have had many anxieties to endure, and a great deal of sickness.

Sixth. That the far greater portion of a life thus tried may nevertheless be remarkable for cheerfulness ; which has been the case with my own.

Seventh. That the value of cheerful opinions is inestimable ; that they will retain a sort of heaven round a man, when every thing else might fail him ; and that, consequently, they ought to be religiously inculcated in children.

Eighth and last. That evil itself has its bright, or at any rate its redeeming side ; probably is but the fugitive requisite of some everlasting good ; and assuredly, in the mean time, and in a thousand obvious instances, is the admonisher, the producer, the increaser, nay, the very adorner and splendid investitor of good ; it is the pain that prevents a worse, the storm that diffuses health, the plague that enlarges cities, the fatigue that sweetens sleep, the discord that enriches harmonies, the calamity that tests affections, the victory and the crown of patience, the enrapturer of the embraces of joy.

I was reminded of the circumstance which gave rise to these reflections, by the mention of the friend of whom I spoke last, and another brother of whom I went to see during my first illness. He was a young and amiable artist, residing at Gainsborough in Lincolnshire. He had no conception of what I suffered ; and one of his modes of entertaining me was his taking me to a friend of his, a surgeon, to see his anatomical preparations, and delight my hypochondriacal eyes with grinnings of skulls and delicacies of injected hearts. I have no more horror now, on reflection, of those frameworks and machineries of the beautiful body in which we live, than I have of the jacks and wires of a harpsichord. The first sight revolts us simply because life dislikes death, and the human being is jarred out of a sense of its integrity by these bits and scraps of the material portion of it. But I know it is no more *me*, than it is the feeling which revolts from it, or than the harpsichord itself is the music that Haydn or Beethoven put into it. Indeed, I did not think otherwise at the time, with the healthier part of me ; nor did this healthier part ever forsake me. I always attributed what I felt to bodily ailment, and talked as reasonably, and for the most part as cheerfully, with my friends as usual, nor did I ever once gainsay the cheerfulness and hopefulness of my opinions. But I could not look comfortably on the bones and the skulls nevertheless, though I made a point of sustaining the exhibition. I bore any thing that came, in order that I might be overborne by nothing ; and I found this practice of patience very useful. I also took part in every diversion, and went into as many different places and new scenes as possible ; which reminds me that I once rode with my Lincolnshire friend from Gainsborough to Doncaster, and that he and I, sick and serious as I was, or rather because I was sick and serious (for such extremes meet, and melan

choly has a good-natured sister in mirth) made, in the course
of our journey, a hundred and fifty rhymes on the word
" philosopher." We stopped at that number, only because
we had come to our journey's end. I shall not apologize to
the reader for mentioning this boy's play, because I take
every reader who feels an interest in this book to be a bit of a
philosopher himself, and therefore prepared to know that boy's
play and man's play are much oftener identical than people
suppose, especially when the heart has need of the pastime.
I need not remind him of the sage, who while playing with
a parcel of schoolboys suddenly stopped at the approach of a
solemn personage, and said, " We must leave off, boys, at
present, for here's a fool coming."

The number of rhymes might be a little more surprising;
but the wonder will cease when the reader considers that
they must have been doggerel, and that there is no end to
the forms in which rhymes can set off from new given points;
as, *go* so far, *throw* so far; *nose* of her, *beaux* of her; *toss*
of her, *cross* of her, &c.

Spirits of Swift and Butler! come to my aid, if any chance
reader, not of our right reading fashion, happen to light upon
this passage, and be inclined to throw down the book. Come
to *his* aid; for he does not know what he is going to do;
how many illustrious jingles he is about to vituperate.

The surgeon I speak of was good enough one day to take
me with him round the country, to visit his patients. I
was startled in a respectable farm-house to hear language
openly talked in a mixed party of males and females, of a
kind that seldom courts publicity, and that would have
struck with astonishment an eulogizer of pastoral innocence.
Yet nobody seemed surprised at it; nor did it bring a blush
on the cheek of a very nice, modest-looking girl. She only
smiled, and seemed to think it was the man's way. Probably it was nothing more than the language which was
spoken in the first circles in times of old, and which thus
survived among the peasantry, just as we find them retaining words that have grown obsolete in cities. The guilt
and innocence of manners very much depend on conventional
agreement; that is to say, on what is thought of them with

respect to practice, and to the harm or otherwise which they are actually found to produce. The very dress which would be shameless in one age or country, is respectable in another; but in neither case is it a moral test. When the shame goes in one respect, it by no means comes in another; otherwise all Turks would be saints, and all Europeans sinners The minds of the people in the Lincolnshire farm-house were "naked and not ashamed." It must be owned, however, that there was an amount of consciousness about them, which savored more of a pagan than a paradisaical state of innocence.

One of this gentleman's patients was v , amusing. He was a pompous old gentleman-farmer, cultivating his gout on two chairs and laying down the law on the state of the nation. Lord Eldon he called "my Lord *Elgin*" (Elgin); and he showed us what an ignorant man this chancellor was, and what a dreadful thing such want of knowledge was for the country. The proof of his own fitness for setting things right, was thus given by his making three mistakes in one word. He took Lord Eldon for Lord Elgin; he took Lord Elgin for the Chancellor; and he pronounced his lordship's name with a soft *g* instead of a hard one. His medical friend was of course not bound to cure his spelling as well as his gout; so we left him in the full-blown satisfaction of having struck awe on the Londoner.

Dr. Young talks of—

"That hideous sight, a naked human heart;"

a line not fit to have been written by a human being. The sight of the physical heart, it must be owned, was trying enough to sick eyes; that of the doctor's moral heart, according to himself, would have been far worse. I don't believe it. I don't believe he had a right thus to calumniate it, much less that of his neighbor, and of the whole human race.

I saw a worse sight than the heart, in a journey which I took into a neighboring county. It was an infant, all over sores, and cased in steel; the result of the irregularities of its father; and I confess that I would rather have seen

the heart of the very father of that child, than I would the
child himself.   I am sure it must have bled at the sight.   I
am sure there would have been a feeling of some sort to vindicate nature, granting that up to that moment the man had
been a fool or even a scoundrel.   Sullenness itself would
have been some amends ; some sort of confession and regret.
As to the poor child, let us trust that the horrible spectacle
prevented more such ;   that he was a martyr, dying soon,
and going to some heaven where little souls are gathered
into comfort.   I never beheld such a sight, before or since,
except in one of the pictures of Hogarth, in his Rake's
Progress ; and I sadden this page with the recollection, for
the same reason that induced him to paint it.

I have mentioned that I got rid of a palpitation of the
heart, which accompanied my first visitation of hypochondria, by riding on horseback.   The palpitation was so strong
and incessant, that I was forced, for some nights, to ·sleep
in a reclining posture, and I expected sudden death ; but
when I began the horseback, I soon found that the more
I rode, and (I used to think) the harder I rode, the less the
palpitation became.   Galloping one day, up a sloping piece
of ground, the horse suddenly came to a stand, by a chalk-
pit, and I was agreeably surprised to find myself not only
unprecipitated over his head (for though a decent, I was not
a skillful rider), but in a state of singular calmness, and self-
possession—a right, proper, masculine state of nerves.   I
might have discovered, as I did afterward, what it was that
so calmed and strengthened me.   I was of a temperament of
body in which the pores were not easily opened ; and the
freer they were kept, the better I was ; but it took me a
long time to discover, that in order to be put into a state of
vigor as well as composure, I required either vigorous exercise or some strong moral excitement connected with the
sense of action.   Unfortunately, I had a tendency to extremes in self treatment.   At one time I thought to cure
myself by cold water baths, in which I persevered through
a winter season ; and, subsequently, I hurt myself by hot
baths.   Late hours at night were not mended by lying in
bed of a morning ; nor incessant reading and writing, by

weeks in which I did little but stroll and visit. It is true, I can hardly be said to have ever been without a book ; for if not in my hand, it was at my side, or in my pocket; but what I needed was ordinary, regular habits, accompanied with a more than ordinary amount of exercise. I was never either so happy or so tranquil, as when I was in a state the most active. I could very well understand the character of an unknown individual, described in the prose works of Ben Jonson, who would sit writing, day and night till he fainted, and then so entirely give himself up to diversion, that people despaired of getting him to work again. But I sympathized still more with one of the Rucellai family, who was so devoted to a sedentary life, that he could not endure the thought of being taken from it ; till being forced, in a manner, to accept a diplomatic mission, he became as vehement for a life of action as he had before been absorbed in indolence, and was never satisfied till he was driving every thing before him, and spinning, with his chariot-wheels, from one court to another. If I had not a reverence, indeed, for whatever has taken place in the ordinance of things, great and small, I should often have fancied that some such business of diplomacy would have been my proper vocation ; for I delight in imagining conferences upon points that are to be carried, or scenes in which thrones are looked upon, and national compliments are to be conveyed ; and I am sure that a great deal of action would have kept me in the finest health. Whatever dries up the surface of my body, intimidates me; but when the reverse has been effected by any thing except the warm bath, fear has forsaken me, and my spirit has felt as broad and healthy as my shoulders.

I did not discover this particular cause of healthy sensation till long after my recovery. I attributed it entirely to exercise in general ; but by exercise, at all events (and I mention the whole circumstance for the benefit of the nervous), health was restored to me ; and I maintained it as long as I persevered in the means.

Not long after convalescence, the good that had been done me was put further to the test. Some friends, among whom were two of my brothers and myself, had a day's boating up the Thames. We were very merry and jovial, and not prepared to think any obstacle, in the way of our satisfaction, possible. On a sudden we perceive a line stretched across the river by some fishermen. We call out to them to lower, or take it away. They say they will not. One of us holds up a knife, and proclaims his intention to cut it. The fishermen defy the knife. Forward goes the knife with the boat, and cuts the line in the most beautiful manner conceivable. The two halves of the line rushed asunder.

"Off," cry the fishermen to one another, " and duck 'em." They push out their boat. Their wives (I forget whence they issued) appear on the bank, echoing the cry of " Duck 'em." We halt on our oars, and are come up with, the fishermen looking as savage as wild islanders, and swearing might and main. My brother and myself, not to let us all be run down (for the fishermen's boat was much larger than ours, and we had ladies with us, who were terrified) told the enemy we would come among them. We did so, going from our boat into theirs.

The determination to duck us now became manifest enough, and the fishermen's wives (cruel with their husbands' lost fishing) seemed equally determined not to let the intention remit. They screamed and yelled like so many furies. The fishermen seized my brother John, whom they took for the cutter of the line, and would have instantly effected their purpose, had he not been clasped round the waist by my brother Robert, who kept him tight down in a corner of the hold. A violent struggle ensued, during which a ruffianly fellow aiming a blow at my brother John's face, whose arms were pinioned, I had the good luck to intercept it. Meanwhile the wives of the boaters were screaming as well as the wives of the fishermen ; and it was asked our antagonists, whether it was befitting brave men to frighten women out of their senses.

The fury seemed to relax a little at this. The word " payment" was mentioned, which seemed to relax it more ; but it was still divided between threat and demand, when, in the midst of a fresh outbreak of the first resolution, beautiful evidence was furnished of the magical effects of the word " law."

Luckily for our friends and ourselves (for the enemy had the advantage of us, both in strength and numbers), the owner of the boat, it seems, had lately been worsted in some action of trespass, probably of the very nature of what they had been doing with their line. I was then living with my brother S., who was in the law. I happened to be dressed in black ; and I had gathered from some words which fell from them during their rage, that what they had been about with their fishing-net, was in all probability illegal. I assumed it to be so. I mentioned the dreaded word " law ;" my black coat corroborated its impression ; and, to our equal relief and surprise, we found them on the sudden converting their rage and extortion into an assumption that we meant to settle with their master, and quietly permitting us to get back to our friends.

Throughout this little rough adventure, which at one time threatened very distressing, if not serious consequences, I was glad to find that I underwent no apprehensions but such as became me. The pain and horror that used to be given me at sight of human antagonism never entered my head. I felt nothing but a flow of brotherhood and determination, and returned in fine breathing condition to the oar. I subsequently found that all corporate occasions of excitement affected me in the same healthy manner. The mere fact of being in a crowd when their feelings were strongly moved, to whatever purpose, roused all that was strong in me ; and from the alacrity, and even comfort and joy, into which I was warmed by the thought of resistance to whatever wrong might demand it, I learned plainly enough what a formidable thing a human being might become if he took wrong for right, and what reverence was due to the training and just treatment of the myriads that compose a nation.

I was now again in a state of perfect comfort and enjoyment, the gayer for the cloud which had gone, though occasionally looking back on it with gravity, and prepared, alas ! or rather preparing myself by degrees to undergo it again in the course of a few years, by relapsing into a sedentary life. Suffer as I might have done, I had not, it seems, suffered enough. However, the time was very delightful while it lasted. I thoroughly enjoyed my books, my walks, my companions, my verses ; and I had never ceased to be ready to fall in love with the first tender-hearted damsel that should encourage me. Now it was a fair charmer, and now a brunette ; now a girl who sang, or a girl who danced ; now one that was merry, or was melancholy, or seemed to care for nothing, or for every thing, or was a good friend, or good sister, or good daughter. With this last, who completed her conquest by reading verses better than I had ever heard, I ultimately became wedded for life; and she reads verses better than ever, to this day, especially some that shall be nameless.

CHAPTER IX.

Establishment of the Examiner.—Albany Fonblanque.—Author's mistakes in setting out in his editorial career.—Objects of the Examiner, and misrepresentations of them by the Tories.—Jeu d'esprit of "Napoleon in his Cabinet."—"Breakfast Sympathies with the Miseries of War."—War dispassionately considered.—Anti-republicanism of the Examiner, and its views in theology.—The Author for some time a clerk in the War Office.—His patron, Mr. Addington, afterward Lord Sidmouth.—Poetry and accounts.

AT the beginning of the year 1808, my brother John and myself set up the weekly paper of the *Examiner* in joint partnership. It was named after the *Examiner* of Swift and his brother Tories. I did not think of their politics. I thought only of their wit and fine writing, which, in my youthful confidence, I proposed to myself to emulate ; and I could find no previous political journal equally qualified to be its godfather. Even Addison had called his opposition paper the *Whig Examiner.*

Some dozen years afterward I had an editorial successor, Mr. Fonblanque, who had all the wit for which I toiled, without making any pretensions to it. He was, indeed, the genuine successor, not of me, but of the Swifts and Addisons themselves ; profuse of wit even beyond them, and superior in political knowledge. Yet, if I labored hard for what was so easy to Mr. Fonblanque, I will not pretend to think that I did not sometimes find it ; and the study of Addison and Steele, of Goldsmith and Voltaire, enabled me, when I was pleased with my subject, to give it the appearance of ease. At other times, especially on serious occasions, I too often got into a declamatory vein, full of what I thought fine turns and Johnsonian antithesis. The new office of editor conspired with my success as a critic to turn my head. I wrote, though anonymously, in the first person, as if, in addition to my theatrical pretensions, I had suddenly become an oracle

1*

in politics ; the words philosophy, poetry, criticism, statesman-
ship, nay, even ethics and theology, all took a final tone in
my lips ; and when I consider the virtue as well as knowledge which I demanded from every body whom I had occasion
to speak of, and of how much charity my own juvenile errors
ought to have considered themselves in need (however they
might have been warranted by conventional allowance), I
will not say I was a hypocrite in the odious sense of the
word, for it was all done out of a spirit of foppery and " fine
writing," and I never affected any formal virtues in private ;
but when I consider all the nonsense and extravagance of
those assumptions—all the harm they must have done me in
discerning eyes, and all the reasonable amount of resentment
which it was preparing for me with adversaries, I blush to
think what a simpleton I was, and how much of the consequences I deserved.   It is out of no " ostentation of candor"
that I make this confession.   It is extremely painful to me.

Suffering gradually worked me out of a good deal of this
kind of egotism.   I hope that even the present most involun-
tarily egotistical book affords evidence that I am pretty well
rid of it ; and I must add, in my behalf, that, in every other
respect, never, at that time or at any after time, was I otherwise than an honest man.   I overrated my claims to public
attention ; I greatly overdid the manner of addressing it ; and
I was not too abundant in either ; but I set out, perhaps,
with as good an editorial amount of qualification as most
writers no older.   I was fairly grounded in English history ;
I had carefully read De Lolme and Blackstone ; I had no
mercenary views whatsoever, though I was a proprietor of
the journal ; and all the levity of my animal spirits, and the
foppery of the graver part of my pretensions, had not de-
stroyed in me that spirit of martyrdom which had been inculcated in me from the cradle.   I denied myself political
as well as theatrical acquaintances ; I was the reverse of a
speculator upon patronage or employment ; and I was prepared, with my excellent brother, to suffer manfully, should
the time for suffering arrive.

The spirit of the criticism on the theatres continued the
same as it had been in the *News*.   In politics, from old

family associations, I soon got interested as a man, though I never could love them as a writer. It was against the grain that I was encouraged to begin them ; and against the grain I ever afterward sat down to write, except when the subject was of a very general description, and I could introduce philosophy and the belles-lettres.

The main objects of the *Examiner* newspaper were to assist in producing Reform in Parliament, liberality of opinion in general (especially freedom from superstition), and a fusion of literary taste into all subjects whatsoever. It began with being of no party ; but Reform soon gave it one. It disclaimed all knowledge of statistics ; and the rest of its politics were rather a sentiment, and a matter of training, than founded on any particular political reflection. It possessed the benefit, however, of a good deal of general reading. It never wanted examples out of history and biography, or a kind of adornment from the spirit of literature ; and it gradually drew to its perusal many intelligent persons of both sexes, who would, perhaps, never have attended to politics under any other circumstances.

In the course of its warfare with the Tories, the *Examiner* was charged with Bonapartism, with republicanism, with disaffection to Church and State, with conspiracy at the tables of Burdett, and Cobbett, and Henry Hunt. Now Sir Francis, though he was for a long time our hero, we never exchanged a word with ; and Cobbett and Henry Hunt (no relation of ours) we never beheld ; never so much as saw their faces. I was never even at a public dinner ; nor do I believe my brother was. We had absolutely no views whatsoever, but those of a decent competence and of the public good ; and we thought, I dare affirm, a great deal more of the latter than of the former. Our competence we allowed too much to shift for itself. Zeal for the public good was a family inheritance ; and this we thought ourselves bound to increase. As to myself, what I thought of, more than either, was the making of verses. I did nothing for the greater part of the week but write verses and read books. I then made a rush at my editorial duties ; took a world of superfluous pains in the writing ; sat up late at night, and was a very

trying person to compositors and newsmen. I sometimes
have before me the ghost of a pale and gouty printer whom
I specially caused to suffer, and who never complained. I
think of him and of some needy dramatist, and wish they
had been worse men.

The *Examiner* commenced at the time when Bonaparte
was at the height of his power. He had the continent at
his feet; and three of his brothers were on thrones. The
reader may judge of our Bonapartist tendencies by the following dramatic sketch, which appeared in the first number:

NAPOLEON IN HIS CABINET.

SCENE—*A Cabinet at St. Cloud.*

NAPOLEON. [*Ruminating before a fire and grasping a poker.*] Who
waits there?

LE M. May it please your majesty, your faithful soldier, Le
Meurtrier.

NAP. Tell Sultan Mustapha that he is the last of the sultans.

LE M. Yes, sire.

NAP. And, hark ye—desire the king of Holland to come to me
directly.

LE M. Yes, sire.

NAP. And the king of Westphalia.—[*Aside*] I must tweak Jerome
by the nose a little, to teach him dignity.

LE M. [*With hesitation.*] M. Champagny, sire, waits to know your
Majesty's pleasure respecting the king of Sweden.

NAP. Oh—tell him, I'll let the boy alone for a month or two. And
stay, Le Meurtrier; go to the editor of the *Moniteur*, and tell him to
dethrone the queen of Portugal. Spain's dethronement is put off to
next year. Where's Bienseance?

[*Exit* LE MEURTRIER, *and enter* BIENSEANCE.

BIEN. May it please your august majesty, Bienseance is before
you.

NAP. Fetch me General F.'s head, and a cup of coffee.

BIEN. [*Smiling with devotion*]. Every syllable uttered by the great
Napoleon convinces Frenchmen that he is their father.

[*Exit* BIENSEANCE.

NAP. [*Meditating with ferocity*]. After driving the Turks out of
Europe [*pokes the fire*], I must annihilate England [*gives a furious
poke*]; but first I shall over-run India; then I shall request America
and Africa to put themselves under my protection; and after making

that great jackass, the Russian emperor, one of my tributaries, crown myself emperor of the east—west—north—and south. Then I must have a balloon army, of which Garnerin shall be field-marshal; for I must positively take possession of the comet, because it makes a noise. That will assist me to conquer the solar system; and then I shall go with my army to the other systems; and then—I think—I shall go to the devil.

I thought of Bonaparte at that time as I have thought ever since; to-wit, that he was a great soldier, and little else; that he was not a man of the highest order of intellect, much less a cosmopolite; that he was a retrospective rather than a prospective man, ambitious of old renown instead of new; and would advance the age as far, and no farther, as suited his views of personal aggrandizement. The *Examiner*, however much it differed with the military policy of Bonaparte's antagonists, or however meanly it thought of their understandings, never overrated his own, or was one of his partisans. What it thought of war and conquest in general may be gathered from another *jeu-d'esprit*—a jest, like many another jest, with laughter on its lips, and melancholy at heart. It was entitled, *Breakfast Sympathies with the Miseries of War*.

TWO GENTLEMEN AND A LADY AT BREAKFAST.

A. [*Reading the newspaper, and eating at every two or three words*]. "The combat lasted twelve hours . . . . . and the two armies separated at nine in the evening . . . . . leaving 30,000 men literally cut to pieces!" (another piece of toast, if you please) "on the field of." . . . . Stop, 30,000 is it? [*looking at the paper closely*]. Egad, I believe, it's 50,000. Tom, is that a three or a five? Oh, a five. That paper's horridly printed.

B. Very indeed.—Well, "leaving 50,000 men on the field of battle." —50,000!—that's a great number to be killed with the bayonet, eh! War's a horrid [*sips*] thing.

THE LADY. Oh, shocking! [*Takes a large bit of toast*].

B. Oh, monstrous! [*Takes a larger*].

A. [*Reading on*]. "One of the French generals of division riding up to the emperor with a sabre covered with blood, after a charge of cavalry, exclaimed,"—stick your fork into that slice of ham for me, Tom—thankye—"exclaimed—There is not a man in my regiment whose sword is not like this. The two armi—"

B. What? What was that about the sword?

A. Why, his own sword, you know, was covered with blood. Didn't you hear me read it? And so he said, There is not a—

B. Ay, ay—whose sword is not like this. I understand you. Gad, what a fellow !

A. [*Sips.*] Oh, horrid !

THE LADY. [*Sips.*] Oh, shocking ! *Dash*, get down : how can you be so ?

A. " The two armi—"

B. By-the-by, have you heard of Mrs. W.'s accident ?

A. AND THE LADY. [*Putting down their cups*]. No ! what can it be ?

A. Poor thing ! her husband's half mad, I suppose.

B. Why, she has broken her arm.

THE LADY. Good God ! I declare you've made me quite sick. Poor dear Mrs. W. ! Why she'll be obliged to wear her arm in a sling ! But she would go out this slippery weather, when the frost's enough to kill one.

B. Well, I must go and tell my father the news. Let's see—how many men killed, Charles ?

A. 50,000.

B. Ah, 50,000. Good-morning. [*Exit.*]

THE LADY. Poor dear Mrs. W., I can't help thinking about her. A broken arm ! Why, it's quite a dreadful thing ! I wonder whether Mrs. F. has heard the news.

B. She'll see it in this morning's paper, you know.

LADY. Oh, what it's in the paper, is it ?

B. [*Laughing.*] Why, didn't you hear Charles read it just now ?

LADY. Oh, that news. No, I mean poor Mrs. W. Poor dear ! [*meditating*] I wonder whether she'll wear a black sling or a blue.* [*Exeunt*].

I now look upon war as one of the fleeting necessities of things in the course of human progress ; as an evil (like all other evils) to be regarded in relation to some other evil that would have been worse without it, but always to be considered as an indication of comparative barbarism—as a necessity, the perpetuity of which is not to be assumed or encouraged—or as a half reasoning mode of adjustment, whether of disputes or of populations, which mankind, on arriving at years of discretion, and coming to a better understanding with one another, may, and must of necessity, do away. It would be as ridiculous to associate the idea of war with an earth covered with railroads and commerce, as a fight between Holborn and the Strand, or between people met in a drawing-room. Wars, like all other evils, have not been without

* *Examiner*, vol. i. p. 748.

their good. They have pioneered human intercourse; have thus prepared even for their own eventual abolition; and their follies, losses, and horrors have been made the best of by adornments and music, and consoled by the exhibition of many noble qualities. There is no evil unmixed with, or unproductive of good. It could not, in the nature of things, exist. Antagonism itself prevents it. But nature incites us to the diminution of evil; and while it is pious to make the best of what is inevitable, it is no less so to obey the impulse which she has given us toward thinking and making it otherwise.

With respect to the charge of republicanism against the *Examiner*, it was as ridiculous as the rest. Both Napoleon and the allies did, indeed, so conduct themselves on the high roads of empire and royalty, and the British sceptre was at the same time so unfortunately wielded, that kings and princes were often treated with less respect in our pages than we desired. But we generally felt and often expressed a wish to treat them otherwise. The *Examiner* was always quoting against them the Alfreds and Antoninuses of old. The "Constitution," with its King, Lords, and Commons, was its incessant watchword. The greatest political change which it desired was Reform in Parliament; and it helped to obtain it, because it was in earnest. As to republics, the United States, notwithstanding our family relationship, were no favorites with us, owing to their love of money and their want of the imaginative and ornamental; and the excesses of the French Revolution we held in abhorrence.

With regard to Church and State, the connection was of course duly recognized by admirers of the English constitution. We desired, it is true, reform in both, being far greater admirers of Christianity in its primitive than in any of its subsequent shapes, and hearty accorders with the dictum of the apostle, who said that the " letter killeth, but the spirit giveth life." Our version of religious faith was ever nearer to what M. Lamartine has called the " New Christianity," than to that of Doctors Horsley and Philpotts. But we heartily advocated the mild spirit of religious government, as exercised by the Church of England, in opposition to the bigoted part of dissent; and in furtherance of this advocacy, the first volume of the *Examiner* contained a series of *Essays on the Folly and Danger of Methodism*, which were afterward collected into a pamphlet. So "orthodox" were these essays, short of points from which common sense and humanity always appeared to us to revolt, and from which the deliverance of the church itself is now, I believe, not far off, that in duty to our hope of that deliverance, I afterward thought it necessary to guard against the conclusions which might have been drawn from them, as to the amount of our assent. A church appeared to me then, as it still does, an instinctive want in the human family. I never to this day pass one, even of a kind the most unreformed, without a wish to go into it and join my fellow-creatures in their affecting evidence of the necessity of an additional tie with Deity and Infinity, with this world and the next. But the wish is accompanied with an afflicting regret that I can not recognize it, free from barbarisms derogatory to both; and I sigh for some good old country church, finally delivered from the corruptions of the Councils, and breathing nothing but the peace and love befitting the Sermon on the Mount. I believe that a time is coming, when such doctrine, and such only, will be preached; and my future grave, by some old ivied tower, seems quieter for the consummation. But I anticipate.

For a short period before and after the setting up of the *Examiner*, I was a clerk in the War Office. The situation was given me by Mr. Addington, then prime minister, afterward Lord Sidmouth, who knew my father. My sorry stock of arithmetic, which I taught myself on purpose, was sufficient for the work which I had to do ; but otherwise I made a bad clerk; wasting my time and that of others in perpetual jesting ; going too late to office ; and feeling conscious that if I did not quit the situation myself, nothing was more likely, or would have been more just, than a suggestion to that effect from others. The establishment of the *Examiner*, and the tone respecting the court and the ministry which I soon thought myself bound to adopt, increased the sense of the propriety of this measure ; and, accordingly, I

sent in my resignation.   Mr. Addington had fortunately
ceased to be minister before the *Examiner* was set up ; and
though I had occasion afterward to differ extremely with the
measures approved of by him as Lord Sidmouth, I never
forgot the personal respect which I owed him for his kindness to myself, to his own amiable manners, and to his un-
doubted, though not wise, conscientiousness.   He had been
Speaker of the House of Commons, a situation for which his
figure and deportment at that time of life admirably fitted
him.   I think I hear his fine voice, in his house at Richmond
Park, good-naturedly expressing to me his hope, in the words
of the poet, that it might one day be said of me,

> "— Not in fancy's maze he wandered long,
> But stoop'd to truth, and moraliz'd his song."

The sounding words, "moralized his song," came *toning* out
of his dignified utterance like "sonorous metal."   This was
when I went to thank him for the clerkship.   I afterward
sat on the grass in the park, feeling as if I was in a dream,
and wondering how I should reconcile my propensity to
verse-making with sums in addition.   The minister, it was
clear, thought them not incompatible : nor are they.   Let
nobody think otherwise, unless he is prepared to suffer for
the mistake, and what is worse, to make others suffer.   The
body of the British Poets themselves shall confute him, with
Chaucer at their head, who was a "comptroller of wool"
and "clerk of works,"

> "Thou hearest neither that nor this,

says the eagle to him in the House of Fame) :

> For when thy labor all done is,
> And hast made *all thy reckonings*,
> Instead of rest and of new things,
> Thou goest home to thine house anon,
> And all so dumb as any stone
> Thou sittest at another book,
> Till fully dazèd is thy look."

Lamb, it is true, though he stuck to it, has complained
of

> "The dry drudgery of the desk's dead wood;'

and how Chaucer contrived to settle his accounts in the
month of May, when as he tells us, he could not help passing whole days in the fields, looking at the daisies, his biographers do not inform us. The case, as in all other matters,
can only be vindicated, or otherwise, by the consequences.
But that is a perilous responsibility; and it involves assumptions which ought to be startling to the modesty of young
rhyming gentlemen not in the receipt of an income.

I did not give up, however, a certainty for an uncertainty.
The *Examiner* was fully established when I quitted the
office.   My friends thought that I should be better able to
attend to it; and it was felt, at any rate, that I could not
with propriety remain.   So I left my fellow-clerks to their
better behavior and quieter rooms ; and set my face in the
direction of stormy polities.

CHAPTER X.

Just after this period I fell in with a new set of acquaintances, accounts of whom may not be uninteresting. I forget what it was that introduced me to Mr. Hill, proprietor of the *Monthly Mirror;* but at his house at Sydenham I used to meet his editor, Du Bois; Thomas Campbell, who was his neighbor; and the two Smiths, authors of *The Rejected Addresses.* I saw also Theodore Hook, and Mathews the comedian. Our host was a jovial bachelor, plump and rosy as an abbot; and no abbot could have presided over a more festive Sunday. The wine flowed merrily and long: the discourse kept pace with it; and next morning in returning to town, we felt ourselves very thirsty. A pump by the roadside, with a plash round it, was a bewitching sight.

Du Bois was one of those wits, who, like the celebrated Eachard, have no faculty of gravity. His handsome hawk's eyes looked blank at a speculation; but set a joke or a piece of raillery in motion, and they sparkled with wit and malice. Nothing could be more trite or commonplace than his serious observations. Acquiescences they should rather have been called; for he seldom ventured upon a gravity, but in echo of another's remark. If he did, it was in defense of orthodoxy, of which he was a great advocate; but his quips and cranks were infinite. He was also an excellent scholar, he, Dr. King and Eachard, would have made a capital trio over a table, for scholarship, mirth, drinking, and religion. He was intimate with Sir Philip Francis, and gave the public a new edition of the Horace of Sir Philip's father. The literary world knew him well also as the writer of a popular novel, in the genuine Fielding manner, entitled *Old Nick*.

Mr. Du Bois held his editorship of the *Monthly Mirror* very cheap. He amused himself with writing notes on Athenæus, and was a lively critic on the theatres; but half the jokes in his magazine were written for his friends, and must have mystified the uninitiated. His notices to correspondents were often made up of this by-play; and made his friends laugh, in proportion to their obscurity to every one else. Mr. Du Bois subsequently became a magistrate in the Court of Requests; and died the other day at an advanced age, in spite of his love of port. But then he was festive in good taste; no gourmand; and had a strong head withal. I do not know whether such men ever last as long as teetotalers; but they certainly last as long and look a great deal younger, than the carking and severe.

They who knew Mr. Campbell only as the author of *Gertrude of Wyoming*, and the *Pleasures of Hope*, would not have suspected him to be a merry companion, overflowing with humor and anecdote, and any thing but fastidious. These Scotch poets have always something in reserve. It is the only point in which the major part of them resemble their countrymen. The mistaken character which the lady formed of Thomson from his *Seasons* is well known. He let part of the secret out in his *Castle of Indolence;* and the more he let out, the more honor it did to the simplicity and cordiality of the poet's nature, though not always to the elegance of it. Allan Ramsay knew his friends Gay and Somerville as well in their writings, as he did when he came to be personally acquainted with them; but Allan, who had bustled up from a barber's shop into a bookseller's was " a cunning shaver ;" and nobody would have guessed the author of the *Gentle Shepherd* to be penurious. Let none suppose that any insinuation to that effect is intended against Campbell. He was one of the few men whom I could at any time have walked half a dozen miles through the snow to spend an evening with; and I could no more do this with a penurious man than I could with a sulky one. I know but of one fault he had, besides an extreme cautiousness in his writings, and that one was national, a matter of words, and amply overpaid by a stream of conversation, lively, piquant, and liberal, not the less interesting for occasionally betraying an intimacy with pain, and for a high and somewhat strained tone of voice, like a man speaking with suspended breath, and in the habit of subduing his feelings. No man felt more kindly toward his fellow-creatures, or took less credit for it. When he indulged in doubt and sarcasm, and spoke contemptuously of things in general, he did it, partly, no doubt, out of actual dissatisfaction, but more perhaps than he suspected, out of a fear of being thought weak and sensitive ; which is a blind that the best men very commonly practice. He professed to be hopeless and sarcastic, and took pains all the while to set up a university (the London).

When I first saw this eminent person, he gave me the idea of a French Virgil. Not that he was like a Frenchman, much less the French translator of Virgil. I found him as handsome, as the Abbé Delille is said to have been ugly. But he seemed to me to embody a Frenchman's ideal notion of the Latin poet ; something a little more cut and dry than I had looked for ; compact and elegant, critical and acute, with a consciousness of authorship upon him ; a taste over-anxious not to commit itself, and refining and diminishing nature as in a drawing-room mirror. This fancy was strengthened in the course of conversation, by his expatiating on the greatness of Racine. I think he had a volume of the French poet in his hand. His skull was sharply cut and fine ; with plenty, according to the phrenologists, both of the reflective and amative organs : and his poetry will bear them out. For a lettered solitude, and a bridal properly got up, both according to law and luxury, commend us to the lovely *Gertrude of Wyoming*. His face and person were rather on a small scale ; his features regular ; his eye lively and penetrating ; and when he spoke, dimples played about his mouth ; which, nevertheless, had something restrained and close in it. Some gentle puritan seemed to have crossed the breed, and to have left a stamp on his face, such as we often see in the female Scotch face, rather than the male. But he appeared not at all grateful for this ;

and when his critiques and his Virgilianism were over, very
unlike a puritan he talked !   He seemed to spite his restrictions ; and out of the natural largeness of his sympathy with
things high and low, to break at once out of Delillo's Virgil
into Cotton's, like a boy let loose from school.   When I had
the pleasure of hearing him afterward, I forgot his Virgil-
ianisms, and thought only of the delightful companion, the
unaffected philanthropist, and the creator of a beauty worth
all the heroines in Racine.

Campbell tasted pretty sharply of the good and ill of the
present state of society, and, for a bookman, had beheld
strange sights.   He witnessed a battle in Germany from the
top of a convent (on which battle he has left us a noble ode) ;
and he saw the French cavalry enter a town, wiping their
bloody swords on the horses' manes.   He was in Germany
a second time, I believe to purchase books ; for in addition
to his classical scholarship, and his other languages, he was
a reader of German.   The readers there, among whom he is
popular, both for his poetry and his love of freedom, crowded
about him with affectionate zeal ; and they gave him, what
he did not dislike, a good dinner.   Like many of the great
men in Germany, Schiller, Wieland, and others, he did not
scruple to become editor of a magazine ; and his name alone
gave it a recommendation of the greatest value, and such as
made it a grace to write under him.

I remember, one day at Sydenham, Mr. Theodore Hook
coming in unexpectedly to dinner, and amusing us very
much with his talent at extempore verse.   He was then a
youth, tall, dark, and of a good person, with small eyes, and
features more round than weak ; a face that had character
and humor, but no refinement.   His extempore verses were
really surprising.   It is easy enough to extemporize in Italian
—one only wonders how, in a language in which every thing
conspires to render verse-making easy, and it is difficult to avoid
rhyming, this talent should be so much cried up—but in English it is another matter.   I have known but one other person besides Hook, who could extemporize in English ; and he
wanted the confidence to do it in public.   Of course, I speak
of rhyming.   Extempore blank verse, with a little practice,

would be found as easy in English as rhyming is in Italian. In Hook the faculty was very unequivocal. He could not have been aware of all the visitors, still less of the subject of conversation when he came in, and he talked his full share till called upon; yet he ran his jokes and his verses upon us all in the easiest manner, saying something characteristic of every body, or avoiding it with a pun; and he introduced so agreeably a piece of village scandal upon which the party had been rallying Campbell, that the poet, though not un-jealous of his dignity, was, perhaps, the most pleased of us all. Theodore afterward sat down to the piano-forte, and enlarging upon this subject, made an extempore parody of a modern opera, introducing sailors and their clap-traps, rus-tics, &c., and making the poet and his supposed flame, the hero and heroine. He parodied music as well as words, giving us the most received cadences and flourishes, and call-ing to mind (not without some hazard to his filial duties) the commonplaces of the pastoral songs and duets of the last half century; so that if Mr. Dignum, the Damon of Vaux-hall, had been present, he would have doubted whether to take it as an affront or a compliment. Campbell certainly took the theme of the parody as a compliment; for having drunk a little more wine than usual that evening, and hap-pening to wear a wig on account of having lost his hair by a fever, he suddenly took off the wig, and dashed it at the head of the performer, exclaiming, "You dog! I'll throw my laurels at you."

I have since been unable to help wishing, perhaps not very wisely, that Campbell would have been a little less care-ful and fastidious in what he did for the public; for, after all, an author may reasonably be supposed to do best that which he is most inclined to do. It is our business to be grateful for what a poet sets before us, rather than to be wishing that his peaches were nectarines, or his Falernian Champagne. Campbell, as an author, was all for refinement and classicality, not, however, without a great deal of pathos and luxurious fancy. His merry *jongleur*, Theodore Hook, had as little propensity, perhaps, as can be imagined, to any of those niceties: yet in the pleasure of recollecting the evening which

I passed with him, I was unable to repress a wish, as little wise as the other ; to-wit, that he had stuck to his humors and farces, for which he had real talent, instead of writing polities.　There was ability in the novels which he subsequently wrote ; but their worship of high life and attacks on vulgarity, were themselves of the vulgarest description.

Mathews, the comedian, I had the pleasure of seeing at Mr. Hill's several times, and of witnessing his imitations, which, admirable as they were on the stage, were still more so in private.　His wife occasionally came with him, with her handsome eyes, and charitably made tea for us.　Many years afterward I had the pleasure of seeing them at their own table ; and I thought that while Time, with unusual courtesy, had spared the sweet countenance of the lady, he had given more force and interest to that of the husband in the very ploughing of it up.　Strong lines had been cut, and the face stood them well.　I had seldom been more surprised than on coming close to Mathews on that occasion, and seeing the bust which he possessed in his gallery of his friend Liston.　Some of these comic actors, like comic writers, are as unfarcical as can be imagined in their interior. The taste for humor comes to them by the force of contrast. The last time I had seen Mathews, his face appeared to me insignificant to what it was then.　On the former occasion, he looked like an irritable, in-door pet : on the latter, he seemed to have been grappling with the world, and to have got vigor by it.　His face had looked out upon the Atlantic, and said to the old waves, " Buffet on ; I have seen trouble as well as you."　The paralytic affection, or whatever it was, that twisted his mouth when young, had formerly appeared to be master of his face, and given it a character of indecision and alarm.　It now seemed a minor thing ; a twist in a piece of old oak.　And what a bust was Liston's ! The mouth and chin, with the throat under it, hung like an old bag ; but the upper part of the head was as fine as possible.　There was a speculation, a look-out, and even an elevation of character in it, as unlike the Liston on the stage, as Lear is to King Pippin.　One might imagine Laberius to have had such a face.

The reasons why Mathews's imitations were still better in private than in public were, that he was more at his ease personally, more secure of his audience ("fit though few"), and able to interest them with traits of private character, which could not have been introduced on the stage. He gave, for instance, to persons who he thought could take it rightly, a picture of the manners and conversation of Sir Walter Scott, highly creditable to that celebrated person, and calculated to add regard to admiration. His commonest imitations were not superficial. Something of the mind and character of the individual was always insinuated, often with a dramatic dressing, and plenty of sauce piquante. At Sydenham he used to give us a dialogue among the actors, each of whom found fault with another for some defect or excess of his own. Kemble objecting to stiffness, Munden to grimace, and so on. His representation of Incledon was extraordinary : his nose seemed actually to become aquiline. It is a pity I can not put upon paper, as represented by Mr. Mathews, the singular gabblings of that actor, the lax and sailor-like twist of mind, with which every thing hung upon him ; and his profane pieties in quoting the Bible ; for which, and swearing, he seemed to have an equal reverence. He appeared to be charitable to every body but Braham. He would be described as saying to his friend Holman, for instance, " My dear George, don't be abusive, George ; don't insult—don't be indecent, by G——d ! You should take the beam out of your own eye—what the devil is it ? you know, in the Bible ; something" (the *a* very broad) " about *a* beam, my dear George ! and——and——and *a* mote ; you'll find it in *any* part of the Bible ; yes, George, my dear boy, the Bible, by G——d ;" (and then with real fervor and reverence) " the Holy Scripture, G——d d——me !" He swore as dreadfully as a devout knight-errant. Braham, whose trumpet blew down his wooden walls, he could not endure. He is represented as saying one day, with a strange mixture of imagination and matter-of-fact, that " he only wished his beloved master, Mr. Jackson, could come down from heaven, and take the Exeter stage to London, to hear that d——d Jew !"

As Hook made extempore verses on us, so Mathews one

day gave an extempore imitation of us all round, with the
exception of a young theatrical critic (*videlicet*, myself), in
whose appearance and manner he pronounced that there was
no handle for mimicry. This, in all probability, was intended as a politeness toward a comparative stranger, but it
might have been policy ; and the laughter was not missed
by it. At all events, the critic was both good-humored
enough, and at that time self-satisfied enough, to have borne
the mimicry ; and no harm would have come of it.

One morning, after stopping all night at this pleasant
house, I was getting up to breakfast, when I heard the noise
of a little boy having his face washed. Our host was a
merry bachelor, and to the rosiness of a priest might, for
aught I knew, have added the paternity ; but I had never
heard of it, and still less expected to find a child in his
house. More obvious and obstreperous proofs, however, of
the existence of a boy with a dirty face, could not have been
met with. You heard the child crying and objecting ; then
the woman remonstrating ; then the cries of the child
snubbed and swallowed up in the hard towel ; and at intervals out came his voice bubbling and deploring, and was
again swallowed up. At breakfast, the child being pitied,
I ventured to speak about it, and was laughing and sympathizing in perfect good faith, when Mathews came in, and I
found that the little urchin was he.

The same morning he gave us his immortal imitation of
old Tate Wilkinson, patentee of the York Theatre. Tate
had been a little too merry in his youth, and was very
melancholy in old age. He had a wandering mind and a
decrepit body ; and being manager of a theatre, a husband,
and a ratcatcher, he would speak, in his wanderings, " vari
ety of wretchedness." He would interweave, for instance
all at once, the subjects of a new engagement at his theatre,
the rats, a veal-pie, Garrick and Mrs. Siddons, and Mrs
Tate and the doctor. I do not pretend to give a specimen :
Mathews alone could have done it ; but one trait I recollect,
descriptive of Tate himself, which will give a good notion
of him. On coming into the room, Mathews assumed the
old manager's appearance, and proceeded toward the window,

to reconnoitre the state of the weather, which was a matter of great importance to him.   His hat was like a hat worn the wrong way, side foremost, looking sadly crinkled and old ; his mouth was desponding, his eye staring, and his whole aspect meagre, querulous, and prepared for objection.   This miserable object, grunting and hobbling, and helping himself with every thing he can lay hold of as he goes, creeps up to the window ; and, giving a glance at the clouds, turns round with an ineffable look of despair and acquiescence, ejaculating " *Uh*, Christ !"

Of James Smith, a fair, stout, fresh-colored man with round features, I recollect little, except that he used to read to us trim verses, with rhymes as pat as butter.   The best of his verses are in the *Rejected Addresses ;* and they are excellent.   Isaac Hawkins Browne with his *Pipe of Tobacco*, and all the rhyming *jeux-d'esprit* in all the Tracts, are extinguished in the comparison ; not excepting the *Probationary Odes.*   Mr. Fitzgerald found himself bankrupt in *non sequiturs ;* Crabbe could hardly have known which was which, himself or his parodist ; and Lord Byron confessed to me, that the summing up of his philosophy, to-wit, that

"Naught is every thing, and every thing is naught,"

was very posing.   Mr. Smith would sometimes repeat after dinner, with his brother Horace, an imaginary dialogue, stuffed full of incongruities, that made us roll with laughter. His ordinary verse and prose were too full of the ridicule of city pretensions.   To be superior to any thing, it should not always be running in one's head.

His brother Horace was delicious.   Lord Byron used to say, that this epithet should be applied only to eatables ; and that he wondered a friend of his (I forget who) that was critical in matters of eating, should use it in any other sense. I know not what the present usage may be in the circles, but classical authority is against his lordship, from Cicero downward ; and I am content with the modern warrant of another noble wit, the famous Lord Peterborough, who, in his fine, open way, said of Fenelon, that he was such a "delicious creature, he was forced to get away from him, else he would have made him pious l", I grant there is something in the word delicious which may be said to comprise a reference to every species of pleasant taste. It is at once a quintessence and a compound ; and a friend, to deserve the epithet, ought, perhaps, to be capable of delighting us as much over our wine, as on graver occasions. Fenelon himself could do this, with all his piety ; or rather he could do it because his piety was of the true sort, and relished of every thing that was sweet and affectionate. A finer nature than Horace Smith's, except in the single instance of Shelley, I never met with in man ; nor even in that instance, all circumstances considered, have I a right to say that those who knew him as intimately as I did the other, would not have had the same reasons to love him. Shelley himself had the highest regard for Horace Smith, as may be seen by the following verses, the initials in which the reader has here the pleasure of filling up :

> " Wit and sense,
> Virtue and human knowledge, all that might
> Make this dull world a business of delight,
> Are all combined in H. S."

Horace Smith differed with Shelley on some points ; but on others, which all the world agree to praise highly and to practice very little, he agreed so entirely, and showed unequivocally that he did agree, that with the exception of one person (Vincent Novello), too diffident to gain such an honor from his friends, they were the only two men I had then met with, from whom I could have received and did receive advice or remonstrance with perfect comfort, because I could be sure of the unmixed motives and entire absence of self-reflection, with which it would come from them.* Shelley said to me once, " I know not what Horace Smith must take me for sometimes : I am afraid he must think me a strange fellow : but is it not odd, that the only truly

---

* Notwithstanding his caprices of temper, I must add Hazlitt, who was quite capable, when he chose, of giving genuine advice, and making you sensible of his disinterestedness. Lamb could have done it, too ; but for interference of any sort he had an abhorrence.

generous person I ever knew, who had money to be generous with, should be a stockbroker! And he writes poetry
too," continued Shelley, his voice rising in a fervor of astonishment; "he writes poetry and pastoral dramas, and yet
knows how to make money, and does make it, and is still
generous!" Shelley had reason to like him. Horace Smith
was one of the few men, who, through a cloud of detraction,
and through all that difference of conduct from the rest of
the world, which naturally excites obloquy, discerned the
greatness of my friend's character. Indeed he became a witness to a very unequivocal proof of it, which I shall mention
by-and-by. The mutual esteem was accordingly very great,
and arose from circumstances most honorable to both parties.
"I believe," said Shelley, on another occasion, "that I have
only to say to Horace Smith that I want a hundred pounds
or two, and he would send it me without any eye to its
being returned; such faith has he that I have something
within me beyond what the world supposes, and that I
could only ask his money for a good purpose." And Shelley
would have sent for it accordingly, if the person for whom
it was intended had not said Nay. I will now mention the
circumstance which first gave my friend a regard for Horace
Smith. It concerns the person just mentioned, who is a man
of letters. It came to Mr. Smith's knowledge, many years
ago, that this person was suffering under a pecuniary trouble.
He knew little of him at the time, but had met him occasionally; and he availed himself of this circumstance to
write him a letter as full of delicacy and cordiality as it
could hold, making it a matter of grace to accept a bank-
note of £100 which he inclosed. I speak on the best authority, that of the obliged person himself; who adds that he not
only did accept the money, but felt as light and happy under
the obligation, as he has felt miserable under the very report
of being obliged to some; and he says, that nothing could
induce him to withhold his name, but a reason, which the
generous, during his life-time, would think becoming.

I have said that Horace Smith was a stockbroker. He
left business with a fortune and went to live in France,
where, if he did not increase, he did not seriously diminish

it; and France added to the pleasant stock of his knowledge.

On returning to England, he set about exerting himself in a manner equally creditable to his talents and interesting to the public.   I would not insult either the
modesty or the understanding of my friend while he was
alive, by comparing him with the author of *Old Mortality*
and *Guy Mannering :* but I ventured to say, and I repeat,
that the earliest of his novels, *Brambletye House*, ran a hard
race with the novel of *Woodstock*, and that it contained more
than one character not unworthy of the best volumes of Sir
Walter.   I allude to the ghastly troubles of the Regicide in
his lone house ; the outward phlegm and merry inward malice of Winkey Boss (a happy name), who gravely smoked a
pipe with his mouth, and laughed with his eyes; and, above
all, to the character of the princely Dutch merchant, who
would cry out that he should be ruined, at seeing a few
nutmegs dropped from a bag, and then go and give a thousand ducats for an antique.   This is hitting the high
mercantile character to a nicety, minute and careful in its
means, princely in its ends.   If the ultimate effect of commerce (*permulti transibunt*, &c.) were not something very
different from what its pursuers imagine, the character
would be a dangerous one to society at large, because it
throws a gloss over the spirit of money-getting ; but, meanwhile, nobody could paint it better, or has a greater right to
recommend it, than he who has been the first to make it a
handsome portrait.

The personal appearance of Horace Smith, like that of
most of the individuals I have met with, was highly indica-
tive of his character.   His figure was good and manly, inclining to the robust ; and his countenance extremely frank
and cordial; sweet without weakness..   I have been told he
was irascible.   If so, it must have been no common offense
that could have irritated him.   He had not a jot of it in his
appearance.

Another set of acquaintances which I made at this time
used to assemble at the hospitable table of Mr. Hunter the
bookseller, in St. Paul's Church-yard.   They were the sur-

vivors of the literary party that were accustomed to dine
with his predecessor, Mr. Johnson. They came, as of old,
on the Friday. The most regular were Fuseli and Bonnycastle. Now and then, Godwin was present: oftener Mr.
Kinnaird the magistrate, a great lover of Horace.

Fuseli was a small man, with energetic features, and a
white head of hair. Our host's daughter, then a little girl,
used to call him the white-headed lion. He combed his
hair up from the forehead; and as his whiskers were large,
his face was set in a kind of hairy frame, which, in addition
to the fierceness of his look, really gave him an aspect of that
sort. Otherwise, his features were rather sharp than round.
He would have looked much like an old military officer,
if his face, besides its real energy, had not affected more.
There was the same defect in it as in his pictures. Conscious of not having all the strength he wished, he endeavored to make out for it by violence and pretension. He carried
this so far, as to look fiercer than usual when he sat for his
picture. His friend and engraver, Mr. Houghton, drew an
admirable likeness of him in this state of dignified extravagance. He is sitting back in his chair, leaning on his hand,
but looking ready to pounce withal. His notion of repose
was like that of Pistol:

" Now, Pistol, lay thy head in Furies' lap."

Agreeably to this over-wrought manner, he was reckoned, I
believe, not quite so bold as he might have been. He painted horrible pictures, as children tell horrible stories; and was
frightened at his own lay figures. Yet he would hardly
have talked as he did about his terrors, had he been as timid
as some supposed him. With the affected, impression is the
main thing, let it be produced how it may. A student of
the Academy told me, that Mr. Fuseli coming in one night,
when a solitary candle had been put on the floor in a corner
of the room, to produce some effect or other, he said it looked " like a damned soul." This was by way of being Dan-
tesque, as Michael Angelo was. Fuseli was an ingenious
caricaturist of that master, making great bodily displays of
mental energy, and being ostentatious with his limbs and

muscles, in proportion as he could not draw them.   A leg or an arm was to be thrust down one's throat, because he knew we should dispute the truth of it.   In the indulgence of this willfulness of purpose, generated partly by impatience of study, partly by want of sufficient genius, and no doubt, also, by a sense of superiority to artists who could do nothing but draw correctly, he cared for no time, place, or circumstance, in his pictures.   A set of prints, after his designs for Shakspeare and Cowper, exhibit a chaos of mingled genius and absurdity, such as, perhaps, was never before seen.   He endeavored to bring Michael Angelo's apostles and prophets, with their super-human ponderousness of intention, into the commonplaces of modern life.   A student reading in a garden is all over intensity of muscle ; and the quiet tea-table scene in Cowper, he has turned into a preposterous conspiracy of huge men and women, all bent upon showing their thews and postures, with dresses as fantastical as their minds.   One gentleman, of the existence of whose trowsers you are not aware till you see the terminating line at the ankle, is sitting and looking grim on a sofa, with his hat on and no waistcoat.   Yet there is real genius in his designs for Milton, though disturbed, as usual, by strainings after the energetic. His most extraordinary mistake, after all, is said to have been on the subject of his coloring.   It was a sort of livid green, like brass diseased.   Yet they say, that when praised for one of his pictures, he would modestly observe, " It is a pretty color."   This might have been thought a jest on his part, if remarkable stories were not told of the mistakes made by other people with regard to color.   Sight seems the least agreed upon, of all the senses.

Fuseli was lively and interesting in conversation, but not without his usual faults of violence and pretension.   Nor was he always as decorous as an old man ought to be ; especially one whose turn of mind is not of the lighter and and more pleasurable cast.   The licenses he took were coarse, and had not sufficient regard to his company.   Certainly they went a great deal beyond his friend Armstrong ; to whose account I believe, Fuseli's passion for swearing was laid.   The poet condescended to be a great swearer, and

Fuseli thought it energetic to swear like him. His friendship with Bonnycastle had something childlike and agreeable
in it. They came and went away together like a couple of
old schoolboys. They, also, like boys, rallied one another,
and sometimes made a singular display of it—Fuseli, at
least, for it was he that was the aggressor. I remember,
one day, Bonnycastle told a story of a Frenchman, whom
he had received at his house at Woolwich, and who invited
him, in return, to visit him in Paris, if ever he should cross
the water. "The Frenchman told me," said he, "that he
had a *superb local.* When I went to Paris I called on him,
and found he had a good prospect out of his window; but
his *superb local* was at a hair-dresser's, up two pair of stairs."

"Vell, vell!" said Fuseli, impatiently (for though he spoke
and wrote English remarkably well, he never got rid of his
Swiss pronunciation), "Vell—vay not? vay not? Vat is
to hinder his local being superb for all *thtat?*"

"I don't see," returned Bonnycastle, "how a barber's
house in an alley can be a superb local."

"You doan't! Vell—but thtat is not the barber's fault,
it is yours."

"How do you make that out? I'm not an alley."

"No; but you're so coarsedly eegnorant."

"I may be as ignorant as you are polite; but you don't
prove any thing."

"Thte thtevil I doan't! Did you not say he had a faine
prospect out of window?"

"Yes, he had a prospect fine enough!"

"Vell, thtat constituted his superb local. A superb local
is not a barber's shop, by Goade! but a faine situation. But
thtat is your coarsed eegnorance of thte language."

Another time, on Bonnycastle's saying that there were
no longer any *auto-da-fés,* Fuseli said he did not know that.
"At all events," said he, if *you* were to go into Spain, they
would have an *auto-da-fé* immediately on the strength of
your appearance.

Bonnycastle was a good fellow, he was a tall, gaunt,
long-headed man, with large features and spectacles, and a
deep internal voice, with a twang of rusticity in it; and he

K*

goggled over his plate, like a horse. I often thought that
a bag of corn would have hung well on him. His laugh
was equine, and showed his teeth upward at the sides.
Wordsworth, who notices similar mysterious manifestations
on the part of donkeys, would have thought it ominous.
Bonnycastle was passionately fond of quoting Shakspeare,
and telling stories; and if the *Edinburgh Review* had just
come out, would give us all the jokes in it. He had once
an hypochondriacal disorder of long duration ; and he told
us, that he should never forget the comfortable sensation
given him one night during this disorder, by his knocking a
landlord, that was insolent to him, down the man's staircase.
On the strength of this piece of energy (having first ascertained that the offender was not killed) he went to bed,
and had a sleep of unusual soundness. Perhaps Bonnycastle
thought more highly of his talents than the amount of them
strictly warranted ; a mistake to which scientific men appear
to be more liable than others, the universe they work in being
so large, and their universality (in Bacon's sense of the word)
being often so small. But the delusion was not only par-
donable, but desirable, in a man so zealous in the performance of his duties, and so much of a human being to all about
him, as Bonnycastle was. It was delightful one day to hear
him speak with complacency of a translation which had
appeared of one of his books in Arabic, and which began
by saying, on the part of the translator, that "it had pleased
God, for the advancement of human knowledge, to raise us
up a Bonnycastle." Some of his stories were a little romantic, and no less authentic. He had an anecdote of a
Scotchman, who boasted of being descended from the Admirable Crichton ; in proof of which, the Scotchman said
he had " a grit quantity of table-leenen in his possassion,
marked A. C., Admirable Creechton."

Kinnaird, the magistrate, was a stout, sanguine man,
under the middle height, with a fine, lamping black eye,
lively to the last, and a person that "had increased, was
increasing, and ought to have been diminished ; which is
by no means what he thought of the prerogative. Next to
his bottle he was fond of his Horace ; and, in the intervals

of business at the police-office, would enjoy both in his arm-chair. Between the vulgar calls of this kind of magistracy, and the perusal of the urbane Horace, there must have been a gusto of contradiction, which the bottle, perhaps, was re-quired to render quite palatable. Fielding did not love his bottle the less for being obliged to lecture the drunken. Nor did his son, who succeeded him in taste and office. I know not how a former poet-laureat, Mr. Pye managed ; another man of letters, who was fain to accept a situation of this kind. Having been a man of fortune and a member of Par-liament and loving his Horace to boot, he could hardly have done without his wine. I saw him once in a state of scorn-ful indignation at being interrupted in the perusal of a manuscript by the monitions of his police-officers, who were obliged to remind him over and over again that he was a magistrate, and that the criminal multitude were in waiting. Every time the door opened, he threatened and implored.

> "Otium divos rogat in patenti
> Prensus."

Had you quoted this to Mr. Kinnaird, his eyes would have sparkled with good-fellowship : he would have finished the verse and the bottle with you, and proceeded to as many more as your head could stand. Poor fellow ; the last time I saw him, he was an apparition formidably substantial. The door of our host's dining-room opened without my hear-ing it, and, happening to turn round, I saw a figure in a great coat, literally almost as broad as it was long, and scarcely able to articulate. He was dying of a dropsy, and was obliged to revive himself, before he was fit to converse, by the wine that was killing him. But he had cares besides, and cares of no ordinary description ; and, for my part, I will not blame even his wine for killing him, unless his cares could have done it more agreeably. After dinner that day, he was comparatively himself again, quoted his Horace as usual, talked of lords and courts with a relish, and begged that *God save the King* might be played to him on the piano-forte ; to which he listened, as if his soul had taken its hat off. I believe he would have liked to die to *God save the King*, and to have " waked and found those visions true."

CHAPTER XI.

THE *Examiner* had been set up toward the close of the reign of George the Third, three years before the appointment of the regency. Pitt and Fox had died two years before; the one, in middle life, of constant ill-success, preying on a sincere but proud, and not very large mind, and unwisely supported by a habit of drinking; the other, of older but more genial habits of a like sort, and of demands beyond his strength by a sudden accession to office. The king—a conscientious but narrow-minded man, obstinate to a degree of disease (which had lost him America), and not always dealing ingenuously, even with his advisers—had lately got rid of Mr. Fox's successors, on account of their urging the Catholic claims. He had summoned to office in their stead Lords Castlereagh, Liverpool, and others, who had been the clerks of Mr. Pitt; and Bonaparte was at the height of his power as French emperor, setting his brothers on thrones, and compelling our Russian and German allies to side with him under the most mortifying circumstances of tergiversation.

It is a melancholy period for the potentates of the earth, when they fancy themselves obliged to resort to the shabbiest measures of the feeble; siding against a friend with his enemy; joining in accusations against him at the latter's dictation; believed by nobody on either side; returning to the friend, and retreating from him, according to the fortunes of war ; secretly hoping, that the friend will excuse them by reason of the pauper's plea, necessity ; and at no time able to give better apologies for their conduct than those "mysterious ordinations of Providence," which are the last refuge of the destitute in morals, and a reference to which they contemptuously deny to the thief and the "king's evidence." It proves to them, "with a vengeance," the "something rotten in the state of Denmark ;" and will continue to prove it, and to be despicable, whether in bad or good fortune, till the world find out a cure for the rottenness.

Yet this is what the allies of England were in the habit of doing, through the whole contest of England with France. When England succeeded in getting, up a coalition against Napoleon, they denounced him for his ambition, and set out to fight him. When the coalition was broken by his armies, they turned round at his bidding, denounced England, and joined him in fighting against their ally. And this was the round of their history : a coalition and a tergiversation alternately ; now a speech and a fight against Bonaparte, who beat them ; then a speech and a fight against England, who bought them off ; then, again, a speech and a fight against Bonaparte, who beat them again ; and then, as before, a speech and a fight against England, who again bought them off. Meanwhile, they took every thing they could get, whether from enemy or friend, seizing with no less greediness whatever bits of territory Bonaparte threw to them for their meanness, than pocketing the millions of Pitt, for which we are paying to this day.

It becomes us to bow, and to bow humbly, to the "mysterious dispensations of Providence ;" but in furtherance of those very dispensations, it has pleased Providence so to constitute us, as to render us incapable of admiring such conduct, whether in king's evidences or in kings ; and some of the meanest figures that present themselves to the imagination in looking back on the events of those times, are the Emperors of Austria and Russia, and the King of Prussia. It is salutary to bear this in mind, for the sake of royalty itself. What has since ruined Louis Philippe, in spite of all his ability, is his confounding royal privileges with base ones, and his not keeping his word as a gentleman.

If it be still asked, what are kings to do under such cir cumstances as those in which they were placed with Bona- parte ? what is their alternative ? it is to be replied, firstly, that the question has been answered already, by the mode in which the charge is put ; and, secondly, that whatever they do, they must either cease to act basely, and like the mean- est of mankind, or be content to be regarded as such, and to leave such stains on their order as tend to produce its down- fall, and to exasperate the world into the creation of republics. Republics, in the first instance, are never desired for their own sakes.　I do not think they will be finally desired at all ; certainly not unaccompanied by courtly graces and good breeding, and whatever can tend to secure to them orna- ment as well as utility.　I do not think it is in human nature to be content with a different settlement of the old question, any more than it is in nature physical to dispense. with her pomp of flowers, and colors.　But sure I am, that the first cravings for republics always originate in some despair created by the conduct of kings.

It might be amusing to bring together a few of the exor- diums of those same speeches, or state papers, of the allies of George the Third ; but I have not time to look for them ; and perhaps they would prove tiresome.　It is more interesting to consider the "state" which Bonaparte kept in those days, and to compare it with his exile in St. Helena.　There are more persons, perhaps, in the present generation who think of Bonaparte as the captive of Great Britain, defeated by Wellington, than as the maker of kings and queens, reigning in Paris, and bringing monarchs about his footstool.　The following is the figure he used to make in the French news- papers at the time when the *Examiner* was set up.

NAPOLEON AND RUSSIA.

"Tilsit, *June* 25, 1807.

" This day at one o'clock, the emperor, accompanied by the Grand Duke of Berg, the Prince of Neufchâtel, Marshal Bessieres, the Grand Marshal of the Palace, Duroc, and the Grand Equery, Caulaincourt, embarked on the banks of the Niemen, in a boat prepared for the purpose. They proceeded to the middle of the river, were General Lariboissiere, commanding the artillery of the guard, had caused a raft to be placed, and a pavilion erected upon it. Close by it was another raft and pavilion for their majesties' suite. At the same moment the Emperor Alexander set out from the right bank, accompanied by the Grand Duke Constantine, General Beningsen, General Ouvaroff, Prince Labanoff, and his principal aid-de-camp, Count Lieven. The two boats arrived at the same instant, and the two emperors embraced each other as soon as they set foot on the raft. - They entered together the saloon which was prepared for them, and remained there during two hours. The conference having been concluded, the persons composing the suite of the two emperors were introduced, The Emperor Alexander paid the handsomest compliments to the officers who accompanied the emperor, who, on his part, had a long conversation with the Grand Duke Constantine and General Beningsen.''

[Note.—That the compliments to officers are all paid by the vanquished man, the Emperor of Russia.]

NAPOLEON AND AUSTRIA.

"Paris, *April* 4, 1810.

"The civil marriage of his majesty the emperor and king, with the archduchess, of Austria, took place at St. Cloud, on the 1st instant, and the public entry into Paris, and the religious ceremony, the next day. Previously to the public entry, the weather had been very unpropitious, but on the firing of the cannon the clouds dispersed, and a serene sky and brilliant sunshine enabled the Parisians to enjoy the pageantry, illuminations, &c. &c., which continued during the whole week. At the civil marriage ceremony, their imperial majesties having taken their seats on the throne, the princes and princesses ranged themselves in the following order :

"To the right of the emperor, Madame ; Prince Louis Napoleon, King of Holland ; Prince Jerome Napoleon, King of Westphalia ; Prince Borghese, Duke of Guastalla ; Prince Joachim Napoleon, King of Naples ; Prince Eugene, Viceroy of Italy ; the Prince Arch-Chancellor ; the Prince Vice Grand Elector. To the left of the empress, the Princess Julia, Queen of Spain ; the Princess Hortense, Queen of Holland ; the Princess Catharine, Queen of Westphalia ; the Princess Eliza, Grand Duchess of Tuscany ; the Princess Pauline ; the Princess Caroline, Queen of Naples ; the Grand Duke of Wurtzburg ; the Princess Augusta, Vice-Queen of Italy ; the Princess Stephanie, Hereditary Grand Duchess of Baden ; the Prince Arch-Treasurer ; the Prince Vice-Constable, &c. &c.''

Look on those pictures, and on the following :

"St. Helena, *December* 17, 1820.

"It is a great crime here to call Bonaparte Emperor.
"He appears very unhappy. The governor will have no communi-

cation with Bertrand, and Bonaparte will not receive any except through him. This system of vexation is said to annoy him considerably ; and combined with the other measures adopted toward him and his follow ers, tends to keep his mind in a state of continual irritation."

"*May* 15, 1821.

" Bonaparte died (on the 5th instant) after an illness of six weeks He must have suffered great pain, though no complaint was uttered For several days previous to his death, he had his son's bust placed at the foot of his bed, and constantly kept his eyes fixed upon it, till he breathed his last."

But the fortunes of Napoleon were on the decline, when they appeared to be at their height. The year 1808 beheld at once their culmination and their descent; and it was the feeblest of his vassals who—by the very excess of his servility —gave the signal for the change. Fortunately, too, for the interests of mankind, the change was caused by a violation of the most obvious principles of justice and good sense. It was owing to the unblushing seizure of Spain. It was owing to the gross and unfeeling farce of a pretended sympathy with the Spanish king's quarrel with his son ; to the acceptance of a throne which the ridiculous father had no right to give away ; and to the endeavor to force the accession on a country, which, instead of tranquilly admitting it on the new principles of indifference to religion and zeal for advancement (as he had ignorantly expected), opposed it with the united vehemence of dogged bigotry and an honest patriotism.

Spain was henceforth the millstone hung round the neck of the conqueror ; and his marriage with a princess of Aus-tria, which was thought such a wonderful piece of success, only furnished him with a like impediment ; for it added to the weight of his unpopularity with all honest and prospect-ive minds. It was well said by Cobbett, that he had much better have assembled a hundred of the prettiest girls in France, and selected the prettiest of them all for his wife. The heads and hearts of the " Young Continent" were hence-forward against the self-seeker, ambitious of the old " shows of things," in contradiction to the honest "desires of the mind." Want of sympathy was prepared for him in case of a reverse; and when, partly in the confidence of his military pride, partly by way of making a final set-off against his difficulties in Spain, and partly in very ignorance of what Russian natures and Russian winters could effect, he went and ran his head against the great northern wall of ice and snow, he came back a ruined man, masterly and surprising as his efforts to reinstate himself might thereafter be. Nothing remained for him but to fume and fret in spirit, get fatter with a vitiated state of body, and see reverse on reverse coming round him, which he was to face to no purpose. The grandest thing he did was to return from Elba : the next, to fight the battle of Waterloo ; but he went to the field, bloated and half asleep, in a carriage. He had already, in body, become one of the commonest of those "emperors" whom he had first laughed at and then leagued with : no great principle stood near him, as it did in the times of the republic, when armies of shoeless youths beat the veteran troops of Austria ; and thus, deserted by every thing but his veterans and his generalship, which came to nothing before the unyieldingness of English, and the advent of Prussian soldiers, he became a fugitive in the " belle France" which he had fancied his own, and died a prisoner in the hands of a man of the name of Lowe.

I do not believe that George the Third, or his minister, Mr. Pitt, speculated at all upon a catastrophe like this. I mean, that I do not believe they reckoned upon Napoleon destroying himself by his own ambition. They looked, it is true, to the chance of "something turning up ;" but it was to be of the ordinary kind. They thought to put him down by paid coalitions, and in the regular course of war. Hence, on repeated failures, the minister's broken heart, and probably the final extinguishment of the king's reason. The latter calamity, by a most unfortunate climax of untimeliness, took place a little before his enemy's reverses.

George the Third was a very brave and honest man. He feared nothing on earth, and he acted according to his convictions. But, unfortunately, his convictions were at the mercy of a will far greater than his understanding ; and hence his courage became obstinacy and his honesty the dupe of his inclinations. He was the son of a father with little brain, and of a mother who had a diseased blood : indeed, neither of his parents was healthy. He was brought up in rigid principles of morality on certain points, by persons who are supposed to have evaded them in their own conduct : he was taught undue notions of kingly prerogative ; he was suffered to grow up, nevertheless, in homely as well as shy and moody habits ; and, while acquiring a love of power tending to the violent and uncontrollable, he was not permitted to have a taste of it, till he became his own master. The consequence of this training were an extraordinary mixture of domestic virtue with official duplicity ; of rustical, mechanical tastes and popular manners, with the most exalted ideas of authority ; of a childish and self-betraying cunning, with the most stubborn reserves ; of fearlessness with sordidness ; good-nature with unforgivingness ; and of the health and strength of temperance and self-denial, with the last weaknesses of understanding, and passions that exasperated it out of its reason. The English nation were pleased to see in him a crowning specimen of themselves—a royal John Bull. They did not discover, till too late (perhaps have not yet discovered), how much of the objectionable, as well as the respectable, lies hidden in the sturdy nickname invented for them by Arbuthnot ; how much the animal predominates in it over the intellectual ; and how terribly the bearer of it may be overdriven, whether in a royal or a national shape. They had much better get some new name for themselves, worthy of the days of Queen Victoria and of the hopes of the world.

In every shape I reverence calamity, and would not be thought to speak of it with levity, especially in connection with a dynasty which has since become estimable, as well as reasonable, in every respect.

If the histories of private as well as public families were known, the race of the Guelphs would only be found, in the person of one of their ancestors, to have shared, in common perhaps with every family in the world, the sorrows of occasioual deterioration. But in the greatest and most tragical examples of human suffering, the homeliest, as well as the loftiest images, are too often forced on the mind together.

George the Third, with all his faults, was a more estimable man than many of his enemies, and, certainly, than any of his wholesale revilers; and the memory of his last days is sanctified by whatever can render the loss of sight and of reason affecting. In one respect, when sensible of his calamity, he must have experienced a great relief. He saw that none of his children were liable to it. They had been saved by the infusion of colder and more judicious blood from another German stock. George the Fourth, though not a wise man, had as sane a constitution as any man in his dominions; and since the accession of his brother William, royalty and reason have never gone more harmoniously together, than they have done on the throne of Great Britain.

Whatever of any kind has taken place in the world, may have been best for all of us in the long run. Nature permits us, retrospectively, and for comfort's sake, though not in a different spirit, to entertain that conclusion among others. But meantime, either because the world is not yet old enough to know better, or because we yet live but in the tuning of its instruments, and have not learned to play the harmonies of the earth sweetly, men feel incited by what is good as well as bad in them, to object and to oppose; and youth being the season of inexperience and of vanity, as well as of enthusiasm otherwise the most disinterested, the *Examiner*, which began its career, like most papers, with thinking the worst of those from whom it differed, and expressing its mind accordingly with fearless sincerity (which was not equally the case with those papers), it speedily excited the anger of government. It did this the more, inasmuch as, according to what has been stated of its opinions on foreign politics, and in matters of church-government, it did not fall into the common and half-conciliating, because degrading error of antagonists, by siding, as a matter of course, with the rest of its enemies.

I need not re-open the questions of foreign and domestic policy, which were mooted with the ruling powers in those days, Reform in particular. The result is well known, and the details in general have ceased to be interesting. I would repeat none of them at all, if personal history did not give a new zest to almost any kind of relation. As such, however, is the case, I shall proceed to observe, that the *Examiner* had not been established a year, when government instituted a prosecution against it, in consequence of some remarks on a pamphlet by a Major Hogan, who accused the Duke of York, as commander-in-chief, of favoritism and corruption.

Major Hogan was a furious but honest Irishman, who had been in the army seventeen years. He had served and suffered bitterly; in the West Indies he possessed the highest testimonials to his character, had been a very active recruiting officer, had seen forty captains promoted over his head in spite of repeated applications and promises, and he desired, after all, nothing but the permission to purchase his advancement, agreeably to every custom.

Provoked out of his patience by these fruitless endeavors to buy, what others who had done nothing, obtained for nothing, and being particularly disgusted at being told, for the sixth time, that he had been " noted for promotion, and would be duly considered, as favorable opportunities offered," the gallant Hibernian went straight, without any further ado, to the office of the commander-in-chief, and there, with a vivacity and plain-speaking which must have looked like a scene in a play, addressed his Royal Highness in a speech that astounded him :

"I submitted (says he) to his Royal Highness's recollection, the long time I had been seeking for promotion, and begged him to take into his consideration the nature of the circumstances under which I was recommended to his notice; particularly pressing upon his attention, that, in the course of the time I had been 'noted' on his Royal Highness's list, upward of forty captains had been promoted without purchase, all of whom were junior to me in rank, and many of them, indeed, were not in the army when I was a captain. I added, almost literally, in these words, 'My applications for promotion have been made in the manner prescribed by the practice of the army, and by the king's regulations; unfortunately without success. Other ways, please your Royal Highness, have been recommended to me; and frequent propositions have been made by those who affected to possess the means of securing that object, that for 600*l.* I could obtain a majority without purchase, which is little more than half the sum {

had lodged to purchase promotion in the regular course.* But I rejected such a proposition; for, even were such a thing possible, I would feel it unworthy of me, as a British officer and a man, to owe the king's commission to low intrigue or petticoat influence!' I expected the instantaneous expression of his Royal Highness's *gratitude* for such a candid declaration. I looked for an immediate demand for explanation, and was prepared with ample evidence to satisfy his Highness, that such proceedings were going on daily, as were disgraceful to the character of the army. But no question was put to me; his royal mind seemed astounded, *vox faucibus hæsit,* and I retired."

Having thus dumfounded the unhappy commander-in-chief, the major, in his pamphlet, turned round upon certain acquaintances of his Royal Highness, and thus further proceeded to astonish the public:

"It has been observed to me (says he), by connoisseurs, that I should have had no reason to complain, if I had proceeded in the proper way to seek promotion. But what is meant by the proper way? I applied to the Duke of York, because he was commander-in-chief. To his Royal Highness I was directed by the King's order to apply; and with these orders alone I felt it consistent with my duty as an officer, and my honor as a gentleman, to comply. But if any other person had been the substitute of the Duke of York, I should have made my application to that person. If a Cooke, a Creswell, a Clarke, a Sinclair, or a Carey, or any other name had been invested by his Majesty with the office of commander-in-chief, to that person I should have applied. Nay, if it had pleased his Majesty to confer upon a female the direct command of the army, I should have done my duty, in applying to the legal depository of power. But to no one other should I condescend to apply; for I scorn undue influence, and feel incapable of enjoying any object, however intrinsically valuable, that should be procured by such means.

"I have that evidence by me (he observes); indeed, I am in possession of such facts, as it would be imprudent in me to write, and as no printer in England perhaps would venture to publish. But if any member of either House of Parliament should be disposed to take up the subject, I can furnish him with materials that would enable him to make such an *exposé,* as shall stagger even the credulity proverbially ascribed to this country.

-----

* "The money paid in the regular course goes into a public fund, which is not tangible by any public officer for private purposes, while the private douceur is wholly applicable to such purposes."—*The Major's Pamphlet.*

" As some proof that I am known to possess materials that are calculated to excite alarm among those who must recollect their own acts, and, if they are at all sensible, must be fully conscious of their objectionable character, I have to state the following extraordinary fact: About dusk on the evening of the first day my advertisement appeared, a lady in a dashing barouche, with two footmen, called at the newspaper-office for my address. She must be, no doubt, one of the vulnerable corps, or their agent; as, upon the following evening, at my lodgings, the waiter delivered me a letter, which I opened in the presence of four gentlemen, whose attestation to the fact appears below. The following is a copy of the letter :

" ' SIR—The inclosed will answer for the deficit of which you complain, and which was not allowed you through mere oversight. I hope this will prevent the publication of your intended pamphlet; and, if it does, you may rely on a better situation than the one you had. When I find that you have given up all your secrets from public view, which would hurt you with all the royal family, I shall make myself known to you, and shall be happy in your future acquaintance and friendship; by which, I promise you, you will reap much benefit. If you recall the advertisment, you shall hear from me, and your claims shall be rewarded as they deserve.

" 'MAJOR HOGAN.'
" ' Saturday, 27th August, 1808.

" ' We, the undersigned, do hereby certify, that we were present when Major Hogan opened this letter and inclosure, containing four bank-notes to the amount of four hundred pounds.

" ' JOHN DANIEL, late Capt. 17th Light Drags.
FRANCIS MOE.
HENRY WHEAT, Lieut. 32d Regt.
LEWIS GASQUET, late Lieut. 20th Light Drags.

' Frank's Coffee-house.'

" ' I do hereby certify, that this letter was delivered to me at the door by a lady, who particularly desired me to be careful to give it to Major Hogan, and instantly went away : it was dusk at the time ; I returned into the coffee-room and delivered the letter.

" 'GEORGE FOZED,
" ' Waiter, Frank's Coffee-house.

" But such expedients shall have no effect upon the revelations of
" D. HOGAN.

" Frank's Hotel, 3, Brook-street, Sept. 2, 1808.

" P. S.—The person who inclosed the four hundred pounds, not having left any address, I can not ascertain to whom I am to return that sum ; but if the numbers of the notes received are sent to No 14 Angel-court, Throgmorton-street, the money will be returned. D. H."

The *Examiner* made comments on these disclosures, of a nature that was to be expected from its ardor in the cause of Reform; not omitting, however, to draw a distinction between the rights of domestic privacy and the claims to indulgence set up by traffickers in public corruption. The government, however, cared nothing for this distinction; neither would it have had the corruption inquired into. Its prosecutions were of a nature that did not allow truth to be investigated; and one of these was accordingly instituted against us, when it was unexpectedly turned aside by a member of Parliament, Colonel Wardle, who was resolved to bring the female alluded to by Major Hogan before the notice of that tribunal.

I say "unexpectedly," because neither then, nor at any time, had I the least knowledge of Colonel Wardle. The *Examiner*, so to speak, lived quite alone. It sought nobody; and its principles in this respect had already become so well understood that few sought it, and no one succeeded in making its acquaintance. The colonel's motion for an investigation came upon us, therefore, like a god-send. The prosecution against the paper was dropped; and the whole attention of the country was drawn to the strange spectacle of a laughing, impudent woman, brought to the bar of the House of Commons, and forcing them to laugh in their turn at the effrontery of her answers. The poor Duke of York had parted with her, and she had turned against him.

The following is a specimen of the dialogue:

Question. Who brought that message?
Answer. A particular friend of the duke's—Mr. Taylor, a shoemaker in Bond-street—(*a laugh*).
Q. Pray, by whom did you send your desires to the duke?
A. By my own pen.
Q. I wish to know who brought the letter?
A. Why, the same Embassador of Morocco—(*loud laughing.*) The witness was here called to order by the Speaker, and admonished to be more circumspect, or she would receive the censure of the House.
Q. What is your husband's name?
A. Clarke.
Q. Where were you married?
A. Mr. W. Adam can tell. (Adam was the duke's agent.)

Q. Did you not say you were married in Berkhampstead church?

A. No; I merely laughed at it, when I heard it.

Q. Did you ever see Mr. Alderman Clarke, or do you now believe that your husband was his nephew?

A. I don't recollect having seen Mr. Alderman Clarke; and as to my husband, I never took any pains to ascertain any thing respecting him, since I quitted him. He is nothing to me, nor I to him.

Q. But what profession was he of?

A. None that I know of; but his father was a builder. (He was understood to be a mason.)

      *   *   *   *   *

Q. Have you not, at various times, received money from Mr. Dowler? (Dowler was Assistant-Commissary of Stores.)

A. At some particular times. I had a thousand pounds from him for his situation.

Q. Do you owe any money to Mr. Dowler?

A. I never recollect my debts to gentlemen—(*a loud burst of laughter*).

The upshot of the investigation was, that Mrs. Clarke had evidently made money by the seekers of military promotion, but that the duke was pronounced innocent of connivance. His Royal Highness withdrew however from office for a time (for he was not long afterward reinstated), and public opinion, as to his innocence or guilt, went meanwhile pretty much according to that of party.

My own impression, at this distance of time, and after better knowledge of the duke's private history and prevailing character, is, that there was some connivance on his part, but not of a systematic nature, or beyond what he may have considered as warrantable toward a few special friends of his mistress, on the assumption that she would carry her influence no farther. His own letters proved that he allowed her to talk to him of people with a view to promotion. He even let her recommend him a clergyman, who (as he phrased it) had an ambition to " preach before royalty." He said he would do what he could to bring it about; probably thinking nothing whatsoever—I mean, never having the thought enter his head—of the secret scandal of the thing, or not regarding his consent as any thing but a piece of good-natured patronizing, acquiescence, after the ordinary fashion of the " ways of the world."

For, in truth, the duke of York was as good-natured a

man as he was far from being a wise one. The investigation gave him a salutary caution ; but I really believe, on
the whole,'that he had already been, as he was afterward,
a very good, conscientious war-offiee clerk. He was a brave
man, though no general ; a very filial, if not a very thinking
politician (for he always voted to please his father); and if
he had no idea of economy, it is to be recollected how easily
princes' debts are incurred—how often encouraged by the
creditors who complain of them; and how often, and how
temptingly to the debtor, they are paid off by governments.

As to his amours, the temptations of royalty that way
are still greater : the duke seems to have regarded a mistress
in a very tender and conjugal point of view, as long as the
lady chose to be equally considerate ; and if people wondered why such a loving man did not love his duchess—who
appears to have been as good-natured as himself—the wonder
ceased when they discovered, that her Royal Highness was
a lady of so whimsical a taste, and possessed such an overflowing amount of benevolence toward the respectable race
of beings, hight dogs, that in the constant occupation of looking after the welfare of some scores of her canine friends, she
had no leisure to cultivate the society of those human ones,
that could better dispense with her attentions.

The ministers naturally grudged the *Examiner* its escape
from the Hogan prosecution, especially as they gained nothing
with the paper, in consequence of their involuntary forbear-
ance. Accordingly, before another year was out, they instituted a second prosecution ; and so eager were they to
bring it, that, in their haste, they again overleaped their
prudence. Readers in the present times, when more libels
have been written in a week by Toryism itself against
royalty, in the most irreverent style, than appeared in those
days in the course of a year from pens the most radical, and
against princes the most provoking, are astonished to hear,
that the offense we had committed consisted of the following
sentence :

" Of all monarchs since the Revolution, the successor of
George the Third will have the finest opportunity of becoming nobly popular."

But the real offense was the contempt displayed toward the ministers themselves. The article in which the sentence appeared, was entitled " Change of Ministry ; " the Duke of Portland had just retired from the premiership ; and the *Examiner* had been long girding him and his associates on the score of general incompetency, as well as their particular unfitness for constitutional government. The ministers cared nothing for the king, in any sense of personal zeal, or of a particular wish to vindicate or exalt him. The tempers, caprices, and strange notions of sincerity and craft, to which he was subject, by neutralizing in a great measure his ordinary good nature and somewhat exuberant style of intercourse on the side of familiarity and gossiping, did not render him a very desirable person to deal with, even among friends. But he was essentially a Tory king, and so far a favorite of Tories ; he was now terminating the fiftieth year of his reign ; there was to be a jubilee in consequence ; and the ministers thought to turn the loyalty of the holiday into an instrument of personal revenge.

The entire passage charged with being libellous in that article, consisted of the words marked in italics, and the framers of the indictment evidently calculated on the usual identification of a special with a Tory jury. They had reckoned, at the same time, so confidently on the effect to be produced with that class of persons, by any objection to the old king, that the proprietor of the *Morning Chronicle*, Mr. Perry, was prosecuted for having extracted only the two concluding sentences ; and as the government was still more angered with the Whigs who hoped to displace them, than with the Radicals who wished to see them displaced, Mr. Perry's prosecution preceded ours. This was fortunate ; for though the proprietor of the *Morning Chronicle* pleaded his own cause, an occasion in which a man is said to have " a fool for his client" (that is to say, in the opinion of lawyers), he pleaded it so well, and the judge (Ellenborough) who afterward showed himself so zealous a Whig, gave him a hearing and construction so favorable, that he obtained an acquittal, and the prosecution against the *Examiner* accordingly fell to the ground.

I had the pleasure of a visit from this gentleman while his indictment was pending. He came to tell me how he meant to conduct his defense. He was a lively, good-natured man, with a shrewd expression of countenance, and twinkling eyes, which he not unwillingly turned upon the ladies. I had lately married, and happened to be sitting with my wife. A chair was given him close to us; but as·he was very near-sighted, and yet could not well. put up his eyeglass to look at her (which purpose, nevertheless, he was clearly bent on effecting), he took occasion, while speaking of the way in which he should address the jury, to thrust his face close upon hers, observing at the same time, with his liveliest emphasis, and, as if expressly for her information, "I mean to be very modest."

The unexpectedness of this announcement, together with the equivocal turn given to it by the vivacity of his movement, had all the effect of a dramatic surprise, and it was with difficulty we kept our countenance.

Mr. Perry subsequently became one of my warmest friends, and, among other services, would have done me one of a very curious nature, which I will mention by-and-by.

As the importance attached to the article by government may give it some interest, and as it is not unamusing, I will here lay the greater part of it before the reader. He will see what a very little figure is made in it by the words that were prosecuted, and in how much greater a degree the writer's mind must have been occupied with the king's ministers, than with the king.

"POLITICAL EXAMINER, No. 92.—*Change of Ministry.*

" The administration is still without a head, but the ministerial papers tells us, it does quite as well as before. There can be no doubt of it. As it is not customary, however, for headless trunks to make their appearance at court, or to walk abroad under pretense of looking after the nation, it feels rather awkward without some show of pericranium; and, accordingly, like the vivacious giant in Ariosto, who dived to recover his head out of the sea, it has exhibited a singular ingenuity in endeavoring to supply its loss. At one moment, it was said to have clapped a great bottle on his shoulders, and called itself Richmond : at another. to have mounted an attorney's bag, under the name of Perceval ; and at a third, to have put on an enormous balloon, and strutted forth under the appellation of Wellesley. The very idea, however, of these repairs appeared so ridiculous in the eyes of the spectators, that the project seems to have been abandoned for a time ; for the trunk instantly set about repairing the additional loss of its arms, which were taken off the other day in a duel.* To this end, it is said to have applied to two great lords for assistance,† who answered, with manifest contempt, that they could not think of separating any of their members from each other to patch up so vile a body. The fragment, therefore, continues in a very desponding way at St. James's, where it keeps itself alive by cutting out articles for the *Morning Post* with its toes, and kicking every Catholic who comes that way, to the great diversion of the court. The other day it was introduced to his Majesty, who was pleased to express great commiseration at its want of brains, and said he would do something for it if he could.

" Such is the picture, and unfortunately no exaggerated one, of the British ministry. What the French must think of it, is too mortifying for reflection. Perhaps there never was an instance in this nation of any set of rulers, who suffered under a contempt so universal. In the general run of politics, people differ with each other on the acts of administration, as so many matters of opinion ; but to admire Perceval and Castlereagh is an enormity reconcilable to no standard of common sense. Wherever there is an intellect, unpolluted by interest, there the contempt of these men is pure and unmixed. They can not even produce a decent hireling to advocate their cause ; their writers have become proverbially wretched ; and I believe the most galling thing that could be said to an author applying for one's opinion of his manuscript, would be to tell him that he writes like the *Post*. As to the contractors and jobbers, who all praise the ministry, there are no doubt some shrewd men in so large a body of people ; but a jobber has no opinion ; his object is to cheat the army and navy, and become a baronet ; and he knows very well, that these things are not done by speaking the truth. A contractor, therefore, should never say, ' It is my opinion,' or, ' I really think,' as Sir William, and Sir Charles, and Sir James are apt to do, by slips of the tongue : he should say, ' My turtle informs me ;'—' I understand by a large order I had the other day ;'— ' I am told by a very accurate bale of goods,' &c. &c. When such men can come forward and render themselves politically prominent by sounding the praises of an administration, it is a sure sign that there is nobody else to do it.

" That Lords Grenville and Grey should have refused to coalesce with such a ministry, can not be matter of surprise. Mere shame, one would think, must prevent them. Accordingly, their lordships are said to have transmitted the same prompt refusal from the country, though at the distance of six hundred miles from each other. Lord Grenville,

---

* Between Canning and Lord Castlereagh.
† Grey and Grenville.

however, having followed his letter to town, caused a 'great sensation' among the coffee-house speculators, who gave him up for lost in the irresistible vortex of place ; but the papers of yesterday tell us, that his journey was in consequence of the artful ambiguity of Mr. Perceval's letter, which was so worded as to render it doubtful whether its proposals came direct from his Majesty, or only from the minister ; his lordship, they say, was inclined to view it in the former light, and therefore thought himself 'bound to be near the court in its emergencies ;' whereas, Lord Grey regarded it entirely as a ministerial trap, and treated it accordingly. *Whatever may be the truth of these statements, it is generally supposed that the mutilated administration, in spite of its tenacity of life, can not exist much longer ; and the Foxites, of course, are beginning to rally round their leaders, in order to give it the* coup-de-grace. *A more respectable set of men they certainly are, with more general information, more attention to the encouragement of intellect, and altogether a more enlightened policy ; and if his Majesty could be persuaded to enter into their conciliatory views with regard to Ireland, a most important and most necessary benefit would be obtained for this country. The subject of Ireland, next to the difficulty of coalition, is no doubt the great trouble in the election of his Majesty's servants ; and it is this, most probably, which has given rise to the talk of a regency, a measure to which the court would never resort while it felt a possibility of acting upon its own principles. What a crowd of blessings rush upon one's mind, that might be bestowed upon the country in the event of such a change ! Of all monarchs, indeed, since the Revolution, the successor of George the Third will have the finest opportunity of becoming nobly popular.*"

Of the ministers, whom a young journalist thus treated with contempt, I learned afterward to think better. Not as ministers ; for I still consider them, in that respect, as the luckiest, and the least deserving their luck, of any statesmen that have been employed by the House of Brunswick. I speak not only of the section at that moment reigning, but of the whole of what was called Mr. Pitt's successors. But with the inexperience and presumption of youth, I was too much in the habit of confounding difference of opinion with dishonest motives. I did not see (and it is strange how people, not otherwise wanting in common sense or modesty, can pass whole lives without seeing) that if I had a right to have good motives attributed to myself by those who differed with me in opinion, I was bound to reciprocate the concession. I did not reflect that political antagonists have generally been born and bred in a state of antagonism, and that for any one

of them to demand identity of opinion from another on pain
of his being thought a man of bad motives, was to demand
that he should have had the antagonist's father and mother
as well as his own—the same training, the same direction
of conscience, the same predilections and very prejudices ; not
to mention, that good motives themselves might have induced
a man to go counter to all these, even had he been bred in
them ; which, in one or two respects, was the case with myself.

Canning, indeed, was not a man to be treated with contempt, under any circumstances, by those who admired wit
and rhetoric; though, compared with what he actually
achieved in either, I can not help thinking that his position
procured him an undue measure of fame.   What has he left
us to perpetuate the amount of it?   A speech or two, and
the *Ode on the Knife-Grinder*.   This will hardly account,
with the next ages, for the statue that occupies the highway
in Westminster ; a compliment, too, unique of its kind ;
monopolizing the parliamentary pavement, as though the
original had been the only man fit to go forth as the representative of Parliament itself, and to challenge the admiration
of the passengers.   The liberal measures of Canning's last
days renewed his claim on the public regard, especially as
he was left, by the jealousy and resentment of his colleagues,
to carry them by himself; jealousy, because small as his wit
was for a great fame, they had none of their own to equal
it ; and resentment, because, in its indiscretions and inoon-
siderateness, it had nicknamed or bantered them all round—
the real cause, I have no doubt, of that aristocratical desertion of his ascendency, which broke his heart at the very
height of his fortunes.   But at the time I speak of, I took
him for nothing but a great sort of impudent Eton boy, with
an unfeelingness that surmounted his ability.   Whereas, he
was a man of great natural sensibility, a good husband and
father, and an admirable son.   Canning continued, as long
as he lived, to write a letter every week to his mother who
had been an actress, and whom he treated, in every respect,
with a consideration and tenderness that may be pronounced
to have been perfect.   "Good son" should have been written
under his statue.   It would have given the somewhat pert

look of his handsome face a pleasanter effect ; and have done him a thousand times more good with the coming generations, than his *Ode on the Knife-Grinder.*

The Earl of Liverpool, whom Madame de Stael is said to have described as having a "talent for silence," and to have asked, in company, what had become of "that dull speaker, Lord Hawkesbury" (his title during his father's lifetime), was assuredly a very dull minister ; but I believe he was a very good man.   His father had been so much in the confidence of the Earl of Bute at the accession of George III., as to have succeeded to his invidious reputation of being the secret adviser of the king : and he continued in great favor during the whole of the reign.   The son, with little interval, was in office during the whole of the war with Napoleon ; and after partaking of all the bitter draughts of disappointment which ended in killing Pitt, had the luck of tasting the sweets of triumph.   I met him one day, not long afterward, driving his barouche in a beautiful spot where he lived, and was so struck with the melancholy of his aspect, that, as I did not know him by sight, I asked a passenger who he was.

The same triumph did not hinder poor Lord Castlereagh from dying by his own hand.   The long burden of responsibility had been too much, even for him ; though, to all appearance, he was a man of a stronger temperament than Lord Liverpool, and had, indeed, a very noble aspect.   He should have led a private life, and been counted one of the models of the aristocracy ; for though a ridiculous speaker, and a cruel politician (out of patience of seeing constant trouble, and not knowing otherwise how to end it), he was an intelligent and kindly man in private life, and could be superior to his position as a statesman.   He delighted in the political satire of the *Beggars' Opera ;* has been seen applauding it from a stage box ; and Lady Morgan tells us, would ask her in company to play him the songs on the piano-forte, and good-humoredly accompany them with a bad voice.   How pleasant it is thus to find one's self reconciled to men whom we have ignorantly undervalued ! and how fortunate to have lived long enough to say so !

The *Examiner*, though it preferred the Whigs to the
Tories, was not a Whig of the school then existing. Its
great object was a reform in Parliament, which the older
and more influential Whigs did not advocate, which the
younger ones (the fathers of those now living) advocated but
fitfully and misgivingly, and which had lately been suffered
to fall entirely into the hands of those newer and more
thorough-going Whigs, which were known by the name of
Radicals, and have since been called Whig-Radicals, and
Liberals. The opinions of the *Examiner*, in fact, both as
to State and Church Government, allowing, of course, for
difference of position in the parties, and tone in their manifestation, were those now swaying the destinies of the country,
in the persons of Queen Victoria and her minister Lord John
Russell. I do not presume to give her Majesty the name of
a partisan ; or to imply that, under any circumstances, she
would condescend to accept it. Her business, as she well
knows and admirably demonstrates, is, not to side with any
of the disputants among her children, but to act lovingly
and dispassionately for them all, as circumstances render
expedient. But the extraordinary events which took place
on the continent during her childhood, the narrow political
views of most of her immediate predecessors, her own finer
and more genial brain, and the training of a wise mother,
whose family appears to have taken healthy draughts of
those ample and fresh fountains of German literature which
are so well qualified to return the good done them by our
own, and set the contracted stream of English thought and
nurture flowing again, as becomes its common Saxon origin
—all these circumstances in combination have rendered her
what no prince of her house has been before her—equal to
the demands not only of the nation and the day, but of the
days to come, and the popular interests of the world. So,
at least, I conceive. I do not pretend to any special knowledge of the court or its advisers. I speak from what I
have seen of her Majesty's readiness to fall in with every
great and liberal measure for the education of the country,
the freedom of trade, and the independence of nations ; and
I spoke in the same manner, before I could be suspected of

confounding esteem with gratitude. She knows how, and nobly dares, to let the reins of restriction in the hands of individuals be loosened before the growing strength and self-government of the many; and the royal house that best knows how to do this, and neither to tighten those reins in anger nor abandon them out of fear, will be the last house to suffer in any convulsion which others may provoke, and the first to be re-assured in their retention, as long as royalty shall exist. May it exist, under the shape in which I can picture it to my imagination, as long as reasonableness can outlive envy, and ornament be known to be one of nature's desires! Excess, neither of riches nor poverty, would then endanger it. I am no republican, nor ever was, though I have lived during a period of history when kings themselves tried hard to make honest men republicans by their apparent unteachableness. But my own education, the love, perhaps, of poetic ornament, and the repulsiveness of a republic itself, even of British origin, with its huffing manners, its frontless love of money, and its slave-holding abuse of its very freedom, kept me within the pale of the loyal. I might prefer, perhaps, a succession of queens to kings, and a simple fillet on their brows to the most gorgeous diadem. I think that men more willingly obey the one, and I am sure that nobody could mistake the cost of the other. But peaceful and reasonable provision for the progress of mankind toward all the good possible to their nature, is the great desideratum in government; and seeing this more securely and handsomely maintained in limited monarchies than republics, I am for English permanency in this respect, in preference to French volatility, and American slave-holding utilitarianism.

The Tory government having failed in its two attacks on the *Examiner*, could not be content, for any length of time, till it had failed in a third. For such was the case. The new charge was again on the subject of the army—that of military flogging. An excellent article on the absurd and cruel nature of that punishment, from the pen of the late Mr. John Scott (who afterward fell in a duel with one of the writers in Blackwood), had appeared in a country paper, the *Stamford News*, of which he was editor. The most striking passages of this article were copied into the *Exam-iner ;* and it is a remarkable circumstance in the history of juries that after the journal which copied it had been ac-quitted in London, the journal which originated the copied matter was found guilty in Stamford ; and this, too, though the counsel was the same in both instances—the present Lord Brougham.

The attorney-general at that time was Sir Vicary Gibbs ; a name, which it appears somewhat ludicrous to me to write at present, considering what a bug-bear it was to politicians, and how insignificant it has since become. He was a little, irritable, sharp-featured, bilious-looking man (so at least he was described, for I never saw him) ; very worthy, I believe, in private ; and said to be so fond of novels, that he would read them after the labors of the day, till the wax-lights guttered without his knowing it. I had a secret regard for him on this account, and wished he would not haunt me in a spirit so unlike Tom Jones. I know not what sort of lawyer he was ; probably none the worse for imbuing himself with the knowledge of Fielding and Smol-lett ; but he was a bad reasoner, and made half-witted charges. He used those edge-tools of accusation which cut a man's own fingers. He assumed, that we could have no motives for writing but mercenary ones ; and he argued, that because Mr. Scott (who had no more regard for Bona-parte than we had) endeavored to shame down the practice of military flogging by pointing to the disuse of it in the armies of France, he only wanted to subject his native country to invasion. He also had the simplicity to ask, why we did not " speak privately on the subject to some member of Parliament," and get him to notice it in a proper man-ner, instead of bringing it before the public in a newspaper? We laughed at him ; and the event of his accusations enabled us to laugh more.

The charge of being friends of Bonaparte against all who differed with Lord Castlereagh and Mr. Canning was a common, and, for too long a time, a successful trick, with such of the public as did not read the writings of the persons accused. I have often been surprised, much later in life, both in relation to this and other charges, at the credulity into which many excellent persons had owned they had been thus beguiled, and at the surprise which they expressed in turn at finding the charges the reverse of true.   To the readers of the *Examiner*, they caused only indignation or merriment.

The last and most formidable prosecution against us remains to be told ; but some intermediate circumstances must be related first.

CHAPTER XII.

The Reflector and the writers in it.—Feast of the Poets.—Its attack on Gifford for his attack on Mrs. Robinson.—Character of Gifford and his writings.—Specimens of the Baviad and Mæviad.—His appearance at the Roxburgh sale of books.—Attack on Walter Scott, occasioned by a passage in his edition of Dryden.—Tory calumny. —Quarrels and recriminations of authors.—The writer's present opinion of Sir Walter.—General offense caused by the Feast of the Poets.—Its inconsiderate treatment of Hayley.—Dinner of the Prince Regent.—Holland House and Lord Holland.—Neutralization of Whig advocacy.—Recollections of Blanco White.

THE *Examiner* had been established about three years, when my brother projected a quarterly magazine of literature and politics, entitled the *Reflector*, which I edited. Lamb, Dyer, Barnes, Mitchell, the present Greek Professor Scholefield (all Christ-Hospital men), together with Dr. Aikin and his family wrote in it; and it was rising in sale every quarter, when it stopped at the close of the fourth number for want of funds. Its termination was not owing to want of liberality in the payments. But the radical reformers in those days were not sufficiently rich or numerous to support such a publication.

Some of the liveliest effusions of Lamb first appeared in this magazine; and in order that I might retain no influential class for my good wishers, after having angered the stage, dissatisfied the Church, offended the State, not very well pleased the Whigs, and exasperated the Tories, I must needs commence the maturer part of my verse-making with contributing to its pages the *Feast of the Poets*.

The *Feast of the Poets* was (perhaps, I may say, is) a *jeu-d'esprit* suggested by the *Session of the Poets* of Sir John Suckling. Apollo gives the poets a dinner; and many

verse-makers, who have no claim to the title, present themselves, and are rejected.

With this effusion, while thinking of nothing but showing
my wit, and reposing under the shadow of my " laurels" (of
which I expected a harvest as abundant as my self-esteem), I
made almost every living poet and poetaster my enemy, and
particularly exasperated those among the Tories. I speak
of the shape in which it first appeared, before time and reflection had moderated its judgment. It drew upon my
head all the personal hostility which had hitherto been held
in a state of suspense by the vaguer daring of the *Examiner;* and I have reason to believe that its inconsiderate, and,
I am bound to confess, in some respects, unwarrantable levity,
was the origin of the gravest and far less warrantable attacks which I afterward sustained from political antagonists,
and which caused the most serious mischief to my fortunes.
Let the young satirist take warning; and consider how much
self-love he is going to wound, by the indulgence of his own.

Not that I have to apologize to the memory of every one
whom I attacked. I am sorry to have had occasion to differ
with any of my fellow-creatures, knowing the mistakes to
which we are all liable, and the circumstances that help to
cause them. But I can only regret it, personally, in proportion to the worth or personal regret on the side of the
enemy.

The *Quarterly Review*, for instance, had lately been set
up, and its editor was Gifford, the author of the *Baviad and
Mæviad.* I had been invited, nay pressed, by the publisher
to write in the new review; which surprised me, considering its politics and the great difference of my own. I was
not aware of the little faith that was held in the politics of
any beginner of the world; and I have no doubt that the
invitation had been made at the instance of Gifford himself,
of whom, as the dictum of a " man of vigorous learning,"
and the "first satirist of his time," I had quoted in the
Critical Essays the gentle observation, that " all the fools
in the kingdom seemed to have risen up with one accord, and
exclaimed, ' let us write for the theatres !' "

Strange must have been Gifford's feelings, when, in the

Feast of the Poets, he found his eulogizer falling as trenchantly on the author of the *Baviad and Mæviad* as the *Baviad and Mæviad* had fallen on the dramatists. The Tory editor discerned plainly enough that if a man's politics were of no consideration with the *Quarterly Review*, provided the politician was his critical admirer, they were very different things with the Editor Radical. He found also that the new satirist had ceased to regard the old one as a " critical authority:" and he might not have unwarrantably concluded, that I had conceived some disgust against him as a man ; for such, indeed, was the secret of my attack.

The reader is perhaps aware, that George the Fourth, when he was Prince of Wales, had a mistress of the name of Robinson. She was the wife of a man of no great character ; had taken to the stage for a livelihood ; was very handsome, wrote verses, and is said to have excited a tender emotion in the bosom of Charles Fox. The Prince allured her from the stage, and lived with her for some years. After their separation, and during her decline, which took place before she was old, she became afflicted with rheumatism ; and as she solaced her pains, and perhaps added to her subsistence, by writing verses, and as her verses turned upon her affections, and she could not discontinue her old vein of love and sentiment, she fell under the lash of this masculine and gallant gentleman, Mr. Gifford, who, in his *Baviad and Mæviad* amused himself with tripping up her " crutches," particularly as he thought her on her way to her last home. This he considered the climax of the fun.

" See," exclaimed he, after a hit or two at other women, like a boy throwing stones in the street,

> "See Robinson forget her state, and move
>   *On crutches tow'rd the grave to* ' Light o' Love.' "

This is the passage which put all the gall into any thing which I said then or afterward, of Gifford, till he attacked myself and my friends. At least it disposed me to think the worst of whatever he wrote : and as reflection did not improve nor suffering soften him, he is the only man I ever attacked, respecting whom I have felt no regret.

It would be easy for me at this distance of time to own that Gifford possessed genius, had such been the case. It would have been easy for me at any time. But he had not a particle. The scourger of poetasters was himself a poetaster. When he had done with his whip, every body had a right to take it up, and lay it over the scourger's shoulders ; for though he had sense enough to discern glaring faults, he abounded in commonplaces. His satire itself, which, at its best never went beyond smartness, was full of them.

The reader shall have a specimen or two, in order that Mr. Gifford may speak for himself; for his book has long ceased to be read. He shall see with how little a stock of his own a man may set up for a judge of others.

The *Baviad and Mæviad*—so called from two bad poets mentioned by Virgil—was a satire imitated from Persius, on a set of fantastic writers who had made their appearance under the title of Della Cruscans. The coterie originated in the meeting of some of them at Florence, the seat of the famous Della Cruscan Academy. Mr. Merry, their leader, who was a member of that academy, and who wrote under its signature, gave occasion to the name. They first published a collection of poems, called the *Florence Miscellany*, and then sent verses to the London newspapers, which occasioned an overflow of contributions in the like taste. The taste was as bad as can be imagined ; full of floweriness, conceits, and affectation ; and, in attempting to escape from commonplace, it evaporated into nonsense :

> " Was it the shuttle of the morn
> That wove upon the cobwebb'd thorn
> Thy airy lay?"

> " Hang o'er his eye the gossamery tear."

> " Gauzy zephyrs, fluttering o'er the plain,
> On twilight's bosom drop their filmy rain."
> &c. &c.

It was impossible that such absurdities could have had any lasting effect on the public taste. They would have died of inanition. But Mr. Gifford, finding the triumph easy and the temptation to show his superiority irresistible, chose to think otherwise ; and hence his determination to scourge the rogues and trample on their imbecility.

The female portion of them particularly offended him. The first name he mentions is that of Mrs. Piozzi, whose presumption in writing books he seémed to consider a personal offense—as though he represented the whole dignity and indignation of literature. His attack on her, which he commences in a note, opens with the following unconscious satire on himself;

" ' Though no one better knows his *own* house' than I the *vanity* of this woman, yet the idea of her undertaking such a work" (*British Synonimes*) "had never entered my head, and I was *thunderstruck* when I first saw it announced."

Mrs. Piozzi was, perhaps, as incompetent to write *British Synonimes* as Mr. Gifford to write poetry ; but what call had he to be offended with the mistake ?

His satire consists, not in a critical exposure—in showing why the objects of his contempt are wrong—but in simply asserting that they are so. He turns a commonplace of his own in his verses, quotes a passage from his author in a note, expresses his amazement at it, and thus thinks he has proved his case, when he has made out nothing but an overweening assumption at the expense of what was not worth noticing. " I was born," says he,

> " To *brand* obtrusive ignorance with scorn.
> On bloated pedantry to *pour my rage*,
> And *hiss preposterous fustian* from the stage."

What commonplace talking is that ?   And so he goes on,

> " Lo ! Della Crusca in his closet pent,
> *He toils to give the crude conceptions vent.*
> Abortive thoughts, that *right and wrong confound*,
> Truth *sacrificed* to letters, [why ' letters '?] *sense to sound ;*
> *False glare*, incongruous images, *combine ;*
> And noise and nonsense clatter through the line."

What is the example of writing here which is shown to the poor Della Cruscans ?   What the masterly novelty of style or imagery ?   What the right evinced to speak in the language of a teacher ?   Yet Gifford never doubted himself on these points. He stood uttering his didactic nothings, as if other literary defaulters were but so many children, whom it taxed his condescension to instruct. Here is some more of the same stuff :

> " Then let your style be brief, your meaning clear,
> Nor, like Lorenzo tire the laboring ear
> With a wild waste of words ; sound without sense,
> And all the florid glare of impotence.
> Still, with your characters, your language change,
> From grave to gay, *as nature dictates*, range :
> Now droop in all the plaintiveness of woe, (! !)
> Now in glad numbers light and airy flow ;
> Now shake the stage with guilt's alarming *tone*, (! !)
> And make the aching bosom *all your own*."

Was there ever a fonder set of complacent old phrases, such as any schoolboy might utter ? Yet this is the man who undertook to despise Charles Lamb, and to trample on Keats and Shelley.

I have mentioned the Roxburgh sale of books. I was standing among the bidders with my friend the late Mr. Barron Field, when he jogged my elbow, and said, " There is Gifford over the way, looking at you with *such* a face !" I met the eyes of my beholder, and saw a little man, with a warped frame and a countenance between the querulous and the angry, gazing at me with all his might. It was, truly enough, the satirist who could not bear to be satirized—the denouncer of incompetencies, who could not bear to be told of his own. He had now learnt, as I was myself to learn, what it was to taste of his own bitter medicaments ; and he never profited by it ; for his *Review* spared neither age nor sex as long as he lived. What he did at first, out of a self-satisfied incompetence, he did at last out of an envious and angry one ; and he was, all the while, the humble servant of power, and never expressed one word of regret for his inhumanity. This mixture of implacability and servility is the sole reason, as I have said before, why I still speak of him as I do. If he secretly felt regret for it, I am sorry— especially if he retained any love for his " Anna," whom I take to have been not only the good servant and friend he describes her, but such a one as he could wish that he had married.   Why did he not marry her, and remain a humbler and a happier man ? or how was it, that the power to have any love at all could not teach him that other people might have feelings as well as himself, especially women and the sick ?

Such were the causes of my disfavor with the Tory critics in England.

To those in Scotland I gave, in like manner, the first cause of offense, and they had better right to complain of me ; though they ended, as far as regards the mode of resentment, in being still more in the wrong.   I had taken a dislike to Walter Scott, on account of a solitary passage in his edition of *Dryden*—nay, on account of a single word. The word, it must be allowed, was an extraordinary one, and such as he must have regretted writing : for a more dastardly or deliberate piece of wickedness than allowing a ship with its crew to go to sea, knowing the vessel to be leaky, believing it likely to founder, and on purpose to destroy one of the passengers, it is not easy to conceive ; yet, because this was done by a Tory king, the relater could find no severer term for it than " ungenerous."   Here is the passage :

" His political principles (the Earl of Mulgrave's) were those of a stanch Tory, which he maintained through his whole life ; and he was zealous for the royal prerogative, although he had no small reason to complain of Charles the Second, who, to avenge himself of Mulgrave, for a supposed attachment to the Princess Anne, sent him to Tangiers, at the head of some troops, in a leaky vessel, *which it was supposed must have perished in the voyage.*   Though Mulgrave was apprized of the danger, he scorned to shun it ; and the Earl of Plymouth, a favorite son of the king, generously insisted upon sharing it along with him. This *ungenerous* attempt to destroy him in the very act of performing his duty, with the refusal of a regiment, made a temporary change in Mulgrave's conduct."—*Notes on Absalom and Achitophel in Dryden's Works,* vol. ix. p. 304.

This passage was the reason why the future great novelist was introduced to Apollo, in the *Feast of the Poets,* after a very irreverent fashion.

I believe, that with reference to high standards of poetry and criticism, superior to mere description, however lively, to the demands of rhyme for its own sake, to prosaical groundworks of style, metaphors of common property, conventionalities in general, and the prevalence of a material over a spiritual treatment, my estimate of Walter Scott's then publications, making allowance for the manner of it, will still be found not far from the truth, by those who have profited by a more advanced age of æsthetical culture.

There is as much difference, for instance, poetically speaking, between Coleridge's brief poem, *Christabel*, and all the narrative poems of Walter Scott, or, as Wordsworth called them, " novels in verse," as between a precious essence and a coarse imitation of it, got up for sale. Indeed, Coleridge, not unnaturally, though not with entire reason (for the story and the characters were the real charm), lamented that an endeavor, unavowed, had been made to catch his tone, and had succeeded just far enough to recommend to unbounded popularity what had nothing in common with it.

But though Walter Scott was no novelist at that time, except in verse, the tone of personal assumption toward him in the *Feast of the Poets* formed a just ground of offense. Not that I had not as much right to differ with any man on any subject, as he had to differ with others ; but it would have become me, especially at that time of life, and in speaking of a living person, to express the difference with modesty. I ought to have taken care also not to fall into one of the very prejudices I was reproving, and think ill or well of people in proportion as they differed or agreed with me in politics. Walter Scott saw the good of mankind in a Tory or retrospective point of view. I saw it from a Whig, a Radical, or prospective one ; and though I still think he was mistaken, and though circumstances have shown that the world think so too, I ought to have discovered, even by the writings which I condemned, that he was a man of a kindly nature ; and it would have become me to have given him credit for the same good motives which I arrogated exclusively for my own side of the question. It is true, it might be supposed, that I should have advocated that side with less ardor, had I been more temperate in this kind of judgment ; but I do not think so. Or if I

had, the want of ardor would probably have been com-
pensated by the presence of qualities, the absence of which
was injurious to its good effect.   At all events, I am now
of opinion, that whatever may be the immediate impression,
a cause is advocated to the most permanent advantage by
persuasive, instead of provoking manners ; and certain I am,
that whether this be the case or not, no human being, be he
the best and wisest of his kind, much less a confident young
man, can be so sure of the result of his confidence, as to
warrant the substitution of his will and pleasure in that
direction, for the charity which befits his common modesty
and his participation of error.

It is impossible for me, in other respects, to regret the
war I had with the Tories.   I rejoice in it as far as I can
rejoice at any thing painful to myself and others, and I am
paid for the consequences in what I have lived to see ; nay,
in the respect and regrets of the best of my enemies.   But
I am sorry, that in aiming wounds which I had no right to
give, I can not deny that I brought on myself others which
they had still less right to inflict ; and I make the amends
of this confession, not only in return for what they have
expressed themselves, but in justice to the feelings which
honest men of all parties experience as they advance in life,
and when they look back calmly upon their common errors.

" I shall put this book in my pocket," said Walter Scott
to Murray, after he had been standing a while at his counter,
reading the *Story of Rimini.*

" Pray do," said the publisher.   The copy of the book
was set down to the author in the bookseller's account, as a
present to Walter Scott.   Walter Scott was beloved by his
friends ; the author of the *Story of Rimini* was an old
offender, personal as well as political ; and hence the fury
with which they fell on him in their new publication.

Gifford, in his *Baviad and Mœviad,* speaking of a daily
paper called the *World,* had said, " In this paper were
given the earliest specimens of those unqualified and auda-
cions attacks on all private character, which the town first
railed at for their quaintness, then tolerated for their absurdity, and now that other papers, equally wicked and more

intelligible, have ventured to imitate it, will have to lament to the last hour of British liberty."

This close of Gifford's remark is one of his commonplaces —a conventional cadence and turn of words. Calumny has been out of fashion for some time. But the example he speaks of was infectious in those days ; and curiously enough, it was destined to be followed up, and carried to excess, by his own side of the question. It is to the honor of the Whigs and Radicals, that they went to no such extremities, even during the height of the warfare. The Priestleys, Aikins, and Gilbert Wakefields, were in too philosophic and suffering a minority for it ; Montgomery the poet (who edited the *Sheffield Iris*), had too much religion for it ; Cobbett, with all his virulence, appears never to have thought of it ; Hazlitt, though his portrait-painting tempted him into minor personalities, disdained it ; and all the notice (as far as I am aware) which any liberal journal took of matters of private life, the *Examiner* included, was confined to circumstances that were forced on the public attention by their connection with matters of state ; as in the instances of the Duke of York's mistress, who trafficked in commissions, and of poor foolish Queen Caroline, who was victimized by an unworthy husband.

Every party has a right side and a wrong. The right side of Whiggism, Radicalism, or the love of liberty, is the love of justice ; the wish to see fair-play to all men, and the advancement of knowledge and competence. The wrong side is the wish to pull down those above us, instead of the desire of raising those who are below. The right side of Toryism is the love of order, and the disposition to reverence and personal attachment ; the wrong side is the love of power for power's sake, and the determination to maintain it in the teeth of all that is reasonable and humane. A strong spice of superstition, generated by the habit of success, tended to confuse the right and wrong sides of Toryism, in minds not otherwise unjust or ungenerous. They seemed to imagine, that heaven and earth would "come together," if the supposed favorites of Providence were to be considered as favorites no longer ; and hence the unbounded license which they gave to

their resentment, and the strange self-permission of a man
like Walter Scott, not only to lament over the progress of
society, as if the future had been ordained only to carry on
the past, but to countenance the border-like forages of his
friends into provinces which they had no business to invade,
and to speculate upon still greater organizations of them
which circumstances, luckily for his fame, prevented. I allude to the intended establishment of a journal, which, as it
never existed, it is no longer necessary to name.

Readers in these kindlier days of criticism have no conception of the extent to which personal hostility allowed itself to be transported, in the periodicals of those times. Personal habits, appearances, connections, domesticities, nothing
was safe from misrepresentations, begun perhaps in the gayety
of a saturnalian license, but gradually carried to an excess
which would have been ludicrous, had it not sometimes produced tragical consequences. It threatened a great many
more, and scattered, meantime, a great deal of wretchedness
among unoffending as well as offending persons, sometimes
in proportion to the delicacy which hindered them from ex-
culpating themselves, and which could only have vindicated
one portion of a family by sacrificing another. I was so
caricatured, it seems, among the rest, upon matters great
and small (for I did not see a tenth part of what was said
of me), that persons, on subsequently becoming acquainted
with me, sometimes expressed their surprise at finding me
no other than I was in face, dress, manners, and very walk ;
to say nothing of the conjugality which they found at my
fireside, and the affection which I had the happiness of enjoying among my friends in general. I never retaliated in
the same way ; first, because I had never been taught to
respect it, even by the jests of Aristophanes ; secondly, because I observed the sorrow it caused both to right and
wrong ; thirdly, because it is impossible to know the truth
of any story if related of a person, without hearing all the
parties concerned ; and fourthly, because, while people thought
me busy with politics and contention, I was almost always
absorbed in my books and verses, and did not, perhaps sufficiently consider the worldly consequences of the indulgence

The quarrels of authors, and the scandals which they have caused one another, were, unfortunately not new to the reading part of the public, though the tone of hostility had hardly before been exceeded, except in religious controversy, and in the disputes between some of the early writers of Italy. " The life of a wit," said Steele, " is a warfare upon earth." He himself was called by an enemy, the " vilest of mankind ;" upon which he said, in the gayety of an honest heart, that " it would be a glorious world if he was." Even Steele, so exasperating is this kind of warfare, allowed himself to be provoked into personalities. Swift abounded in it, though he lived in one of the most perilous of " glass-houses," and miraculously escaped retribution ; probably from the very pity which he denied. But why multiply examples on this painful subject ? Clarke and Cudworth have been called " atheists"; and Fenelon, who was " only a little lower than the angels," a "ferocious brute!" I do not pretend to compare myself with the least of such men ; and I am willing to have paid the penalty of what was really faulty in me, in suffering for what was not : but as I do not claim to be considered better than my neighbors, or to have been so at any time, so I may be allowed to comfort myself with thinking I am no worse. I may even presume so far in copying the jovial self-reconcilement of Steele, as to believe that the world would be no very great vale of tears, if all the men in it were no worse disposed.

If Sir Walter Scott was a poet of a purely conventional order, warmed with a taste for old books, and if he was a critic more agreeable than subtle, and a bitter and not very large-minded politician, unwilling, and perhaps unable to turn his eyes from the past to the future, and to look with patience on the prospects of the many, he was a man of singular and admirable genius in the points in which he excelled, great in some respects, and charming almost in all. I beg leave to think that he did not possess that attribute of genius, which is said to partake of the feminine as well as the masculine ; if feminine only it be to excel in sweet as well as strong, to be musical and graceful, and he able to paint women themselves ; and I will not do such discredit to his memory,

in this or in any masculine respect, as to repeat the comparisons of him with Shakspeare, who painted both women and
men to admiration, and was a great poet, and a profound
universalist, and excelled as much in nature as in manners ;
for certainly Scott was in all these respects (and rare is the
excellence that can be put even to such a disadvantage) but
a half, or even a third or fourth kind of Shakspeare, with all
the poetry (so to speak) taken out of him, and all the expression and the quotability besides ; Sir Walter being, perhaps,
the least quotable for sententiousness or wit, or any other
memorable brevity, in the whole circle of illustrious writers.
But he was an agreeable and kindly biographer, a most entertaining selector from history, an exquisite antiquary, a
charming companion, a warm hearted friend, a good father,
husband, and man ; and though his novels, as works of art
and style, were inferior to Fielding, and I think it was a
want of imagination in him, and a self-abasement, to wish
to build a great house and be a feudal lord, instead of being
content to write about houses and lords, and living among
us all to this day in a cottage that still would have been a
shrine for princes to visit ; yet, assuredly, he was the most
wonderful combiner of the novel and romance that ever existed.   He was Shakspearian in the abundance and variety
of his characters, unsurpassed, if ever equaled, in the substantial flow of his pen ; and in spite of admirable Burns
and delightful Thomson, and all the historical and philosophical names of Edinburgh during the last and present century,
was upon the whole the greatest writer that Scotland has
produced.

It can be of no consequence to the memory of such a man
what I said or thought of him, whether before his death or
after ; but for my own sake, since I am forced to speak of
such things in a work like the present, I may be allowed to
state, that whatever hostility I was forced to maintain with
his politics, and so far with himself, I had the pleasure of
expressing my regret for the mistakes which I had made
about him, long before I experienced their ill effects.   I
will add, that long after those effects, and when he was
lying sick in London on his way to his last home, I called

every morning at his door (anonymously ; for I doubted whether my name would please him) to furnish a respectful bulletin of his health to a daily paper, in which I suggested its appearance ; and I will not conceal, that as I loved the humanities in his wonderful pages, in spite of the politics which accompanied them, so I mourned for his closing days, and shed tears at his death.

To return to the *Feast of the Poets.* I offended all the critics of the old or French school, by objecting to the monotony of Pope's versification, and all the critics of the new or German school, by laughing at Wordsworth, with whose writings I was then unacquainted, except through the medium of his deriders. On reading him for myself, I became such an admirer, that Lord Byron accused me of making him popular upon town. I had not very well pleased Lord Byron himself, by counting him inferior to Wordsworth. Indeed, I offended almost every body whom I noticed; some by finding any fault at all with them ; some, by not praising them on their favorite points ; some, by praising others on any point ; and some, I am afraid, and those among the most good-natured, by needlessly bringing them on the carpet, and turning their very good-nature into a subject for caricature. Thus I introduced Mr. Hayley, whom I need not have noticed at all, as he belonged to a by-gone generation. He had been brought up in the courtesies of the old school of manners, which he ultra-polished and rendered caressing, after the fashion of my Arcadian friends of Italy ; and as the poetry of the *Triumphs of Temper* was not as vigorous in style as it was amiable in its moral and elegant in point of fancy, I chose to sink his fancy and his amiableness, and to represent him as nothing but an effeminate parader of phrases of endearment and pickthank adulation. I looked upon him as a sort of powder-puff of a man, with no real manhood in him, but fit only to suffocate people with his frivolous vanity, and be struck aside with contempt. I had not yet learned, that writers may be very " strong " and huffing on paper, while feeble on other points, and, *vice versâ*, weak in their metres, while they are strong enough as regards muscle. I remember my astonishment, years afterward, on finding that the "gentle Mr. Hayley," whom I had taken for

"A puny insect, shivering at a breeze,"

was a strong-built man, famous for walking in the snow before daylight, and possessed of an intrepidity as a horseman amounting to the reckless. It is not improbable, that the feeble Hayley, during one of his equestrian passes, could have snatched up the "vigorous" Gifford, and pitched him over the hedge into the next field.

Having thus secured the enmity of the Tory critics north and south, and the indifference (to say the least of it) of the gentlest lookers on, it fell to the lot of the better part of my impulses, to lose me the only counteracting influence which was offered me in the friendship of the Whigs. I had partaken deeply of Whig indignation at the desertion of their party by the Prince Regent. The *Reflector* contained an article on his Royal Highness, bitter accordingly, which bantered, among other absurdities, a famous dinner given by him to "one hundred and fifty particular friends." There was a real stream of water running down the table at this dinner, stocked with gold fish. It had banks of moss and bridges of pasteboard; the salt-cellars were panniers borne by "golden-asses;" every thing, in short, was as unlike the dinners now given by the sovereign, in point of taste and good sense, as effeminacy is different from womanhood; and the *Reflector* in a parody of the complaint of the shepherd, described how

"Despairing, beside a clear stream,
    The bust of a cod-fish was laid;
And while a false taste was his theme,
    A drainer supported his head."

A day or two after the appearance of this article, I met in the street the late estimable Blanco White, whom I had the pleasure of being acquainted with. He told me of the amusement it had given at Holland House; and added that Lord Holland would be glad to see me among his friends there, and that he (Blanco White) was commissioned to say so.

I did not doubt for an instant, that any thing but the most disinterested kindness and good-nature dictated the invitation which was thus made me. It was impossible, at any future time, that I could speak with greater respect and admiration of his lordship, than I had been in the habit of doing already. Never had an unconstitutional or illiberal measure taken place in the House of Lords, but his protest was sure to appear against it; and this, and his elegant literature and reputation for hospitality, had completely won my heart. At the same time, I did not look upon the invitation as any return for this enthusiasm. I considered his lordship (and now at this moment consider him) as having been as free from every personal motive as myself; and this absence of all suspicion, prospective or retrospective, enabled me to feel the more confident and consoled in the answer which I felt bound to make to his courtesy.

I said to Mr. Blanco White, that I could not sufficiently express my sense of the honor that his lordship was pleased to do me; that there was not a man in England at whose table I should be prouder or happier to sit; that I was fortunate in having a conveyer of the invitation, who would know how to believe what I said, and to make a true representation of it; and that with almost any other person, I should fear to be thought guilty of immodesty and presumption, in not hastening to avail myself of so great a kindness; but that the more I admired and loved the character of Lord Holland, the less I dared to become personally acquainted with him; that being a far weaker person than he gave me credit for being, it would be difficult for me to eat the mutton and drink the claret of such a man, without falling into any opinion into which his conscience might induce him to lead me; and that not having a single personal acquaintance, even among what was called my own party (the Radicals), his lordship's goodness would be the more easily enabled to put its kindest and most indulgent construction on the misfortune which I was obliged to undergo, in denying myself the delight of his society.

I do not say that these were the very words, but they convey the spirit of what I said to Mr. Blanco White; and

I should not have doubted his giving them a correct report, even had no evidence of it followed. But there did ; for Lord Holland courteously sent me his publications, and never ceased, while he lived, to show me all the kindness in his power.

Of high life in ordinary, it is little for me to say that I might have had a surfeit of it, if I pleased. Circumstances, had I given way to them, might have rendered half my existence a round of it. I might also have partaken no mean portion of high life extraordinary. And very charming is its mixture of softness and strength, of the manliness of its taste and the urbanity of its intercourse. I have tasted, if not much of it, yet some of its very essence, and I cherish, and am grateful for it at this moment. What I have said, there fore, of Holland House, is mentioned under no feelings, either of assumption or servility. The invitation was made, and declined, with an equal spirit of faith on both sides in far better impulses.

Far, therefore, am I from supposing, that the silence of the Whig critics respecting me was owing to any hostile influence which Lord Holland would have condescended to exercise. Not being among the visitors at Holland House, I dare say I was not thought of; or if I was thought of I was regarded as a person who, in shunning Whig connection, and, perhaps, in persisting to advocate a reform toward which they were cooling, might be supposed indifferent to Whig advocacy. And, indeed, such was the case, till I felt the want of it.

Accordingly the *Edinburgh Review* took no notice of the *Feast of the Poets,* though my verses praised it at the expense of the *Quarterly,* and though some of the reviewers, to my knowledge, liked it, and it echoed the opinions of others. It took no notice of the pamphlet on the *Folly and Danger of Methodism,* though the opinions in it were, perhaps, identical with its own. And it took as little of the *Reformist's Answer to an Article in the Edinburgh Review*—a pamphlet which I wrote in defense of it own re forming principles, which it had lately taken it into its head to renounce as impracticable. Reform had been apparently given up for ever by its originators ; the Tories were increasing in strength every day; and I was left to battle with them as I could. Little did I suppose, that a time would come when I should be an Edinburgh reviewer myself; when its former editor, agreeably to the dictates of his heart, would be one of the kindest of my friends; and when a cadet of one of the greatest of the Whig houses, too young at that time to possess more than a prospective influence, would carry the reform from which his elders recoiled, and gift the prince-opposing Whig-Radical with a pension, under the gracious countenance of a queen whom the Radical loves. I think the *Edinburgh Review* might have noticed my books a little oftener. I am sure it would have done me a great deal of worldly good by it, and itself no harm in these progressing days of criticism. But I said nothing on the subject, and may have been thought indifferent.

Of Mr. Blanco White, thus brought to my recollection, a good deal is known in certain political and religious quarters; but it may be new to many readers, that he was an Anglo-Spaniard, who was forced to quit the Peninsula for his liberal opinions, and who died in his adopted country not long ago, after many years' endeavor to come to some positive faith within the Christian pale. At the time I knew him he had not long arrived from Spain, and was engaged, or about to be engaged, as tutor to the present Lord Holland. Though English by name and origin, he was more of the Spaniard in appearance, being very unlike the portrait prefixed to his *Life and Correspondence*. At least, he must have greatly altered from what he was when I knew him, if that portrait ever resembled him. He had a long pale face, with prominent drooping nose, anxious and somewhat staring eyes, and a mouth turning down at the corners. I believe there was not an honester man in the world, or one of an acuter intellect, short of the mischief that had been done it by a melancholy temperament and a superstitious training. It is distressing, in the work alluded to, to see what a torment the intellect may be rendered to itself by its own sharpness, in its efforts to make its way to conclusions, equally unnecessary to discover and impossible to be arrived at.

But, perhaps, there was something naturally self-torment-ing in the state of Mr. White's blood. The first time I met him at a friend's house, he was suffering under the calumnies of his countrymen ; and though of extremely gentle manners in ordinary, he almost startled me by sud-denly turning round, and saying, in one of those incorrect foreign sentences which force one to be relieved while they startle, " If they proceed more, I will go mad." ·

In like manner, while he was giving me the Holland-house invitation, and telling me of the amusement derived from the pathetic cod's head and shoulders, he looked so like the piscatory bust which he was describing, that with all my respect for his patriotism and his sorrows, I could not help partaking of the unlucky tendency of my countrymen to be amused, in spite of myself, with the involuntary bur-lesque.

Mr. White, on his arrival in England, was so anxious a student of the language, that he noted down in a pocket-book every phrase which struck him as remarkable. Ob-serving the words " Cannon Brewery" on premises then standing in Knightsbridge, and taking the figure of a can-non which was over them, as the sign of the commodity dealt in, he put down as a nicety of speech, " The English *brew* cannon."

Another time, seeing maid-servants walking with children in a nursery-garden, he rejoiced in the progeny-loving char-acter of the people among whom he had come, and wrote down, "Public gardens provided for nurses, in which they take the children to walk."

This gentleman, who had been called " Blanco" in Spain —which was a translation of his family name " White," and who afterward wrote an excellent English book of enter-taining letters on the Peninsula, under the Græco-Spanish appellation of Don Leucadio Doblado (White doubled)—was author of a sonnet which Coleridge pronounced to be the best in the English language. I know not what Mr. Wordsworth said on this judgment. Perhaps he wrote fifty sonnets on the spot to disprove it. And in truth it was a bold sentence, and probably spoken out of a kindly, though not conscious, spirit of exaggeration. The sonnet, never-theless, is truly beautiful.

As I do not like to have such things referred to without being shown them, in case I have not seen them before, I shall·do as I would be done by, and lay it before the reader :

"Mysterious night! when our first parent knew
   Thee, from report divine, and heard thy name,
   Did he not tremble for this lovely frame—
   This glorious canopy of light and blue?
Yet, 'neath a curtain of translucent dew,
   Bathed in the rays of the great setting flame
   Hesperus, with the host of heaven, came,
   And, lo! creation widened in Man's view.
Who could have thought such darkness lay concealed
   Within thy beams, O sun! or who could find,
Whilst fly, and leaf, and insect stood revealed,
   That to such countless orbs thou mad'st us blind!
Why do we then shun death with anxious strife?
If light can thus deceive, wherefore not life?"

CHAPTER XIII.

THE REGENT AND THE EXAMINER.

"The Prince on St. Patrick's Day."—Indictment for an attack on the Regent in that article.—Present feelings of the writer on the subject.—Real sting of the offense in the article.—Sentence of the proprietors of the Examiner to an imprisonment for two years.—Their rejection of two proposals of compromise.—Lord Ellenborough, Mr. Garrow, and Mr. Justice Grose.

EVERY thing having been thus prepared by myself, as well as by others, for a good blow at the *Examiner*, the ministers did not fail to strike it.

There was an annual dinner of the Irish on St. Patrick s Day, at which the Prince of Wales's name used to be the reigning and rapturous toast, as that of the greatest friend they possessed in the United Kingdom. He was held to be the jovial advocate of liberality in all things, and sponsor in particular for concession to the Catholic claims. But the Prince of Wales, now become Prince Regent, had retained the Tory ministers of his father; he had broken life-long engagements; had violated his promises, particular as well as general, those to the Catholics among them; and led *in toto* a different political life from what had been expected. The name, therefore, which used to be hailed with rapture, was now, at the dinner in question, received with hisses.

An article appeared on the subject in the *Examiner;* the attorney-general's eye was swiftly upon the article; and the result to the proprietors was two years' imprisonment, with a fine, to each, of five hundred pounds. I shall relate the story of my imprisonment a few pages onward. Much as it injured me, I can not wish that I had evaded it, for I believe that it did good, and I should have suffered far worse in the self-abasement. Neither have I any quarrel, at this distance of time, with the Prince Regent; for though his frivolity, his tergiversation, and his treatment of his wife, will not allow me to respect his memory, I am bound to pardon it as I do my own faults, in consideration of the circumstances which mould the character of every human being.   Could I meet him in some odd corner of the Elysian fields, where charity had room for both of us, I should first apologize to him for having been the instrument in the hand of events for attacking a fellow-creature, and then expect to hear him avow as hearty a regret for having injured myself, and unjustly treated his wife.

Having made these acknowledgments, I here repeat the article in which the libel appeared, in order that people may see how far it was excusable or otherwise under the circumstances, and whether the acknowledgments are sufficing.   I would rather, for obvious reasons, both personal to myself and otherwise, have repeated nothing whatsoever against any individual of her Majesty's kindred, however differently constituted from herself, or however strong and obvious the line which every body can draw between portions of the same family at different periods of time, and under different circumstances of breeding and connection.   A man may have had a quarrel with Charles the Second (many a man did have one), without bringing into question his loyalty to Queen Mary or Queen Anne.   Nay, his loyalty may have been greater, and was ; nor (as I have said elsewhere) could I have felt so much respect, and done my best to show it, for the good qualities of Queen Victoria had I not been impressed in a different manner by the faults of her kinsmen. But having committed myself to the task of recording these events in the history of the *Examiner*, I could not but render the narrative complete.

THE PRINCE ON ST. PATRICK'S DAY.

(*Examiner*, *No.* 221; *Sunday, March* 22, 1812.)

The Prince Regent is still in every body's mouth; and unless he is as insensible to biting as to bantering, a delicious time he has of it in that remorseless ubiquity ! If a person takes in a newspaper, the first thing he does, when he looks at it, is to give the old groan, and say,

"Well! what of the Prince Regent now?" If he goes out after breakfast, the first friend he meets is sure to begin talking about the Prince Regent; and the two always separate with a shrug. He who is lounging along the street will take your arm, and turn back with you to expatiate on the Prince Regent; and he in a hurry, who is skimming the other side of the way, hallooes out as he goes, "Fine things these of the Prince Regent!" You can scarcely pass by two people talking together, but you shall hear the words, "Prince Regent;" "If the Prince Regent has done that, he must be—" or such as, "The Prince Regent and Lord Yar—" the rest escapes in the distance. At dinner, the Prince Regent quite eclipses the goose or the calf's-head; the tea-table, of course, rings of the Prince Regent; if the company go to the theatre to see *The Hypocrite*, or the new farce of *Turn Out*, they can not help thinking of the Prince Regent; and, as Dean Swift extracted philosophical meditations from a broom-stick, so it would not be surprising if any serious person, in going to bed, should find in his very nightcap something to remind him of the merits of the Prince Regent. In short, there is no other subject but one that can at all pretend to a place in the attention of our country-men, and that is their old topic, the weather; their whole sympathies are at present divided between the Prince Regent and the barometer.

> "Nocte pluit totâ; redeunt spectacula manè;
> Divisum imperium cum Jove Cæsar habet."
>
> VIRGIL.

> All night the weeping tempests blow;
> All day our state surpasseth show;
> Doubtless a blessed empire share
> The Prince of Wales and Prince of Air.

But the ministerial journalists, and other creatures of government, will tell you that there is nothing in all this; or, rather, they will insist that it is to be taken in a good sense, and that the universal talk respecting the Prince Regent is highly to his advantage; for it is to be remarked that these gentlemen have a pleasant way of proving to us that we have neither eyes nor ears, and would willingly persuade us in time, that to call a man an idiot or a profligate is subscribing to his wisdom and virtue; a logic, by-the-by, which enables us to dis-cover how it is they turn their own reputation to account, and contrive to have so good an opinion of themselves. Thus, whenever they per-ceive an obnoxious sensation excited among the people by particular measures, they always affect to confine it to the organs by which it is expressed, and cry out against what they are pleased to term "a few factious individuals," who are represented as a crafty set of fellows, that get their living by contradicting and disgusting every body else! How such a trade can be thriving, we are not informed: it is certainly a very different one from their own, which, however it may disgust other people, succeeds by echoing and flattering the opinions of men in power. It is in vain that you refer them to human nature, and to the opinions that are naturally created by profligate rulers : they are not acquainted with human nature, and still less with any such rulers ; it is in vain that you refer them to companies ; it is in vain that you refer them to popular meetings, to common-halls of their own. Be it so, then ; let us compound with them, and agree to consider all direct political meetings as party-assemblages, particularly those of the Reformists, who, whatever room they may occupy on the occasion, and whatever advocates they may possess from one end of the kingdom to another, shall be nothing but a few factious individuals, as contemptible for their numbers and public effect, as for their bad writing and worse principles. Nay, let us even resort on this occasion to persons, who, having but one great political object, unconnected with the abstract merits of party, persisted for so many years in expressing an ardent and hopeful attachment to the Prince Regent, and in positively shutting their eyes to such parts of his character as might have shaken their dependence upon him, looking only to his succession in the government as the day of their country's happiness, and caring not who should surround his throne, provided he would only be true to his own word. An assembly of such persons—such, at least, was their composition for the much greater part—met the other day at the Freemasons' Tavern, to celebrate the Irish anniversary of Saint Patrick ; and I shall proceed to extract from the *Morning Chronicle* such passages of what passed on the occasion as apply to his Royal Highness, in order that the reader may see at once what is now thought of him, not by Whigs and Pittites, or any other party of the state, but by the fondest and most trusting of his fellow-subjects, by those whose hearts have danced at his name, who have caught from it inspiration to their poetry, patience to their afflictions, and hope to their patriotism.

"The anniversary of this day—a day always precious in the estimation of an Irishman—was celebrated yesterday at the Freemasons' Tavern by a numerous and highly respectable assemblage of individuals. The Marquis of Lansdowne presided at the meeting, supported by the Marquis of Downshire, the Earl of Moira, Mr. Sheridan, the Lord Mayor, Mr. Sheriff Heygate, &c. &c. When the cloth was removed, *Non Nobis Domine* was sung, after which the Marquis of Lansdowne, premising that the meeting was assembled for purposes of charity, rather than of party or political feeling, gave 'the health of the King,' which was drunk with enthusiastic and rapturous applause. This was followed by *God save the King*, and then the Noble Marquis gave 'the health of the Prince Regent,' which was drunk with partial applause, and *loud and reiterated hisses.* The next toast, which called forth great and continued applause, lasting nearly five minutes, was ' the Navy and Army.' "

The interests of the Charity were then considered, and, after a procession of the children (a sight worth all the gaudy and hollow flourish of military and courtly pomps), a very handsome collection was made from the persons present. Upon this, the Toasts were resumed :

and ' Lord Moira's health being drunk with loud and reiterated cheering,' his lordship made a speech, in which *not a word was uttered of
the Regent.* Here let the reader pause a moment and consider what
a quantity of meaning must be wrapped up in the silence of such a
man with regard to his old companion and prince.   Lord Moira uni-
versally bears the character of a man who is generous to a fault; he
is even said to be almost unacquainted with the language of denial or
rebuke; and if this part of his character has been injurious to him, it
has, at least, with his past and his present experience, helped him to a
thorough knowledge of the prince's character.   Yet this nobleman,
so generous, so kindly affectioned, so well experienced—even he has
nothing to say in favor of his old acquaintance.   The Prince has had
obligations from him, and therefore his lordship feels himself bound, in
gentlemanly feeling, to say nothing in his disparagement; and, in spite
of the additional tenderness which that very circumstance would give
him for the better side of his Royal Highness's character, he feels himself bound in honesty to say nothing in his praise—not a word—not a
syllable! No more need be observed on this point.   His Lordship
concluded with proposing the health of the Marquis of Lansdowne,
who, upon receiving the applause of the company, expressed himself
' deeply sensible of such an honor, coming from men whose national
character it was to be generously warm in their praise, but not more
generously warm than faithfully sincere.' This elegant compliment was
justly received, and told more perhaps, than every body imagined; for
those who are ' faithfully sincere' in their praise are apt to be equally
so in their censure, and thus the hisses bestowed were put on an equal
footing of sincerity with the applause.   The health of the Vice-Pres-
idents was then given, and after a short speech from Lord Mountjoy,
and much *anticipating* clamor with ' Mr. Sheridan's health,' Mr.
Sheridan *at length* arose, and in a low tone of voice returned his thanks
for the honorable notice by which so large a meeting of his countrymen
thought proper to distinguish him. (*Applause.*) He had ever been
proud of Ireland, and hoped that his country might never have cause
to be ashamed of him. (*Applause.*) Ireland never forgot those who
did all they could do, however little that might be, in behalf of her best
interests.   All allusion to politics had been industriously deprecated
by their noble Chairman.   He was aware that charity was the immediate object of their meeting; but standing as he did, before an assembly of his countrymen, he could not affect to disguise his convic-
tion, that at the present crisis Ireland involved in itself every consideration dear to the best interests of the empire. (*Hear, hear.*) It
was, therefore, that he was most anxious that nothing should transpire
in that meeting calculated to injure those great objects, or to visit
with undeserved censure the conduct of persons whose love to Ireland
was as cordial and as zealous as it ever had been.   He confessed
frankly, that, knowing as he did the unaltered and unalterable sentiments of one *illustrious personage* toward Ireland, he could not conceal
from the meeting that he had felt considerably shocked at the *sulky*

coldness and *surly discontent* with which they had on that evening drunk the health of the Prince Regent. (Here we are sorry to observe that Mr. S. was interrupted by *no very equivocal* symptoms of disapprobation.)   When silence was somewhat restored, Mr. Sheridan said that he *knew the Prince Regent well*—(hisses)—he knew his *principles* —(hisses)—they would at least, he hoped, give him credit for believing that he knew them when he said he did.   (*Applause.*)   He repeated, that he knew well the principles of the Prince Regent, and that so well satisfied was he that they were all that Ireland could wish, that he (Mr. Sheridan) hoped, that as he had lived up to them, so he might die in the principles of the Prince Regent.   (*Hisses and applause.*) He should be sorry personally to have merited their disapprobation. (*General applause*, with cries of ' Change the subject, and speak out.') He could only assure them that the Prince Regent remained unchangeably true to those principles.   (*Here the clamors became so loud and general that we could collect nothing mo*re.)

Although the company, however, refused to give a quiet hearing to Mr. Sheridan while he talked in this manner, yet the moment he sat down they rose up, it seems, and, as a mark that they were not personally offended, gave him a general clap : the *Chronicle* says it was 'to mark their peculiar respect and esteem for him ;' and as the rest of the above report is taken from that paper, it is fit that this encomiastic assertion should accompany it ; but, however the reporter might choose to interpret it, there appears to be no reason for giving it a livelier construction, than the one before mentioned.   We know well enough what the Irish think of Mr. Sheridan.   They believe he has been, and is their friend ; and on that account their gratitude will always endeavor to regard him as complacently as possible, and to separate what his masters can do from what he himself can not : it even prevents them, perhaps, from discerning the harm which a man of his lax turn of thinking, in countenancing the loose principles of another, may have done to the cause which he hoped to assist ; but they are not blind to his defects in general any more than the English ; and after the terrible example that has been furnished us for the bad effects of those principles, 'peculiar respect and esteem' are words not to be prostituted to every occasion of convivial good temper.   It is too late to let a contingent and partial good-will exaggerate in this manner, and throw away the panegyrics that belong to first-rate worthiness.

But to return to the immediate subject.   Here is an assembly of Irishmen, respectable for their rank and benevolence, and desirous, for years, of thinking well of the Prince of Wales, absolutely loading with contempt the very mention of his ' principles,' and shutting their ears against a repetition of the word—so great is their disdain and their indignation.   Principles !   How are we to judge of principles but by conduct ?   And what, in the name of common sense, does Mr. Sheridan mean by saying that the prince adheres to his principles ?   Was it a principle then in his Royal Highness, not to adhere to his professions and promises? And is it in keeping to such a principle, that Mr. Sheridan informs us and 'the public in general,' that he means to live and die in the principles of his master? What did Lord Moira, the Marquis Lansdowne, or the Duke of Devonshire say to these praises? Did they anticipate or echo them? No; *they kept a dead silence;* and for this conscientiousness they are reproved by the ministerial papers, which pathetically tell us how good his Royal Highness had been to the charity, and what a shame it was to mingle political feelings with the objects of such a meeting! Political candor, they mean: had it been political flattery, they would not have cared what had been said of the Prince Regent, nor how many foreign questions had been discussed. It might have been proper in the meeting, had it been possible, to distinguish between the Prince of Wales as a subscriber to the Irish charity, and the Prince of Wales as a clincher of Irish chains; but when the health of such a personage is proposed to such a meeting, political considerations are notoriously supposed to be implied in the manner of its reception, and had the reception been favorable, the ministerialists would have been as eager to take advantage of it as they now are to take umbrage. So much for the inevitable disclosure of truth, in one way or another; and thus has the very first utterance of the public opinion, *vivâ voce,* been loud and unequivocal in rebuke of the Prince Regent.

It is impossible, however, before the present article is closed, to resist an observation or two on the saddest of these ministerial papers. Our readers are aware that the *Morning Post,* above all its rivals, has a faculty of carrying its nonsense to a pitch that becomes amusing in spite of itself, and affords relief to one's feelings in the very excess of its inflictions. Its paper of Thursday last, in answer to a real or pretended correspondent, contained the following paragraph: 'The publication of the article of a friend, relative to the ungenerous, unmanly conduct, displayed at a late public meeting though evidently well meant, would only serve to give consequence to a set of worthless beings, whose imbecile efforts are best treated with sovereign contempt.' *Worthless beings* and *sovereign contempt!* Who would not suppose that some lofty and exemplary character was here speaking of a set of informers and profligates? One, at any rate, whose notice was an honor, and whose silent disdain would keep the noisiest of us in obscurity? Yet this is the paper, notorious above all others in the annals of perfidy, scandal, imbecility, and indecency—the paper which has gone directly from one side to another, and which has levied contributions upon this very prince, which has become a byword for its cant and bad writing, and which has rioted in a doggrel, an adulation, and a ribaldry, that none but the most prostituted pens would consent to use—the paper, in short, of the Stuarts, the Benjafields, the Byrnes, and the Rosa Matildas! and this delicious compound is to 'give consequence' to a society, consisting of the most respectable Irishmen in London, with rank and talent at their head! Help us, benevolent compositors, to some mark or other—some significant and comprehensive index—that shall denote a laugh of an hour's duration.   If any one of our readers should not be so well acquainted as another with the taste and principles of this bewitching *Post*, he may be curious to see what notions of praise and political justice are entertained by the person whose contempt is so overwhelming. .

He shall have a specimen, and when he is reading it, let him lament, in the midst of his laughter, that a paper, capable of such sickening adulation, should have the power of finding its way to the table of an English prince, and of helping to endanger the country by polluting the sources of its government.   The same page, which contained the specimen of contempt above-mentioned, contained also a set of wretched commonplace lines in French, Italian, Spanish, and English, *literally* addressing the prince regent in the following terms, among others : '-You are the *Glory of the people*'—' You are the *Protector of the arts*'—' You are the *Mæcnus of the age*'—' Wherever you appear *you conquer all hearts,* wipe away tears, excite *desire and love,* and win *beauty* toward you'—' You breathe *eloquence*'—' You inspire the Graces'—' You are *Adonis in loveliness !*'   ' Thus gifted,' it proceeds in English,

> ' Thus gifted with each grace of mind,
> Born to delight and bless mankind ;
> Wisdom, with Pleasure in her train,
> Great prince ! shall signalize thy reign :
> To Honor, Virtue, Truth allied ;
> The nation's safeguard and its pride ;
> With monarchs of immortal fame
> Shall bright renown enroll the name.'

What person, unacquainted with the true state of the case, would imagine, in reading these astounding eulogies, that this ' *Glory of the people*' was the subject of millions of shrugs and reproaches ! that this ' *Protector of the arts*' had named a wretched foreigner his historical painter, in disparagement or in ignorance of the merits of his own countrymen ! that this ' *Mæcnus of the age*' patronized not a single deserving writer ! that this ' *Breather of eloquence*' could not say a few decent extempore words—if we are to judge, at least, from what he said to his regiment on its embarkation for Portugal ! that this ' *Conqueror of hearts*' was the disappointer of hopes ! that this ' *Exciter of desire*' [bravo ! Messieurs of the *Post !*]—this ' *Adonis in loveliness*' was a corpulent man of fifty ! in sort, that this *delightful, blissful, wise, pleasurable, honorable, virtuous, true,* and *immortal* prince, was a violator of his word, a libertine, over head and ears in disgrace, a despiser of domestic ties, the companion of gamblers and demireps, a man who has just closed half a century without one single claim on the gratitude of his country, or the respect of posterity !

These are hard truths; but are they *not* truths ?   And have we not suffered enough—are we not now suffering bitterly—from the disgusting flatteries of which the above is a repetition ?   The minis-

ters may talk of the shocking boldness of the press, and may throw out
their wretched warnings about interviews between Mr. Perceval and
Sir Vicary Gibbs; but let us inform them, that such vices as have
just been enumerated are shocking to all Englishmen who have a just
sense of the state of Europe; and that he is a bolder man, who, in
times like the present, dares to afford reason for the description.
Would to God, the *Examiner* could ascertain that difficult, and perhaps undiscoverable point, which enables a public writer to keep clear
of an appearance of the love of scandal, while he is hunting out the
vices of those in power! Then should one paper, at least, in this
metropolis, help to rescue the nation from the charge of silently
encouraging what it must publicly rue; and the Sardanapalus, who
is now afraid of none but informers, be taught to shake, in the midst
of his minions, in the very drunkenness of his heart, at the voice of
honesty. But if this be impossible, still there is one benefit which
truth may derive from adulation—one benefit which is favorable to
the former in proportion to the grossness of the latter, and of which
none of his flatterers seem to be aware—the opportunity of contradicting its assertions. Let us never forget this advantage, which
adulation can not help giving us; and let such of our readers as are
inclined to deal insincerely with the great, from a false notion of policy
and of knowledge of the world, take warning from what we now see
of the miserable effects of courtly disguise, paltering, and profligacy.
Flattery in any shape is unworthy a man and a gentleman; but
political flattery is almost a request to be made slaves. If we would
have the great to be what they ought, we must find some means or
other to speak of them as they are.

This article, no doubt, was very bitter and contemptuous;
therefore, in the legal sense of the term, very libelous; the
more so, inasmuch as it was very true. There will be no
question about the truth of it, at this distance of time, with
any class of persons, unless, possibly, with some few of the
old Tories, who may think it was a patriotic action in the
Prince to have displaced the Whigs for their opponents. But
I believe, that under all the circumstances, there are few
persons indeed nowadays, of any class, who will not be of
opinion, that, bitter as the article was, it was more than
sufficiently avenged by two years' imprisonment and a fine
of a thousand pounds. For it did but express what all the
world were feeling, with the exception of the Prince's once
bitterest enemies, the Tories themselves, then newly become
his friends; and its very sincerity and rashness, had the
Prince possessed greatness of mind enough to think so, might

have furnished him such a ground for pardoning it, as would have been the best proof he could have given us of our having mistaken him, and turned us into blushing and grateful friends. An attempt to bribe us on the side of fear, did but further disgust us. A free and noble waiving of the punishment would have bowed our hearts into regret. We should have found in it the evidence of that true generosity of nature paramount to whatsoever was frivolous or appeared to be mean, which his flatterers claimed for him, and which would have made us doubly blush for the formal virtues to which he seemed to be attached, when, in reality, nothing would have better pleased us than such a combination of the gay and the magnanimous. I say doubly blush, for I now blush at ever having been considered, or rather been willing to be considered, an advocate of any sort of conventionality, unqualified by liberal exceptions and prospective enlargement; and I am sure that my brother, had he been living, who was one of the best natured and most indulgent of men, would have joined with me in making the same concession; though I am bound to add, that, with all his good sense, and all his indulgence of others, I have no reason to believe that he had ever stood in need of that pardon for even conventional license, from the necessity of which I can not pretend to have been exempt. I had never, to be sure, affected to denounce poor Mrs. Robinson and others, as Gifford had done; nor did I afterward condescend to make concessions about poor Queen Caroline, while I denounced those who had no right to demand them. All the airs which I gave myself as a censor were over men; and I should have blushed indeed at any time, to have given myself those, had the men combined any thing like generosity with license.

I now think, that although for many reasons connected with a long career of literature as well as politics, and for the general spirit of both, I fully deserve the pension which a liberal minister and a gracious queen have bestowed on me, I had no right in particular instances, and in my own person, to demand more virtues from any human being than nature and education had given him, or to denounce his faults without giving him the excuse of those circumstances,

and freely confessing my own. I think that the world is
best served in any respect, in proportion as we dig into the
first roots of error, and cease blaming the poor boughs which
they injure. No man has any more right than another to

> " Compound for sins he is inclined to,
>   By damning those he has no mind to."

If I thought the Prince of Wales a coxcomb in one sense of
the word, he might have been fully justified in thinking me
one in another. If I seemed to demand, that his life should
be spotless, he might reasonably have turned upon me, and
asked whether I was spotless myself. If I disliked him because he was selfish and ungenerous, he might have asked
where was the generosity of forgetting the luxury in which
he had been brought up, my own poverty of nurture, on the
other hand, and the master, who was ready to flog instead
of flatter me, whenever I did not behave as I ought.

It is understood, after all, that the sting of the article lay
not in the gravest portion of it, but in the lightest; in the
banter about the " Adonis" and the " corpulent gentleman of
fifty." The serious remarks might have been endured, on
the assumption that they themselves were an assumption;
but to be touched where the claim to admiration was at
once obvious and preposterous, was intolerable. Hence the
general impression, was, and is, that we were sent to prison,
because we said the Prince Regent was fat. Now, the
truth is, I had no wish to speak of his fat, or to allude to
his person in any way. Nor did I intend even to banter him
in a spirit of levity. I was very angry with the flattery,
and ridicule was the natural answer to it. It was natural
enough in the Prince not to like to give up his fine dressing
and his youthful pretensions; for he was not wise, and he
had been very handsome;

> " The glass of fashion, and the mould of form."

But his adulators had no such excuse; and I was provoked
to see them encouraging the weakest of his mistakes, when
the most important questions of state were demanding his
attention, and meeting, I thought, with nothing but the un-
handsomest tergiversation.

I have spoken of an attempt to bribe us. We were given

to understand, through the medium of a third person, but in a manner emphatically serious and potential, that if we would abstain in future from commenting upon the actions of the royal personage, means would be found to prevent our going to prison. The same offer was afterward repeated, as far as the payment of a fine was concerned, upon our going thither. I need not add, that we declined both. We do not mean to affirm, that these offers came directly or indirectly from the quarter in which they might be supposed to originate ; but we know the immediate quarter from which they did come ; and this we may affirm, that of all the " two hundred and fifty particular friends," who dined on a former occasion at Carlton House, his Royal Highness had not one more zealous or liberal in his behalf.

The expectation of a prison was in one respect very formidable to me ; for I had been a long time in a bad state of health. I was suffering under the worst of those hypochondriacal attacks which I have described in a former chapter ; and when notice was given that we were to be brought up for judgment, I had just been advised by the physician to take exercise every day on horseback, and go down to the sea-side. I was resolved, however, to do no disgrace either to the courage which I really possessed, or to the example set me by my excellent brother. I accordingly put my countenance in its best trim ; I made a point of wearing my best apparel ; and descended into the legal arena to be sentenced gallantly. As an instance of the imagination which I am accustomed to mingle with every thing, I was at that time reading a little work, to which Milton is indebted, the *Comus* of Erycius Puteanus ; and this, which is a satire on "Bachusses and their revelers," I pleased myself with having in my pocket.

It is necessary on passing sentence for a libel, to read over again the words that composed it. This was the business of Lord Ellenborough, who baffled the attentive audience in a very ingenious manner by affecting every instant to hear a noise, and calling upon the officers of the court to prevent it. Mr. Garrow, the attorney-general (who had succeeded Sir Vicary Gibbs at a very cruel moment,

for the indictment had been brought by that irritable per
son, and was the first against us which took effect), behaved
to us with a politeness that was considered extraordinary.
Not so Mr. Justice Grose, who delivered the sentence. To
be didactic and oldwomanish seemed to belong to his nature ;
but to lecture us on pandering to the public appetite for
scandal, was what we could not so easily bear. My brother,
as I had been the writer, expected me, perhaps, to be the
spokesman ; and speak I certainly should have done, had I
not been prevented by the dread of that hesitation in my
speech, to which I had been subject when a boy, and the
fear of which (perhaps idly, for I hesitated at that time
least among strangers, and very rarely do' so at all), has
been the main cause, perhaps, why I have appeared and
acted in public less than any other public man. There is
reason to think, that Lord Ellenborough was still less easy
than ourselves. He knew that we were acquainted with
his visits to Carlton-house and Brighton (sympathies not
eminently decent in a judge), and with the good things
which he had obtained for his kinsmen ; and we could not
help preferring our feelings at the moment to those which
induced him to keep his eyes fixed on his papers, which he
did almost the whole time of our being in court, never turning them once to the place on which we stood. There
were divers other points, too, on which he had some reason
to fear that we might choose to return the lecture of the
bench. He did not even look at us, when he asked, in the
course of his duty, whether it was our wish to make any
remarks. I answered, that we did not wish to make any
there; and Mr. Justice Grose proceeded to pass sentence.
At the sound of two years' imprisonment in separate jails,
my brother and myself instinctively pressed each other's
arm. It was a heavy blow; but the pressure that acknowledged it, encouraged the resolution to bear it ; and I do not
believe that either of us interchanged a word afterward on
the subject.

CHAPTER XIV.

IMPRISONMENT.

Author's imprisonment.—Curious specimen of a jailer, an under-jailer, and an under-jailer's wife.—Mr. Holme Sumner.—Conversion of a room in a prison into a fairy bower.—Author's visitors.—A heart-rending spectacle.—Felons and debtors.—Restoration to freedom.

WE parted in hackney-coaches to our respective abodes, accompanied by two tipstaves apiece.

They prepared me for a singular character in my jailer. His name was Ives. I was told he was a very self-willed personage, not the more accommodating for being in a bad state of health; and that he called every body *Mister* " In short," said one of the tipstaves, "he is one as may be led, but he'll never be *druv*."

The sight of the prison-gate and the high wall was a dreary business. I thought of my horseback and the downs of Brighton; but congratulated myself, at all events, that I had come thither with a good conscience. After waiting in the prison-yard as long as if it had been the ante-room of a minister, I was ushered into the presence of the great man. He was in his parlor, which was decently furnished, and had a basin of broth before him, which he quitted on my appearance, and rose with much solemnity to meet me. He seemed about fifty years of age. He had a white night-cap on, as if he was going to be hung, and a great red face, which looked ready to burst with blood. Indeed, he was not allowed by his physician to speak in a tone above a whisper.

The first thing which this dignified person said was, " Mister, I'd ha' given a matter of a hundred pounds, that you had not come to this place—a hundred pounds!" The emphasis which he had laid on the word " hundred" was ominous.

I forget what I answered. I endeavored to make the

best of the matter ; but he recurred over and over again to
the hundred pounds ; and said he wondered, for his part,
what the Government meant by sending me there, for the
prison was not a prison fit for a gentleman.   He often
repeated this opinion afterward, adding, with a peculiar nod
of his head, and "Mister, they knows it."

I said, that if a gentleman deserved to be sent to prison,
he ought not to be treated with a greater nicety than any
one else : upon which he corrected me, observing very properly (though, as the phrase is, it was one word for the gentleman and two for the letter of prison lodgings), that a
person who had been used to a better mode of living than
"low people," was not treated with the same justice, if
forced to lodge exactly as they did.

I told him his observation was very true ; which gave
him a favorable opinion of my understanding : for I had
many occasions of remarking, that he looked upon nobody
as his superior, speaking even of the members of the royal
family as persons whom he knew very well, and whom
he estimated no more than became him.   One royal duke
had lunched in his parlor, and another he had laid under some polite obligation.   "They knows me," said he,
"very well, mister ; and, mister, I knows them."   This
concluding sentence he uttered with great particularity and
precision.

He was not proof, however, against a Greek Pindar,
which he happened to light upon one day among my books.
Its unintelligible character gave him a notion that he had
got somebody to deal with who might really know something which he did not.   Perhaps the gilt leaves and red
morocco binding had their share in the magic.   The upshot
was, that he always showed himself anxious to appear well
with me, as a clever fellow, treating me with great civility
on all occasions but one, when I made him very angry by
disappointing him in a money amount.   The Pindar was a
mystery that staggered him.   I remember very well, that
giving me a long account one day of something connected
with his business, he happened to catch with his eye the
shelf that contained it, and whether he saw it or not,

abruptly finished by observing, " But, mister, you knows all these things as well as I do."

Upon the whole, my new acquaintance was as strange a person as I ever met with. A total want of education, together with a certain vulgar acuteness, conspired to render him insolent and pedantic. Disease sharpened his tendency to fits of passion, which threatened to suffocate him ; and then in his intervals of better health he would issue forth, with his cock-up-nose and his hat on one side, as great a fop as a jockey. I remember his coming to my rooms, about the middle of my imprisonment, as if on purpose to insult over my ill health with the contrast of his convalescence, putting his arms in a gay manner a-kimbo, and telling me I should never live to go out, whereas he was riding about as stout as ever, and had just been in the country. He died before I left prison.

The word *jail*, in deference to the way in which it is sometimes spelt, this accomplished individual pronounced *gole ;* and Mr. Brougham he always spoke of as Mr. *Bruffam.* He one day apologized for this mode of pronunciation, or rather gave a specimen of vanity and self-will, which will show the reader the high notions a jailer may entertain of himself. " I find," said he, " that they calls him *Broom ;* but, mister" (assuming a look from which there was to be no appeal), " *I* calls him *Bruffam !*"

Finding that my host did not think the prison fit for me, I asked if he could let me have an apartment in his house. He pronounced it impossible ; which was a trick to enhance the price. I could not make an offer to please him ; and he stood out so long, and, as he thought, so cunningly, that he subsequently overreached himself by his trickery ; as the reader will see. His object was to keep me among the prisoners, till he could at once sicken me of the place, and get the permission of the magistrates to receive me into his house ; which was a thing he reckoned upon as a certainty. He thus hoped to secure himself in all quarters ; for his vanity was almost as strong as his avarice. He was equally fond of getting money in private, and of the approbation of the great men whom he had to deal with in public ; and it so happened that there had been no prisoner, above the poorest condition, before my arrival, with the exception of Colonel Despard. From abusing the prison, he then suddenly fell to speaking well of it, or rather of the room occupied by the colonel; and said, that another corresponding with it would make me a capital apartment. "To be sure," said he, " there is nothing but bare walls, and I have no bed to put in it." I replied, that of course I should not be hindered from having my own bed from home. He said, " No; and if it rains," observed he, " you have only to put up with want of light for a time." " What!" exclaimed I, " are there no windows?" " Windows, mister!" cried he; " no windows in a prison of this sort; no glass, mister: but excellent shutters."

It was finally agreed, that I should sleep for a night or two in a garret of the jailer's house, till my bed could be got ready in the prison, and the windows glazed. A dreary evening followed, which, however, let me completely into the man's character, and showed him in a variety of lights, some ludicrous, and others as melancholy. There was a full length portrait in the room, of a little girl, dizzened out in her best. This, he told me, was his daughter, whom he had disinherited for her disobedience. I tried to suggest a few reflections, capable of doing her service; but disobedience, I found, was an offense doubly irritating to his nature, on account of his sovereign habits as a jailer; and seeing his irritability likely to inflame the plethora of his countenance, I desisted. Though not allowed to speak above a whisper, he was extremely willing to talk; but at an early hour I pleaded my own state of health, and retired to bed.

On taking possession of my garret, I was treated with a piece of delicacy, which I never should have thought of finding in a prison. When I first entered its walls, I had been received by the under-jailer, a man who seemed an epitome of all that was forbidding in his office. He was short and very thick, had a hook nose, a great severe countenance, and a bunch of keys hanging on his arm. A friend stopped short at sight of him, and said in a melancholy tone, " And this is the jailer!"

Honest old *Cave!* thine outside would have been unworthy of thee, if upon further acquaintance I had not
found it a very hearty outside—ay, and in my eyes, a very
good-looking one, and as fit to contain the milk of human-
kindness that was in thee, as the husk of a cocoa.   To show
by one specimen the character of this man, I could never
prevail on him to accept any acknowledgment of his kindness,
greater than a set of tea-things, and a piece or two of old
furniture which I could not well carry away.   1 had, indeed
the pleasure of leaving him in possession of a room which I
had papered ; but this was a thing unexpected, and
which neither of us had supposed could be done.   Had
I been a prince, I would have forced on him a pension ;
being a journalist, I made him accept an *Examiner* weekly, which he lived for some years to relish his Sunday pipe
with.

This man, in the interval between my arrival and introduction to the head-jailer, had found means to give me farther
information respecting my condition, and to express the interest he took in it.   I thought little of his offers at the time.
He behaved with the greatest air of deference to his principal ; moving as fast as his body would allow him, to execute
his least intimation ; and holding the candle to him while
he read, with an obsequious zeal.   But he had spoken to his
wife about me, and his wife I found to be as great a curiosity
as himself.   Both were more like the romantic jailers drawn
in some of our modern plays, than real Horsemonger-lane
palpabilities.   The wife, in her person, was as light and
fragile as the husband was sturdy.   She had the nerves of
a fine lady, and yet went through the most unpleasant duties
with the patience of a martyr.   Her voice and look seemed
to plead for a softness like their own, as if a loud reply would
have shattered her.   Ill health had made her a Methodist,
but this did not hinder her from sympathizing with an invalid who was none, or from loving a husband who was as
little of a saint as need be.   Upon the whole, such an extraordinary couple, so apparently unsuitable, and yet so fitted
for one another ; so apparently vulgar on one side, and yet
so naturally delicate on both ; so misplaced in their situation,

and yet for the good of others so admirably put there, I have never met with before or since.

It was the business of this woman to lock me up in my garret ; but she did it so softly the first night, that I knew nothing of the matter. The night following, I thought I heard a gentle tampering with the lock. I tried it, and found it fastened. She heard me as she was going down-stairs, and said the next day, " Ah, sir, I thought I should have turned the key so as for you not to hear it ; but I found you did." The whole conduct of this couple toward us, from first to last, was of a piece with this singular delicacy.

My bed was shortly put up, and I slept in my new room. It was on an upper story, and stood in a corner of the quadrangle, on the right hand as you enter the prison-gate. The windows (which had now been accommodated with, glass, in addition to their " excellent shutters") were high up, and barred ; but the room was large and airy, and there was a fireplace. It was intended to be a common room for the prisoners on that story ; but the cells were then empty. The cells were ranged on either side of the arcade, of which the story is formed, and the room opened at the end of it. At nighttime the door was locked ; then another on the top of the staircase, then another on the middle of the staircase, then a fourth at the bottom, a fifth that shut up the little yard belonging to that quarter, and how many more, before you got out of the gates, I forget : but I do not exaggerate when I say there were ten or eleven. The first night I slept there, I listened to them, one after the other, till the weaker part of my heart died within me. Every fresh turning of the key seemed a malignant insult to my love of liberty. I was alone, and away from my family ; I, who to this day have never slept from home above a dozen weeks in my life. Furthermore, the reader will bear in mind that I was ill. With a great flow of natural spirits, I was subject to fits of nervousness, which had latterly taken a more continued shape. I felt one of them coming on, and having learned to anticipate and break the force of it by exercise, I took a stout walk by pacing backward and forward for the space of three hours. This threw me into a state in which rest, for rest's sake, became pleasant. I got hastily into bed, and slept without a dream till morning.

By the way, I never dreamt of prison but twice all the time I was there, and my dream was the same on both occasions. I fancied I was at the theatre, and that the whole house looked at me in surprise, as much as to say, " How could he get out of prison ?"

I saw my wife for a few minutes after I entered the jail, but she was not allowed on that day to stop longer. The next day she was with me for some hours. To say that she never reproached me for these and the like taxes upon our family prospects, is to say little. A world of comfort for me was in her face. There is a note in the fifth volume of my Spenser, which I was then reading, in these words : "February 4th, 1813." The line to which it refers is this :

" Much dearer be the things which come through hard distresse."

I now applied to the magistrates for permission to have my wife and children constantly with me, which was granted. Not so my request to move into the jailer's house. Mr Holme Sumner, on occasion of a petition from a subsequent prisoner, told the House of Commons that my room had a view over the Surrey hills, and that I was very well content with it. I could not feel obliged to him for this postliminious piece of enjoyment, especially when I remembered that he had done all in his power to prevent my removal out of the room, precisely (as it appeared to us), because it looked upon nothing but the felons, and because I was *not* contented. In fact, you could not see out of the windows at all, without getting on a chair ; and then, all that you saw, was the miserable men whose chains had been clanking from daylight. The perpetual sound of these chains wore upon my spirits in a manner to which my state of health allowed me reasonably to object. The yard, also, in which I took exercise, was very small. The jailer proposed that I should be allowed to occupy apartments in his house, and walk occasionally in the prison garden ; adding, that I should certainly die if I did not ; and his opinion was seconded by that of the medical man. Mine host was sincere in this, if it nothing else. Telling us, one day, how warmly he had put it to the magistrates, and how he insisted that I should not survive, he turned round upon me, and, to the doctor's astonishment, added, "Nor, mister, will you." I believe it was the opinion of many; but Mr. Holme Sumner argued otherwise; perhaps from his own sensations, which were sufficiently iron. Perhaps he concluded, also, like a proper old Tory, that if I did not think fit to flatter the magistrates a little, and play the courtier, my wants could not be very great. At all events, he came up one day with the rest of them, and after bowing to my wife, and piteously pinching the cheek of an infant in her arms, went down and did all he could to prevent our being comfortably situated.

The doctor then proposed that I should be removed into the prison infirmary; and this proposal was granted. Infirmary had, I confess, an awkward sound, even to my ears. I fancied a room shared with other sick persons, not the best fitted for companions; but the good-natured doctor (his name was Dixon) undeceived me. The infirmary was divided into four wards, with as many small rooms attached to them. The two upper wards were occupied, but the two on the floor had never been used : and one of these, not very providently (for I had not yet learned to think of money) I turned into a noble room. I papered the walls with a trellis of roses; I had the ceiling colored with clouds and sky; the barred windows I screened with Venetian blinds; and when my bookcases were set up with their busts, and flowers and a pianoforte made their appearance, perhaps there was not a handsomer room on that side the water. I took a pleasure, when a stranger knocked at the door, to see him come in and stare about him. The surprise on issuing from the Borough, and passing through the avenues of a jail, was dramatic. Charles Lamb declared there was no other such room, except in a fairy tale.

But I possessed another surprise; which was a garden. There was a little yard outside the room, railed off from another belonging to the neighboring ward. This yard I shut in with green palings, adorned it with a trellis, bordered it with a thick bed of earth from a nursery, and even contrived to have a grass-plot. The earth I filled with flowers and young trees. There was an apple-tree, from which we managed to get a pudding the second year. As to my flowers, they were allowed to be perfect. Thomas Moore, who came to see me with Lord Byron, told me he had seen no such heart's-ease. I bought the *Parnaso Italiano* while in prison, and used often to think of a passage in it, while looking at this miniature piece of horticulture :

" Mio picciol orto,
A me sei vigna, e campo, e selva, e prato."—BALDI.

" My little garden,
To me thou'rt vineyard, field, and meadow, and wood."

Here I wrote and read in fine weather, sometimes under an awing. In autumn, my trellises were hung with scarlet runners, which added to the flowery investment. I used to shut my eyes in my arm-chair, and affect to think myself hundreds of miles off.

But my triumph was in issuing forth of a morning. A wicket out of the garden led into the large one belonging to the prison. The latter was only for vegetables ; but it contained a cherry-tree, which I saw twice in blossom. I parcelled out the ground in my imagination into favorite districts. I made a point of dressing myself as if for a long walk ; and then, putting on my gloves, and taking my book under my arm, stepped forth, requesting my wife not to wait dinner if I was too late. My eldest little boy, to whom Lamb addressed some charming verses on the occasion, was my constant companion, and we used to play all sorts of juvenile games together. It was, probably, in dreaming of one of these games (but the words had a more touching effect on my ear) that he exclaimed one night in his sleep, " No : I'm not lost ; I'm found." Neither he nor I were very strong at that time ; but I have lived to see him a man of forty ; and wherever he is found, a generous hand and a great understanding will be found together.

I entered prison the 3d of February 1813, and removed to my new apartments the 16th of March, happy to get out of the noise of the chains. When I sat amidst my books, and saw the imaginary sky overhead, and my paper roses about me, I drank in the quiet at my ears, as if they were thirsty. The little room was my bedroom. I afterward made the two rooms change characters, when my wife lay-in. Permission for her continuance with me at that period was easily obtained of the magistrates, among whom a new-comer made his appearance. This was another good-natured man, Lord Leslie, afterward Earl of Rothes.* He heard me with kindness; and his actions did not belie his countenance. My eldest girl (now, alas! no more) was born in prison. She was beautiful, and for the greatest part of an existence of thirty years, she was happy. She was christened Mary after my mother, and Florimel after one of Spenser's heroines. But Mary we called her. Never shall I forget my sensations when she came into the world; for I was obliged to play the physician myself, the hour having taken us by surprise. But her mother found many unexpected comforts; and during the whole time of her confinement, which happened to be in very fine weather, the garden door was set open, and she looked upon trees and flowers. A thousand recollections rise within me at every fresh period of my imprisonment, such as I can not trust myself with dwelling upon.

These rooms, and the visits of my friends, were the bright side of my captivity. I read verses without end, and wrote almost as many. I had also the pleasure of hearing that my brother had found comfortable rooms in Coldbath-fields, and a host who really deserved that name as much as a jailer could. The first year of my imprisonment was a long pull up-hill; but never was metaphor so literally verified, as by the sensation at the turning of the second. In the first year, all the prospect was that of the one coming: in the second, the days began to be scored off, like those of children at school preparing for a holiday. When I was fairly settled in my new apartments, the jailer could hardly give sufficient vent to his spleen at my having escaped his clutches, his astonishment was so great. Besides, though I treated him

* George William, twelfth earl of that name. He died a few years afterward.

handsomely, he had a little lurking fear of the *Examiner* upon him; so he contented himself with getting as much out of me as he could, and boasting of the grand room which he would fain have prevented my enjoying.

My friends were allowed to be with me till ten o'clock at night, when the under-turnkey, a young man with his lantern, and much ambitious gentility of deportment, came to see them out. I believe we scattered an urbanity, about the prison, till then unknown. Even William Hazlitt, who there first did me the honor of a visit, would stand interchanging amenities at the threshold, which I had great difficulty in making him pass. I know not which kept his hat off with the greater pertinacity of deference, I to the diffident cutter-up of Tory dukes and kings, or he to the amazing prisoner and invalid who issued out of a bower of roses. There came my old friends and school-fellows, Pitman, whose wit and animal spirits still keep him alive; Mitchell, who translated Aristophanes; and Barnes, who always reminded me of Fielding. It was he that introduced me to the late Mr. Thomas Alsager, the kindest of neighbors, a man of business, who contrived to be a scholar and a musician. He loved his leisure, and yet would start up at a moment's notice to do the least of a prisoner's biddings.

My now old friend, Cowden Clarke, with his ever young and wise heart, was good enough to be his own introducer, paving his way, like a proper invester of prisons, with baskets of fruit.

The Lambs came to comfort me in all weathers, hail or sunshine, in daylight and in darkness, even in the dreadful frost and snow of the beginning of 1814.

My physician, curiously enough, was Dr. Knighton (afterward Sir William), who had lately become physician to the prince. He, therefore, could not, in decency, visit me under the circumstances, though he did again afterward never failing in the delicacies due either to his great friend or to his small. Meantime, another of his friends, the late estimable Dr. Gooch, came to me as his substitute, and he came often.

Great disappointment and exceeding viciousness may talk

as they please of the badness of human nature. For my part, I am now in my sixty-fifth year, and I have seen a good deal of the world, the dark side as well as the light, and I say that human nature is a very good and kindly thing, and capable of all sorts of virtues. Art thou not a refutation of all that can be said against it, excellent Sir John Swinburne ? another friend whom I made in prison, and who subsequently cheered some of my greatest passes of adversity.

To evils I have owed some of my greatest blessings. It was imprisonment that brought me acquainted with my friend of friends, Shelley. I had seen little of him before ; but he wrote to me, making me a princely offer, which at that time I stood in no need of.

Some other persons, not at all known to us, offered to raise money enough to pay the fine of £1000. We declined it, with proper thanks ; and it became us to do so. But, as far as my own feelings were concerned, I have no merit ; for I was destitute, at that time, of even a proper instinct with regard to money. It was not long afterward that I was forced to call upon friendship for its assistance ; and nobly (as I shall show by-and-by) was it afforded me !

To some other friends, near and dear, I may not even return thanks in this place for a thousand nameless attentions, which they make it a business of their existence to bestow on those they love. I might as soon thank my own heart. But one or two others, whom I have not seen for years, and who by some possibility (if, indeed, they ever think it worth their while to fancy any thing on the subject) might suppose themselves forgotten, I may be suffered to remind of the pleasure they gave me. M. S., who afterward saw us so often near London, has long, I hope, been enjoying the tranquillity he so richly deserved ; and so, I trust is C. S., whose face, or rather something like it (for it was not easy to match her own), I continually met with afterward in the land of her ancestors. Her vail, and her baskets of flowers, used to come through the portal like light.

I must not omit the honor of a visit from the venerable Bentham, who was justly said to unite the wisdom of a sage with the simplicity of a child. He found me playing at battledore, in which he took a part, and with his usual eye toward improvement, suggested an amendment in the constitution of shuttlecocks. I remember the surprise of the governor at his local knowledge and his vivacity. "Why, mister," said he, "his eye is every where at once."

All these comforts were embittered by unceasing ill-health, and by certain melancholy reveries, which the nature of the place did not help to diminish. During the first six weeks, the sound of the felons' chains, mixed with what I took for horrid execrations or despairing laughter, was never out of my ears. When I went into the infirmary, which stood between the jail and the prison walls, gallows were occasionally put in order by the side of my windows, and afterward set up over the prison gates, where. they remained visible. The keeper one day, with an air of mystery, took me into the upper ward, for the purpose, he said, of gratifying me with a view of the country from the roof. Something prevented his showing me this; but the spectacle he did show me I shall never forget. It was a stout country girl, sitting in an absorbed manner, her eyes fixed on the fire. She was handsome, and had a little hectic spot in either cheek, the effect of some gnawing emotion. He told me, in a whisper, that she was there for the murder of her bastard child. I could have knocked the fellow down for his unfeelingness in making a show of her; but, after all, she did not see us. She heeded us not. There was no object before her but what produced the spot in her cheek. The gallows, on which she was executed, must have been brought out within her hearing : but perhaps she heard that as little.

To relieve the reader's feelings, I will here give him another instance of the delicacy of my friend the under-jailer. He always used to carry up her food to this poor girl himself; because, as he said, he did not think it a fit task for younger men.

This was a melancholy case. In general, the crimes were not of such a staggering description, nor did the criminals appear to take their situations to heart. I found by

degrees, that fortune showed fairer play than I had supposed
to all classes of men, and that those who seemed to have
most reason to be miserable, were not always so.   Their
criminality was generally proportioned to their want of
thought.   My friend Cave, who had become a philosopher
by the force of his situation, said to me one day, when a
new batch of criminals came in, " Poor ignorant wretches,
sir !"   At evening, when they went to bed, I used to stand
in the prison garden, listening to the cheerful songs with
which the felons entertained one another.   The beaters of
hemp were a still merrier race.   Doubtless the good hours
and simple fare of the prison contributed to make the blood
of its inmates run better, particularly those who were forced
to take exercise.   At last, I used to pity the debtors more
than the criminals ; yet even the debtors had their gay
parties and jolly songs.   Many a time (for they were my
neighbors) have I heard them roar out the old ballad in
Beaumont and Fletcher ;

> " He that drinks, and goes to bed sober,
>   Falls as the leaves do, and dies in October."

To say the truth, there was an obstreperousness in their
mirth, that looked more melancholy than the thoughtlessness
of the lighter-feeding felons.

On the 3d of February 1815, I was free.   When my
family, the preceding summer, had been obliged to go down
to Brighton for their health, I felt ready to dash my head
against the wall, at not being able to follow them.   I would
sometimes sit in my chair, with this thought upon me, till
the agony of my impatience burst out at every pore.   I would
not speak of it, if it did not enable me to show how this kind
of suffering may be borne, and in what sort of way it terminates.   I learned to prevent it by violent exercise.   All fits
of nervousness ought to be anticipated as much as possible
with exercise.   Indeed, a proper healthy mode of life would
save most people from these effeminate ills, and most likely
cure even their inheritors.

It was now thought that I should dart out of my cage like
a bird, and feel no end in the delight of ranging.   But partly
from ill-health, and partly from habit, the day of my libera

tion brought a good deal of pain with it. An illness of a long standing, which required very different treatment, had by this time been burnt in upon me by the iron that enters into the soul of the captive, wrap it in flowers as he may; and I am ashamed to say, that after stopping a little at the house of my friend Alsager, I had not the courage to continue looking at the shoals of people passing to and fro, as the coach drove up the Strand. The whole business of life seemed a hideous impertinence. The first pleasant sensation I experienced was when the coach turned into the New Road, and I beheld the old hills of my affection standing where they used to do, and breathing me a welcome.

It was very slowly that I recovered any thing like a sensation of health. The bitterest evil I suffered was in consequence of having been confined so long in one spot. The habit stuck to me on my return home, in a very extraordinary manner, and made, I fear, some of my friends think me ungrateful. They did me an injustice; but it was their fault; nor could I wish them the bitter experience which alone makes us acquainted with the existence of strange things. This weakness I outlived; but I have never thoroughly recovered the shock given my constitution. My natural spirits, however, have always struggled hard to see me reasonably treated. Many things give me exquisite pleasure, which seem to affect other men in a very minor degree; and I enjoyed, after all, such happy moments with my friends, even in prison, that in the midst of the beautiful climate which I afterward visited, I was sometimes in doubt whether I would not rather have been in jail than in Italy.

END OF VOLUME THE FIRST.

Printed in Great Britain
by Amazon

11077926R00174